U.S. MARINE GUIDEBOOK

U.S. MARINE GUIDEBOOK

UNITED STATES MARINE CORPS

SKYHORSE PUBLISHING

Skyhorse Publishing books may be purchased in bulk at special discounts for sales promotion, corporate gifts, fund-raising, or educational purposes. Special editions can also be created to specifications. For details, contact the Special Sales Department, Skyhorse Publishing, 307 West 36th Street, 11th Floor, New York, NY 10018 or info@skyhorsepublishing.com.

www.skyhorsepublishing.com

10 9 8

Library of Congress Cataloging-in-Publication Data

U.S. Marine guidebook / by United States Marine Corps.
p. cm.
ISBN 978-1-60239-941-9
1. United States. Marine Corps--Handbooks, manuals, etc. 2. United States. Marine Corps--Regulations. I. United States. Marine Corps. II. Title: US Marine guidebook. III. Title: United States Marine guidebook.
VE153.U18 2009
359.9'60973--dc22

2009039693

Printed in the United States of America

CONTENTS*

**Throughout this order the words HE, HIS, HIM, and HIMSELF will be considered to include the meaning of SHE, HERS, HER, and HERSELF except in chapter 10 which, by regulation, is restricted to male Marines only.*

Chapter 1. Code of Conduct, Military Law/UCMJ, and Conduct in War

Section I. Code of Conduct

***Objective:** Provided with a list of the six articles of the Code of Conduct, explain the meaning of each article.*

A. CODE OF CONDUCT ARTICLES

1. **Article I.** "I am an American fighting man. I serve in the forces which guard my country and our way of life. I am prepared to give my life in their defense."

INTERPRETATION: I am a Marine. I will fight and, if necessary, die for my country and our way of life.

EXAMPLE: Resistance can demand the ultimate sacrifice—your life. Lance Corporal Jimenez made that sacrifice while serving as a Fire Team Leader with Company K, Third Battalion, Seventh Marines, First Marine Division in operations against the enemy in the Republic of Vietnam on 28 August 1969. On that date Lance Corporal Jimenez's unit came under heavy attack by North Vietnamese Army soldiers concealed in well-camouflaged emplacements. Lance Corporal Jimenez reacted by seizing the initiative and plunging forward toward the enemy position. He personally destroyed several enemy personnel and silenced an antiaircraft weapon. Shouting encouragement to his companions, Lance Corporal Jimenez continued his aggressive forward movement. He slowly maneuvered to within ten feet of hostile soldiers who were firing automatic weapons from a trench and, in the face of vicious enemy fire, destroyed the position. Although he was by now the target of concentrated fire from hostile gunners intent upon halting his assault, Lance Corporal Jimenez continued to press forward. As he moved to attack another enemy soldier, he was mortally wounded. Because of his unconquerable courage, aggressive fighting spirit, and unfaltering devotion to duty, Lance Corporal Jimenez was awarded the Medal of Honor posthumously.

2. **Article II.** "I will never surrender of my own free will. If in command, I will never surrender my men while they still have the means to resist."

INTERPRETATION: I will never surrender as long as I can fight, nor will I surrender my men if they can fight. If they lose the means to fight, they will take all possible steps to evade capture.

EXAMPLE: During the Vietnam War, Captain Walsh, an aviator, ejected from his stricken aircraft, and parachuted to the ground. He landed in the midst of a sizeable enemy unit. He immediately drew his service revolver and fired on the opposing force, inflicting a casualty. Taking cover, he continued to engage his adversaries until he ran out of ammunition, at which time he was captured. Placed in a boat en route to a POW camp, he attempted to escape, but was unsuccessful. Once formally imprisoned Captain Walsh maintained his high degree of courage by resisting his captors' efforts to secure any information from him. By his steadfast policy of noncooperation with the enemy, he provided leadership by example for his fellow POW's. For his courage, resourcefulness, and devotion to duty he was awarded the Bronze Star Medal.

NOTE: Suppose a man surrenders while he still has the means to fight back or can remain in hiding. What can he expect to gain in captivity? During the Korean War, four out of every ten Americans who became prisoners of the communists died. Untold numbers were coldly executed shortly after laying down their arms, and these were not included in the "prisoner" statistics. The odds are in favor of the man who "sticks by his guns." Since many of the deaths in a prison camp result from lack of will, the person who surrenders to the enemy is even less likely to survive.

3. Article III. "If I am captured, I will continue to resist by all means available. I will make every effort to escape and aid others to escape. I will accept neither parole nor special favors from the enemy."

INTERPRETATION: If I am captured, I will not take any favors from the enemy, but I will resist and escape, if possible.

EXAMPLE: One prisoner who escaped against great odds was Lieutenant Charles F. Klusmann, a U.S. Navy pilot, shot down over Laos and captured by the communists in June 1964. Lieutenant Klusmann at once decided to escape, if possible. After 2 months of solitary confinement, he was moved in August to another building where some Laotians were imprisoned. Here, he and two other prisoners cautiously mapped out an escape plan.

Their moment came in late August and they succeeded in breaking out of the prison compound. Throughout the night, the three escapees traveled through rice paddies and along wooded trails. A communist patrol recaptured one of the Laotians the next day, but the other two escapees evaded the patrol in the brush. After running for 2 hours, they slowed to a walk keeping to animal trails.

A chilling rain that night added to their misery. At dawn the following day they were on their way again, heading toward friendly troops which they believed to be beyond a high mountain. Keeping a close watch for communist patrols, the two succeeded in crossing over the mountain by late afternoon. That night they risked a small fire to cook some squash they had found. Early the next morning, after finishing the remains of the squash, they resumed their march. Since their escape, Lieutenant Klusmann and his companion had been bothered by painful leech bites which caused their legs to swell. Klusmann's right leg was in such bad shape that he could not lift it without using his hand to lever it along, but by midafternoon the two reached a friendly outpost. That evening a plane was called in to fly Lieutenant Klusmann to safety, capping his escape with a final triumph.

4. **Article IV.** "If I become a prisoner of war, I will keep faith with my fellow prisoners. I will give no information nor take part in any action which might be harmful to my comrades. If I am senior, I will take command. If not, I will obey the lawful orders of those appointed over me and will back them up in every way."

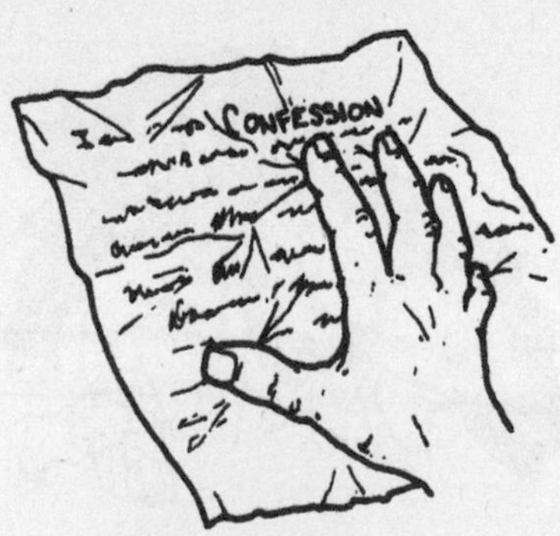

INTERPRETATION: If I am a prisoner I will help my fellow prisoners and not sell them out for favors from the enemy. If senior, I will take charge; if not, I will follow the orders of the senior prisoner, regardless of his branch of service (U.S. or allied nation).

EXAMPLE: While interned as a Prisoner of War by the Viet Cong in Vietnam from December 1964 to December 1967, Colonel (then Captain) Cook answered the call for leadership. Repeatedly assuming more than his share of manual labor in order that the other Prisoners of War could improve the states of their health, Colonel Cook willingly and unselfishly put the interests of his comrades before that of his own well-being and, eventually, his life. Giving more needy men his medicine and drug allowance while constantly nursing them, he risked infections from contagious diseases while his health deteriorated rapidly. This unselfish and exemplary conduct, coupled with his refusal to stray even the slightest from the Code of Conduct, earned him the deepest respect from not only his fellow prisoners, but his captors as well. Rather than negotiate for his own release or better treatment, he steadfastly frustrated attempts by the Viet Cong to break his unconquerable spirit, and passed the same resolve on to the men with whose wellbeing he so closely associated himself. Knowing his refusals would prevent his release prior to the end of the war, and also knowing his chances for prolonged survival would be small in the event of continued refusal, he chose nevertheless to adhere to a Code of Conduct far above that which could be expected. Colonel Cook was awarded the Medal of Honor posthumously.

5. Article V. "When questioned, should I become a prisoner of war, I am required to give name, rank, service number, and date of birth (fig 1-1). I will evade answering further questions to the utmost of my ability. I will make no oral or written statements disloyal to my country and its allies or harmful to their cause."

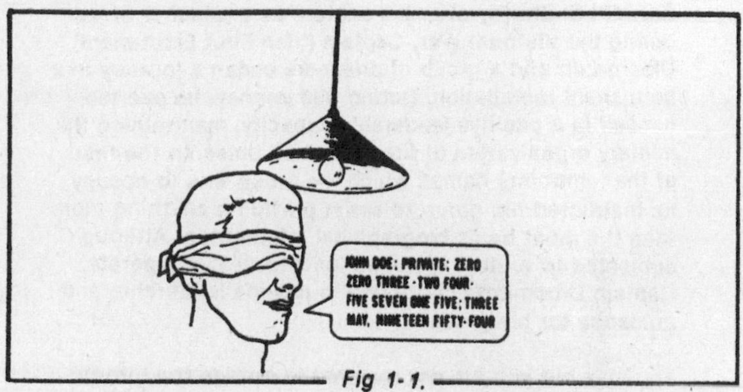

Fig 1-1.

INTERPRETATION: If a prisoner, I will give my service number (social security number), name, rank, and date of birth. I may fill out a Geneva Convention Capture Card, (fig 1-1) but I am not required to. I may also write letters home and talk with the enemy about matters of health and welfare. I will say or sign nothing that may hurt my fellow prisoners, my country, or its allies.

Fig 1-1. Contd

EXAMPLE: Shortly after his capture as a prisoner of war during the Vietnam War, Captain (then First Lieutenant) Dibernardo and a group of prisoners began a journey to a permanent installation. During this journey, he exerted himself in a positive leadership capacity, maintaining the military organization of the men at all times. In the first of the temporary camps which the group was to occupy, he instructed his group to resist providing anything more than the most basic biographical information. Although subjected to routine cruelties for refusal to cooperate, Captain Dibernardo continued to provide leadership and guidance for his group.

You may but you are **not** required to provide the information requested on this card. Be especially aware that the enemy may include unauthorized questions on the Capture Card that they offer you.

CAPTURE CARD FOR PRISONER OF WAR — FRONT

PRISONER OF WAR MAIL — POSTAGE FREE

CAPTURE CARD FOR PRISONER OF WAR

IMPORTANT
THIS CARD MUST BE COMPLETED BY EACH PRISONER IMMEDIATELY AFTER BEING TAKEN PRISONER AND EACH TIME HIS ADDRESS IS CHANGED (BY REASON OF TRANSFER TO A HOSPITAL OR TO ANOTHER CAMP).

THIS CARD IS DISTINCT FROM THE SPECIAL CARD WHICH EACH PRISONER IS ALLOWED TO SEND TO HIS RELATIVES.

CENTRAL PRISONERS OF WAR AGENCY

INTERNATIONAL COMMITTEE OF THE RED CROSS

GENEVA
SWITZERLAND

Fig 1-2. Geneva Convention Capture Card.

CAPTURE CARD REVERSE SIDE

WRITE LEGIBLY AND IN BLOCK LETTERS

1. POWER ON WHICH THE PRISONER DEPENDS__________

2. NAME 3. FIRST NAME (IN FULL) 4. FIRST NAME OF FATHER

5. DATE OF BIRTH__________ 6. PLACE OF BIRTH__________

7. RANK__________

8. SERVICE NUMBER__________

9. ADDRESS OF NEXT OF KIN__________

*10. TAKEN PRISONER ON: (OR) COMING FROM (CAMP NO., HOSPITAL, ETC)__________

*11. (A) GOOD HEALTH____ (B) NOT WOUNDED ____ (C) RECOVERED ____ (D) CONVALESCENT____ (E) SICK ____ (F) SLIGHTLY WOUNDED____ (G) SERIOUSLY WOUNDED____

12. MY PRESENT ADDRESS IS: PRISONER NO.__________ NAME OF CAMP__________

13. DATE__________ 14. SIGNATURE__________

*STRIKE OUT WHAT IS NOT APPLICABLE--DO NOT ADD ANY REMARKS--SEE EXPLANATIONS OVERLEAF.

Fig 1-2. Contd

WRITE LEGIBLY AND IN BLOCK LETTERS

1. POWER ON WHICH THE PRISONER DEPENDS U.S. GOVERNMENT

13. DATE__________ 14. SIGNATURE JOHN DOE

* STRIKE OUT WHAT IS NOT APPLICABLE - - DO NOT ADD ANY REMARKS - - SEE EXPLANATIONS OVERLEAF.

6. **Article VI.** "I will never forget that I am an American fighting man, responsible for my actions, and dedicated to the principles which made my country free. I will trust in my God and in the United States of America."

INTERPRETATION: I am a Marine fighting for my country. I will be responsible for my conduct, and I will trust in my God and my country.

EXAMPLE: In 1966 Lieutenant (JG) Dieter Dengler, a U.S. Navy pilot, added another illustrious chapter to the traditions of U.S. fighting men. While on a mission over North Vietnam near the Laotian border on 1 February, his plane was crippled by ground fire and crashed. Unable to avoid capture, Lieutenant Dengler repeatedly refused to give his captors any military information or to sign a propaganda statement condemning the United States. He was severely mistreated for refusing to comply. Months later on 29 June, Lieutenant Dengler and another prisoner, U.S. Air Force First Lieutenant Duane Martin, a helicopter pilot, escaped. The two men, barefoot and weakened by malnutrition and illness, traveled by foot and raft toward safety. Lieutenant Martin was killed by a villager, but Lieutenant Dengler managed to signal a friendly plane and was rescued by helicopter on the 22nd day of his trek to freedom.

B. POW DO'S AND DON'TS

Every American Fighting man must face the fact that he might be captured, even if he does his best to avoid it. Here are some situations to avoid should you fall into enemy hands.

1. Don't be pressured into "confessing" anything, verbally or in writing. A false confession of guilt can brand you as a "War Criminal" and cost you your POW status; this will deny you the protection of the Geneva Convention and may prevent your return to the U.S. when the war ends.

2. Don't sign petitions and other documents offered by the enemy. These could be used against you, the United States, or its allies. Even a blank sheet of paper with your signature can be filled in and used by the enemy. (This

does not apply, of course, to authorized forms notifying your family and proper authorities of your capture, address, and state of health.)

3. Don't make oral statements, publicly or privately, which could be useful to the enemy.

4. Don't allow yourself to be drawn into conversation with the enemy. One slip of the tongue could be deadly.

5. Don't pose for photographs other than an official identification photograph. Photographs can be used as "proof" of almost anything the enemy wants to prove.

6. Don't invent lies when being interrogated. It is better to reply "I don't know" than to lie.

7. Don't accept parole or favors from the enemy. You can be sure that such "favors" would place you under an obligation to the enemy.

8. Do be firm but polite in your contacts with the enemy. Yielding to the impulse to take a punch at the interrogator could bring you harsher treatment.

9. Do plan your escape under the guidance and supervision of the senior military person and the POW organization, even if this means a long wait for the right opportunity. In your escape plan, consider the welfare of the POW'S left behind.

10. Do take command if you are senior. If you can't do it openly, do it secretly.

11. Do bear in mind at all times that discipline and unity are powerful weapons in a POW camp.

12. Do retain hope. DON'T yield to despair or indulge in self-pity.

NOTE: The UCMJ applies to members of the Armed Services even in a POW situation.

Section II. Military Law/UCMJ

Objectives:

1. State the purpose and function of the military justice system.

2. Describe the rights of an accused before a court-martial and before any administrative and nonjudicial proceeding.

A. PURPOSE AND FUNCTION OF THE MILITARY JUSTICE SYSTEM

The purpose of the military justice system is to establish a means for insuring good order and discipline within the military community. The system serves the same function as criminal statutes in a civilian community. Obedience to military law is the responsibility of each Marine.

B. RIGHTS OF THE ACCUSED

An accused person has certain rights before a court-martial and also before any judicial or non-judicial proceeding in which the accused is subject to charges or in which his conduct is subject to inquiry. Nowhere in any legal system is a person given more protection of his rights than he is under the Uniform Code of Military Justice (UCMJ). The Code is of great importance to you because it explains your legal responsibilities while protecting and guaranteeing your rights. Listed below are some of the rights to which every Marine is entitled.

1. **JUDICIAL RIGHTS.**

a. **Innocent until proven guilty.** The basic principle of law, both in and out of the service, is that an accused person is considered to be innocent until proven guilty beyond a reasonable doubt. The burden to prove guilt beyond a reasonable doubt is always on the prosecution. Unless at least two-thirds of the court (or the military judge where the accused elects trial by the military judge) are convinced beyond any reasonable doubt by the prosecution in court, then the accused is acquitted (set free), even though he may not have presented any evidence in his own defense.

b. **Right to remain silent.** This is a protection against self-incrimination. In other words, you cannot be forced to say anything that might be used to help convict you. The prosecution has to prove the case against you on its own. The right to remain silent about a crime applies to investigations as well as to a court-martial. Under the UCMJ, anyone who is investigating a crime is required to advise you of this right before he can ask you any questions about the crime. If you decide to answer the questions, you are warned that your answers can be used as evidence against you in a subsequent trial.

c. **Right to be represented by a lawyer.** You have the right to consult with a lawyer before being questioned about a crime in which you are suspect and to have your lawyer present during questioning. A military lawyer will be appointed to defend you at no expense, unless you wish to hire a civilian attorney at your own expense.

d. **Protection against double jeopardy.** Every Marine is protected against former jeopardy (double jeopardy). This means that once a person has been declared innocent of wrongdoing by a court-martial, he can never be tried again by a court-martial for the same crime.

e. **Right to call witnesses.** The accused has the right to be able to compel witnesses to appear in court who can present evidence favorable to him. If the witness is a civilian, he can be issued a subpoena which is an order from the court-martial to appear. He must appear or be in violation of Federal law. If the witness is in the military, then his service will prepare orders sending him to testify.

f. **Right to sentence review.** Every Marine has the right to have a conviction and sentence reviewed by a higher authority. In the military, every case is reviewed automatically by higher authority. The sentence can never be increased, but may be decreased or left as is.

g. **Right to speedy public trial.** The accused has the right to a speedy and public trial.

h. **Right to be informed of charges.** A Marine has the right to be informed of charges preferred against him for any type court-martial. The immediate commander will inform him of the charges against him. Further, at the beginning of an investigation of charges that may result in trial by a general court-martial, the accused Marine must be informed of the offense charged against him, the name of the accuser, and the names of known witnesses against him.

i. **Right to an interpreter.** Any Marine who does not fully understand the English language has the right to have an interpreter present at any court-martial proceedings to translate all questions or statements.

j. **Protection against illegal search or seizure.** Evidence obtained through illegal search or seizure cannot be used against an accused.

k. **Right to challenge members of the court.** You may challenge for cause the right of any member of the court to sit in judgment of you. You may also challenge one member of the court peremptorily. (You do not have to state the reason for challenging this member.)

l. **Right to have enlisted representation on the court.** When tried by a general or special court-martial, and no enlisted members have been appointed to the court, you may request in writing that enlisted members be so assigned. If enlisted membership is requested, at least one-third of the court membership must be enlisted.

m. **Right to be tried by a military judge.** If you are the accused in a general or special court-martial, you may request, in writing, to be tried by a military judge alone rather than by a court-martial.

n. **Right to trial by court-martial.** You have the right to refuse Article 15 punishment (office-hours) and demand trial by court-martial instead, unless embarked upon a vessel. You also have the right to object to trial by a summary court-martial. You may then be awarded a special or general court-martial by the appropriate convening authority.

2. NON-JUDICIAL RIGHTS.

a. **Right to appear before boards.** You have the right to appear before an administrative discharge board.

b. **Right to appear before fact-finding bodies.** When you are a party before a fact-finding body, you have the right to be present during the proceedings of the body except when the investigation is cleared for deliberations. Your presence before the fact-finding body, in addition to several other rights, affords you the following specific rights of considerable importance:

- To examine and object to the introduction of physical and documentary evidence and written statements.
- To object to the testimony of witnesses and to cross-examine witnesses other than your own.
- To introduce evidence in your own behalf.
- To testify as a witness in your own behalf.
- To make a voluntary statement for the official record.

For additional training in this area, references are provided below:

1.	Judge Advocate General Manual
2. MCO P1900.16B	Marine Corps Separation and Retirement Manual

Section III. Request Mast

Objective: Define "Request Mast" and describe the procedures involved.

A. DEFINITION

Request mast is a procedure in which an individual can discuss any matter with commanding officers in the chain of command. The Marine Corps uses the chain of command to accomplish its mission and see to the morale, physical well-being, and general welfare of Marines.

B. PURPOSE

1. Request mast procedures are designed to provide timely and appropriate responses to petitions of individual Marines by commanding officers in the chain of command. These procedures are meant to create confidence in request mast as a way to solve problems. Compliance with the spirit and intent of these procedures will maintain this confidence and encourage the resolution of personal problems at the lowest possible level.

2. Marines may not be prohibited from speaking with their commanding officers at a proper time and place. Persons who try to prevent access to the commanding officer may be subject to disciplinary action. However, a commanding officer can deny request mast if disciplinary action is pending concerning the matter and the request mast would improperly affect the pending reviewing action of the officer who began the disciplinary action.

3. Every Marine also has the right to be granted request mast with commanders up to and including the immediate commanding general within the chain of command who is located at the same base or immediate geographic location. An individual may write to higher commanders including the Commandant of the Marine Corps and the Secretary of the Navy and ask for request mast, but does not have a right to personally meet with either.

C. PROCEDURES

Marine Corps chains of command are clear; however, a few commands are dispersed over a wide area, and this has caused some confusion concerning who should be the commanding general for the purpose of request mast. Also, it is not always possible for a Marine to request mast with the commanding general when the commanding general is in another geographic area. To identify the commanding general for purposes of request mast for areas where there is no general officer immediately assigned, you should refer to the current edition of MCO 1700.23, request mast.

1. REQUESTING MAST BELOW THE COMMANDING GENERAL LEVEL.

a. Requests will be submitted at the lowest echelon and forwarded via the chain of command to the commander before whom the requestor wishes to appear.

b. The requestor does not have to state the matter of concern either orally or in writing, to anyone in the chain of command except to the officer with whom the Marine wishes to request mast.

c. There should be no more than a 24 hour delay at any level, whenever possible.

d. Marines may request mast without fear of prejudice to their interest.

e. Upon completion of request mast, the requestor must make a written statement regarding his degree of satisfaction with the outcome.

f. If a request mast petition with a higher commander is resolved by a lower commander, the requestor will make a witnessed, written statement in the record indicating his satisfaction with the action taken and his willingness to withdraw his request mast to the higher commander.

g. Request mast will be conducted at the earliest reasonable time and not later than 72 hours after submission of the request, whenever possible. Emergency cases will be heard as soon as possible, usually within 24 hours from preparation of the request mast.

2. REQUESTING MAST WITH A COMMANDING GENERAL.

a. The requestor must prepare a complete written statement about the reasons for the request mast, to include a list of witnesses with a summary of the expected testimony of each.

b. If applicable, documents to support the request mast must be attached.

c. The written statement must also include a list of persons in the chain of command whom the requestor has seen at request mast and the action taken by these individuals.

For additional training in this area, the following reference is provided below:

1. MCO 1700.23A Request Mast

Section IV. Conduct in War

Objective: Explain the nine principles governing Marines' conduct as stated by the Law of War.

A. PURPOSES OF THE LAW OF WAR

The conduct of armed hostilities on land is regulated by the law of land warfare which is both written and unwritten. It is inspired by the desire to diminish the evils of war by:

- Protecting both combatants and noncombatants from unnecessary suffering;
- Safeguarding certain fundamental human rights of persons who fall into the hands of the enemy, particularly prisoners of war, the wounded, the sick, and civilians; and
- To help bring peace.

B. BACKGROUND

The Secretary of Defense has directed the Armed Forces of the United States to comply with the Law of War in the conduct of military operations and to establish programs to prevent violations of the Law of War as required by those international treaties which regulate armed conflicts.

C. BASIC PRINCIPLES OF THE LAW OF WAR

Discipline in combat is essential. Disobedience to the Law of War dishonors the nation, the Marine Corps, and the individual Marine; and, far from weakening the enemy's will to fight, it strengthens it. The following basic principles require the Marine's adherence in the accomplishment of any mission:

- Marines fight only enemy combatants.
- Marines do not harm enemies who surrender. Disarm them and turn them over to your superior.
- Marines do not kill or torture prisoners.
- Marines collect and care for the wounded, whether friend or foe.
- Marines do not attack medical personnel, facilities, or equipment.
- Marines destroy no more than the mission requires.
- Marines treat all civilians humanely.
- Marines do not steal. Marines respect private property and possessions.
- Marines should do their best to prevent violations of the Law of War. Report all violations of the Law of War to your superior.

Violations of these principles detract from the commander's ability to accomplish his mission, have an adverse impact on public opinion (both national and international), have on occasion served to prolong conflict by inciting an opponent to continue resistance, and in most cases constitute violations of the UCMJ.

These principles are consistent with the principles of war, principles of leadership, and tactical considerations. Violations of these principles disregard these basic military tenets and prejudice the good order and discipline essential to success in combat.

D. SOURCES OF THE LAW OF WAR

The Law of War is derived from two principal sources:

- Lawmaking treaties (or conventions) and
- Custom.

Under the Constitution, treaties constitute part of the "Supreme Law of the Land" and have a force equal to laws enacted by Congress. Although some of the Law of War is not incorporated in any treaty or convention to which the United States is a party, this body of unwritten or customary law is firmly established by the custom of nations. It is also part of the law of the United States and is binding upon the United States, its citizens, and persons serving in the Armed Forces of this country.

For additional training in this area, the following reference is provided below:

1. MCO 3300.2 Law of War Training in the Marine Corps

Chapter 2. Marine Corps History, Customs, and Courtesies

Section I. Marine Corps History

Objectives:

1. Explain the origin of the terms "Devil Dog" and "Leatherneck."

2. Name the World War II battle in which the famous flag raising by Marines occurred.

3. State the basic mission of the Marine Corps.

4. Give four examples where the Marine Corps mission has been accomplished.

A. DEVIL DOG

The term "Devil Dog" came into use during World War I, and is said to have originated as follows: During interrogation, a captured German soldier was asked his opinion of U.S. Marines in the bitter fighting in Belleau Wood during June, 1918. He replied that the Marines fought like **teufel hunden**, legendary wild, devil dogs that at one time roamed the forests of northern Germany.

B. LEATHERNECK

On 25 March 1804 the first official uniform order was issued by the Marine Corps and approved by the Secretary of the Navy directing Marine officers to wear "black leather stock (collars) when on duty." The wearing of these heavy leather collars is believed to be the foundation of the nickname "Leathernecks" for the U.S. Marines. While the leather stock, worn by Marines from 1775 to 1881, was intended to resemble the high stocks and collars of the early years, it was retained by the Marine Corps to make the Marine keep his head erect while in uniform.

C. FLAG RAISING ON IWO JIMA

The raising of the American flag at Mt. Suribachi became perhaps the most famous single photograph ever taken. It was immortalized in the largest bronze statue in the world—the Marine Corps War Memorial in Arlington, VA.

D. MARINE CORPS MISSION

Historically, Marine Corps preparedness has generally been characterized by the phrase, "The First to Fight." Marines are trained, organized, and equipped for offensive amphibious employment and as a "force in readiness." Officially, the mission of the Marine Corps is set forth in the National Security Act of 1947 as amended (1952). The key parts of the act are listed below.

1. To seize or defend advanced naval bases and to conduct such land operations as may be essential to the prosecution of a naval campaign.

2. To provide detachments and organizations for service in armed vessels of the Navy or for protection of naval property on naval stations and bases.

3. To develop, with the other Armed Forces, the tactics, techniques, and equipment employed by landing forces in amphibious operations.

4. To train and equip, as required, Marine forces for airborne operations.

5. To develop, with the other Armed Forces, doctrine, procedures, and equipment of interest to the Marine Corps for airborne operations which are not provided for by the Army.

6. To be able to expand from peacetime components to meet the needs of war in accordance with mobilization plans.

D. MARINE CORPS PARTICIPATION IN WARS AND CONFLICTS

Our mission and readiness has caused us, throughout our history, to take part in many wars and conflicts in the defense of freedom. Some of the more prominent examples where the Marine Corps' mission has been accomplished are listed below:

1. 1775-1940.

a. Revolutionary War
b. Naval War with France
c. War with Tripoli
d. War of 1812
e. Florida Indian War
f. Mexican War
g. Civil War
h. Spanish-American War
i. Philippine Insurrection
j. Boxer Rebellion
k. World War I
l. Banana Wars in Haiti, Dominican Republic, and Nicaragua

2. World War II.

a. Wake
b. Midway
c. Solomon Islands
(1) Guadalcanal
(2) New Georgia
(3) Bougainville
d. Gilbert Islands, Tarawa
e. Marshall Islands
(1) Roi-Namur
(2) Kwajalein
f. Marianas Islands
(1) Saipan
(2) Tinian
(3) Guam
g. Palau Islands, Pelelieu
h. Iwo Jima
i. Okinawa

3. Post World War II.

a. Korea
b. Dominican Republic
c. Republic of Vietnam
d. Seizure of the Mayaguez

For additional training in this area, the following references are provided below:

1. Marine Corps Museum Historical Pamphlets

2. Marine Corps Manual

Section II. Marine Corps Customs

Objectives:

1. Name the birthplace and birthdate of the Marine Corps.

2. Name the three elements of the Marine Corps emblem and state the meaning of each.

3. State the motto of the Marine Corps and what it means.

The Marine Corps is rich in customs and traditions. These are the things that make the Marine Corps what it is. You begin your knowledge of customs and traditions in recruit training and continue this education throughout your life as a Marine. Every Marine should know the following important facts.

A. BIRTHDAY

The birthday of the Marine Corps is 10 November 1775. The legendary birthplace of the Marine Corps was Tun Tavern (fig 2-1) a favorite meeting place in 18th century Philadelphia.

Fig 2-1. Tun Tavern.

B. EMBLEM

The emblem (fig 2-2) of the Marine Corps consists of the eagle, globe, and anchor. The globe and anchor signify worldwide service and sea traditions. The spread eagle is a symbol of the nation itself. The emblem was adopted by Brigadier General Jacob Zeilin, 7th Commandant, in 1868.

Fig 2-2. Marine Corps emblem.

C. MOTTO

The motto of the Corps is "Semper Fidelis" which is Latin for "always faithful."

Section III. Marine Corps Courtesies

Objectives:

1. Demonstrate the correct honors to be observed to officers, uncased colors, during morning and evening colors, and during the playing of the National Anthem and the Marine's Hymn.

2. Demonstrate the correct honors to be observed when embarking and debarking a naval vessel.

A. SALUTING OFFICERS

1. When meeting an officer who is either walking (fig 2-3) or riding (fig 2-4), salute between 6-30 paces to give him or her time to return your salute before you are abreast of the officer. Hold the salute until it is returned, and accompany the salute with "Good morning, sir or ma'am" or some other appropriate greeting.

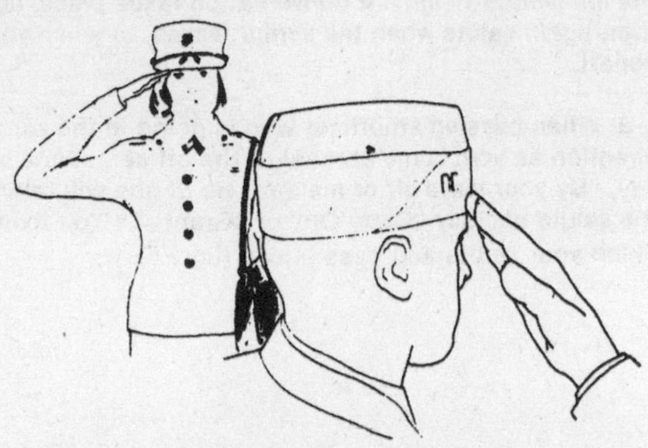

Fig 2-3. Saluting an officer at six paces.

Fig 2-4. Saluting an officer in a vehicle.

2. Render the salute but once if the senior remains in the immediate vicinity. If conversation takes place, however, again salute when the senior leaves, or when you depart.

3. When passing an officer who is going in the same direction as you, come abreast of the officer, salute and say, "By your leave sir or ma'am." He or she will return the salute and say "Carry On" or "Granted." You then finish your salute and pass ahead (fig 2-5).

Fig 2-5. Saluting when overtaking an officer.

4. When armed with a rifle, the rifle salute is executed except when on guard duty when Present Arms is rendered (fig 2-6).

Fig 2-6. Saluting when armed with a rifle.

5. Do not salute if you are engaged in work or play unless spoken to directly.

6. Members of the Naval Service are required to render a salute to officers, regular and reserve, of the Navy, Army, Air Force, Marine Corps, Coast Guard, members of the Army Nurse Corps and Navy Nurse Corps, and to foreign military and naval officers whose governments are formally recognized by the Government of the United States.

7. In general, one does not salute when: at work, indoors (except when under arms, fig 2-7), guarding prisoners, under battle conditions, or when a prisoner.

Fig 2-7. Saluting an officer when indoors and under arms.

8. Individuals not armed with a rifle and in formations do not salute, except at the command "Present Arms."

9. Upon the approach of a superior officer, individuals of a group not in formation are called to attention by the first person noticing the officer and all come smartly to attention and salute (fig 2-8).

Fig 2-8. Group not in formation saluting an officer.

B. REPORTING TO AN OFFICER

1. When ordered to report to an officer, either outdoors or indoors, if under arms, approach the officer at attention and halt about 2 paces from the officer, render the appropriate salute and say "Sir or Ma'am, reporting as ordered," using your name and grade. For example: Sir or Ma'am, Private Jones reporting as ordered." Hold the salute until it is acknowledged. When the business is completed, salute and after the salute has been returned, take one step backward, execute about face and depart at attention.

2. When reporting to an officer indoors when not under

arms, follow the same procedure except remove your headgear before approaching the officer and do not salute.

C. SALUTING WHILE STANDING GUARD AS A SENTRY

1. If you are walking a post, halt and salute by presenting arms (fig 2-9) when you carry a rifle with a parade sling. If you are otherwise armed, or if you are carrying your rifle at sling arms, give the hand salute (Fig 2-10). If you are touring a roving post, you do not halt unless spoken to, but you give the rifle salute when armed with a rifle and the hand salute when otherwise armed.

Fig 2-9. Present arms.

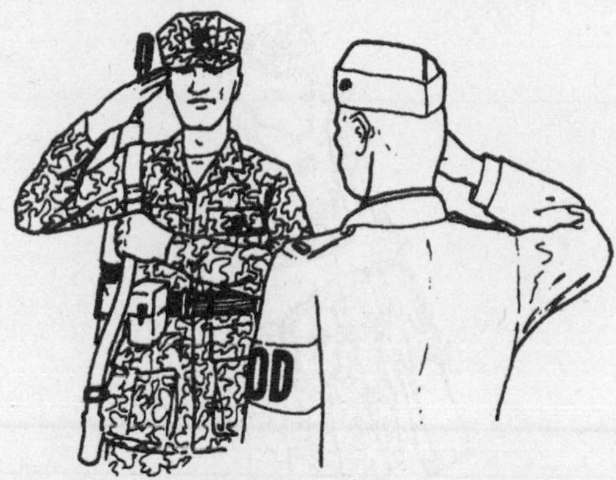

Fig 2-10. Hand Salute when rifle is at sling arms.

2. During the hours when you are required to challenge, salute an officer as soon as he is recognized. If your orders require you to come to the position of raise pistol while challenging, you will not salute (fig 2-12).

3. You salute an officer as he comes to your post. If the officer stops to hold a conversation with you, assume the position of port arms, if armed with a rifle (fig 2-11), or the position of attention (fig 2-12) throughout the conversation. You salute again when the officer leaves.

Fig 2-11. Port arms while talking to an officer.

Fig 2-12. Position of raised pistol.

4. If you are in a conversation with an officer, do not interrupt the conversation to salute another officer. In case the officer to whom you are talking salutes a senior, you also salute.

5. When the flag is raised at morning colors or lowered at evening colors, you stand at attention at the first note of the National Anthem or "To the Colors" (Standard) and render the prescribed salute. If you are engaged in some duty which would be hampered, you need not salute. You usually face the flag while saluting, but if your duty requires it, you can face in another direction. When the music sounds "Carry On" you resume regular duties.

D. RENDERING HONORS DURING COLORS AND PLAYING OF NATIONAL ANTHEM

1. Whenever the National Anthem or To the Colors is played and you are not in formation and not in a vehicle, come to attention at the first note, face the flag, and render the prescribed salute. Hold the salute until the last note of music is sounded.

2. If no flag is near, face the music and salute.

3. If in formation, salute only on the order, "Present Arms."

4. Vehicles in motion are brought to a halt. Troops riding in vehicles do not disembark. They and the driver remain seated at attention and do not salute. Drivers and passengers riding either in military or private vehicles remain seated at attention and do not salute.

5. If outdoors and uncovered, stand at attention and face the direction of the flag or music. When the National

Anthem is played indoors, officers and enlisted men will stand at attention and face the music or flag if one is present.

6. When passing or being passed by an uncased color which is being paraded, presented, or is on formal display, salute at six paces distance and hold the salute until six paces beyond it or until it has passed you by six paces (fig 2-13).

7. If uncovered, stand or march at attention when passing or being passed by an uncased color. The marks of respect shown above are also rendered to the national anthem of any friendly country when played upon official occasions.

Fig 2-13. Saluting during the National Anthem, morning and evening Colors, and saluting uncased colors.

E. RENDERING HONORS DURING THE PLAYING OF THE MARINE'S HYMN

An important part of Marine traditions is the Marine's Hymn. During the playing of this music, all Marines stand at attention whether in uniform or civilian attire. This tradition also applies to former Marines.

F. PROCEDURES FOR ENTERING VEHICLES AND BOARDING NAVAL VESSELS

1. When entering an automobile, small boat, or ship the junior goes first and the others follow in inverse order of rank. In leaving, the senior goes first and the others follow in order of rank.

2. When boarding a naval ship, upon reaching the top of the gangway (brow) face aft and salute the National Ensign (fig 2-14). After completing this salute, salute the officer of the deck who will be standing on the quarterdeck at the head of the gangway (brow) and request permission to come aboard. When leaving the ship, render the salutes in reverse order (fig 2-14). First salute the officer of the deck and request permission to go ashore. Then salute the National Ensign and leave the ship.

BOARDING—0800 to Sunset

a. First, salute the National Ensign at top of gangway brow).

Fig 2-14. Boarding and departing a naval vessel.

b. Second, turn and salute OOD and request permission to come aboard.

Fig 2-14. Contd

DEPARTING-0800 to sunset (reverse procedure)

a. First, salute OOD and request permission to go ashore.

b. Second, go to top of gangway (brow), turn aft, and salute the National Ensign.

BOARDING AND DEPARTING SUNSET TO 0800

Follow the above procedure but do not turn aft and salute the National Ensign.

Chapter 3. Close Order Drill

This text will not attempt to duplicate the NAVMC 2691, but will present highlights or key points.

Section I. The Purpose of Close Order Drill

Objective: State the purpose of close order drill.

PURPOSE. A unit leader uses drill to:

- Move a unit from one place to another in a standard, orderly manner.
- Provide simple formations from which combat formations may be readily assumed.
- Teach discipline by instilling habits of precision and automatic response to orders.
- Increase the confidence of subordinate leaders through the exercise of command, by the giving of proper commands, and by the control of drilling Marines.
- Give Marines an opportunity to handle individual weapons.

For additional training in this area, the following reference is provided:

1. NAVMC 2691 Drill and Ceremonies Manual

Section II. Drill Movements Without Arms

Objective: Individually or in formation, execute on command, all of the drill movements without arms.

A. STATIONARY

1. **ATTENTION** (fig 3-1). Come to attention at the command FALL IN or ATTENTION. Thereafter, move only as ordered until given AT EASE, REST, or FALL OUT.

2. **RESTS.** There are four positions of rest for halted Marines. All are executed from the position of attention.

a. **PARADE REST.** Left foot is moved smartly 12 inches to the left. Join hands behind your back, right hand inside left, palms to rear just below the belt, right hand loosely holding left thumb, fingers extended and joined. Do not move. Do not talk.

b. **AT EASE.** Keep right foot in place. Move, but do not talk.

c. **REST.** Move and talk, but keep your right foot in place.

d. **FALL OUT.** You may leave your position in ranks, but remain nearby. When FALL IN is given, resume your position in ranks at attention.

Fig 3-1. Attention.

Fig. 3-2. Hand salute.

3. **EYES RIGHT.** When RIGHT is given, turn your head smartly and look 45° to the right. At the command READY, FRONT, turn your head and eyes smartly to the front. When a reviewing officer troops the line, READY, FRONT will not be given after EYES, RIGHT. As the reviewing officer passes your unit, follow him with your head and eyes until you are looking directly to the front.

4. **HAND SALUTE** (fig 3-2). Execute the movement at the command HAND, SALUTE or PRESENT, ARMS. Hold it until given the command ORDER, ARMS or READY, TWO.

5. **FACINGS.** All facing movements are done from the position of attention and in the cadence of quick time. The three facing movement are:

- Right face,
- Left face,
- About face,

B. STEPS AND MARCHING

With the exception of RIGHT STEP, all steps in marching which begin from a halt, start with the left foot.

1. **QUICK TIME.** From the halt, command is FORWARD, MARCH. Step is 30 inches at 120 steps per minute.

2. **DOUBLE TIME.** Command is DOUBLE TIME, MARCH. Take 180, 36-inch steps per minute. To resume normal cadence, command is QUICK TIME, MARCH.

3. **HALT.** Command is SQUAD (or appropriate unit), HALT.

4. **MARK TIME.** Command is MARK TIME, MARCH. May be given from the halt, marching at quick time, half step, or double time in place. Ball of foot is raised approximately 2 inches from the deck at a cadence of 120 steps per minute. To resume the quick time, the command is FORWARD, MARCH.

5. **DOUBLE TIME IN PLACE.** Command is IN PLACE, DOUBLE TIME, MARCH.

6. **HALF STEP.** To march with 15-inch steps, the command is HALF-STEP, MARCH. To resume a 30-inch step, the command is FORWARD, MARCH.

7. **SIDE STEP.** The command RIGHT (LEFT) STEP, MARCH is given only at the halt. At the command, MARCH, move your right foot 12 inches to the right, then place your left foot beside your right. Continue until command is given, SQUAD, HALT.

8. **BACK STEP.** Command is BACKWARD, MARCH. Given only from the halt. Continue until command is given, SQUAD, HALT.

9. **TO FACE IN MARCHING OR MARCH BY THE FLANK.** Except for instructional purposes, the command is given only while marching. Command is BY THE RIGHT (LEFT) FLANK, MARCH. To resume marching in column another flanking movement is used.

10. **TO FACE ABOUT WHILE MARCHING.** The command is TO THE REAR, MARCH.

11. **TO CHANGE STEP.** Command is CHANGE STEP, MARCH.

12. **TO MARCH AT EASE.** Command is AT EASE, MARCH. Maintain distance and interval. Don't talk.

13. **TO MARCH AT ROUTE STEP.** Command is ROUTE STEP, MARCH. Maintain interval and distance. You may talk.

14. **TO RESUME QUICK TIME FROM AT EASE OR ROUTE STEP.** The command is SQUAD, ATTENTION.

For additional training in this area, the following reference is provided:

1. NAVMC 2691 Drill and Ceremonies Manual

Section III. Manual of Arms

Objective: Individually or in formation, execute on command, all of the drill movements with the M16 rifle.

All male Marines must be able to execute the manual of arms with the M16 rifle while stationary or on the march. Figure 3-3 illustrates the M16 rifle prepared for drill. Note the position of the sling.

Fig 3-3. M16 prepared for drill.

A. STATIONARY

1. **ORDER ARMS** (fig 3-4). Order arms is the basic position from which a Marine may execute other drill movements. All facing movements must be executed from order arms.

2. **TRAIL ARMS** (fig 3-5). The command is given when the unit is to move short distances. It is given only from order arms. To assume the position of trail arms, the command is TRAIL, ARMS.

Fig 3-4. Order arms. Fig 3-5. Trail arms.

3. PARADE REST (fig 3-6).

Fig 3-6. Parade rest.

4. **PRESENT ARMS.** Present arms is given in formation to render honors. It is also the proper salute given by an armed sentry.

a. Present arms from order arms (fig 3-7).

Fig 3-7. Order arms to present arms.

b. Present arms to order arms (fig 3-8).

Fig 3-8. Present arms to order arms.

5. **PORT ARMS.** From port arms the Marine may return to order arms or continue to right (left) shoulder arms. It is basically an intermediate movement between order arms and shoulder movements.

a. Order arms to port arms (fig 3-9).

Fig 3-9. Order arms to port arms

b. Port arms to order arms (fig 3-10).

Fig 3-10. Port arms to order arms.

c. Port arms to right shoulder arms (fig 3-11).

Fig 3-11. Port arms to right shoulder arms

d. Port arms to left shoulder arms (fig 3-12).

Fig 3-12. Port arms to left shoulder arms.

6. RETURN TO ORDER ARMS.

a. Right shoulder arms to order arms (fig 3-13).

Fig 3-13. Right shoulder arms to order arms.

b. Left shoulder arms to order arms (fig 3-14).

Fig 3-14. Left shoulder arms to order arms.

7. RIFLE SALUTES.

a. Rifle salute from right shoulder arms (fig 3-15).

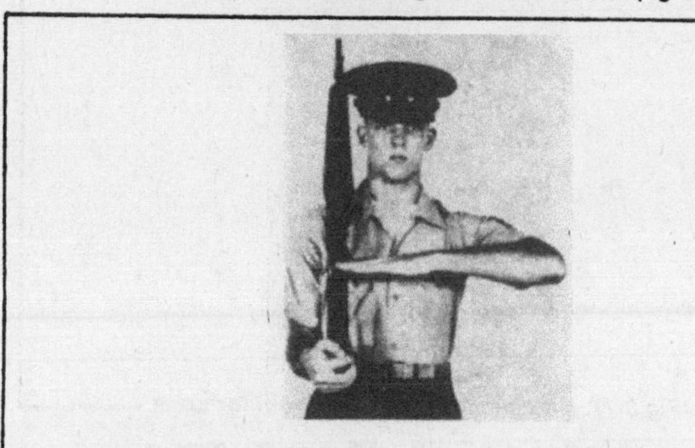

Fig 3-15. Rifle salute from right shoulder arms.

b. Rifle salute from order arms (fig 3-16).

Fig 3-16. Rifle salute from order arms.

c. **Rifle salute from left shoulder arms (fig 3-17).**

Fig 3-17. Rifle salute from left shoulder arms.

d. **Rifle salute from trail arms (fig 3-18).**

Fig 3-18. Rifle salute from trail arms.

8. **INSPECTION ARMS.**

a. Order arms to inspection arms (fig 3-19).

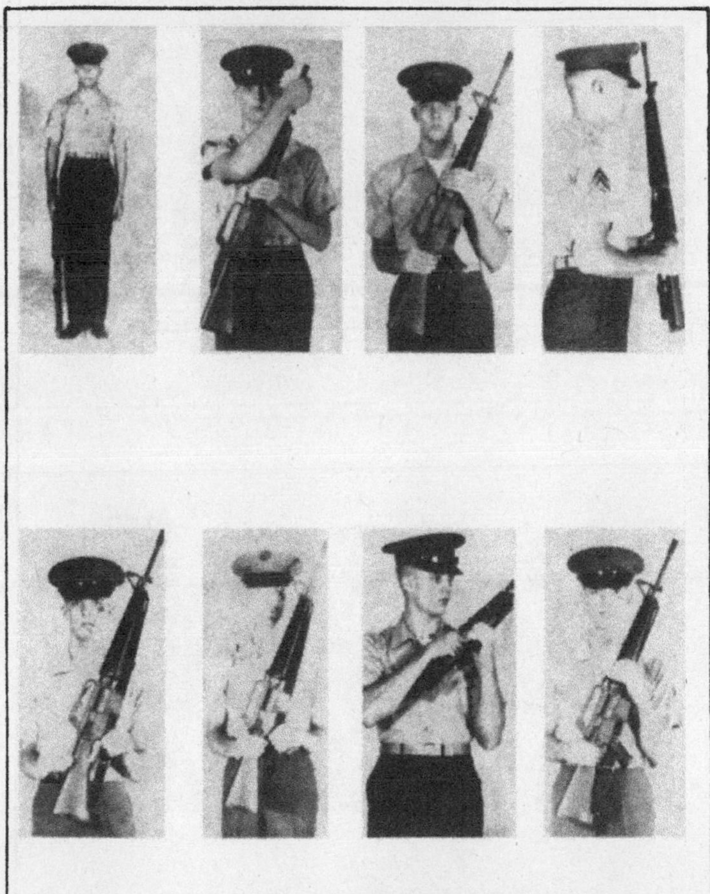

Fig 3-19. Order arms to inspection arms.

b. Inspection arms to port arms (fig 3-20).

Fig 3-20. Inspection arms to port arms.

B. MARCHING

1. The manual of arms may be executed while on the march. In each case, the command of execution will be given on the same foot as the direction of the movement of the rifle. For example, to move from right shoulder arms to port arms, the command would be given as the left foot strikes the deck. The command to move from port arms to left shoulder arms is also given on the left foot. To return to right shoulder arms or port arms from left shoulder arms, the command is given on the right foot.

2. The rifle movements shown above may be combined in a number of ways while on the march. The basic movements must be learned separately, then combined during drill in order to ensure knowledge and proficiency by your unit.

3. The normal cadence for rifle movements is quick time.

For additional training in this area, the following reference is provided:

1. NAVMC 2691 Drill and Ceremonies Manual

Section IV. Execution of Drill Movements

Objective: As a member of a squad or platoon, execute all of the drill movements relating to the squad or platoon.

A. SQUAD DRILL

1. GENERAL. The normal formation of a squad is a rank (line) or file (column) (fig 3-21). The squad marches in line for minor changes of position only.

When the squad is armed with rifles the command RIGHT SHOULDER, ARMS or SLING, ARMS is given before giving a command to move the squad. If the squad is only to be moved a short distance it may be done at trail arms which will be assumed automatically at the command MARCH. The squad will automatically come to order arms on HALT.

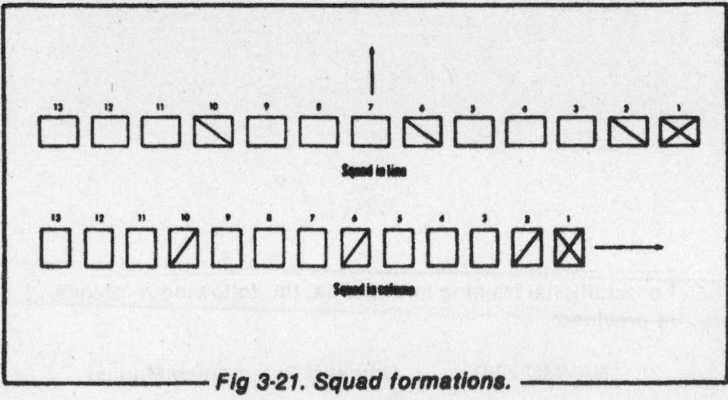

Fig 3-21. Squad formations.

NOTE: ***Symbols used in the figures showing drill movements in this chapter are taken from the Marine Corps Drill and Ceremonies Manual and are reproduced below.***

Platoon Commander

Platoon Sergeant

Platoon Guide

Squad Leader

Fire Team Leader

2. TO FORM THE SQUAD.

a. To form at normal interval (fig 3-22), the command is FALL IN. As soon as each man has obtained interval, he returns to attention.

Fig 3-22. Normal interval.

b. To form at close interval (fig 3-23) the command is AT CLOSE INTERVAL, FALL IN.

c. If the squad is armed, fall in at order arms.

Fig 3-23. Close interval.

3. TO DISMISS THE SQUAD.

a. The squad is dismissed only from a line at attention.

b. Armed troops are given the commands, INSPECTION, ARMS; PORT, ARMS; DISMISSED.

C. Unarmed troops are given the command, DISMISSED.

4. TO COUNT OFF.

a. In line the command is COUNT, OFF. All men except the right flank man turn their heads smartly to the right. The right flank man shouts ONE. The next man turns his head to the front and shouts TWO, the next THREE, and so on down the line. Cadence is quick time.

b. In column, the command is FROM FRONT TO REAR, COUNT OFF. Each man in succession, starting with the front man turns his head to the right and shouts his number as he turns his head back to the front.

5. TO ALINE THE SQUAD.

a. In line, the command is DRESS RIGHT, DRESS or AT CLOSE INTERVAL, DRESS RIGHT, DRESS. Alinement and interval are obtained as in FALL IN (figs 3-22 and 3-23). All men except the squad leader position themselves by short side steps until their right shoulder touch the fingertips of the men on their right. At close interval the right arms touch the elbows of the men on the right as in figure 3-23. The instructor or leader places himself on line with the squad one pace from the right flank man and faces down the line. He orders the men to move backward or forward as necessary.

b. When alinement is correct, the leader faces to the right in marching and moves 3 paces forward, halts, faces to the left and commands, READY, FRONT.

c. In column, the command is COVER. Men move as necessary to place themselves directly behind the man in front of them, still maintaining a 40-inch distance.

6. TO OBTAIN CLOSE INTERVAL FROM NORMAL INTERVAL IN LINE.

The command is CLOSE, MARCH. All men, except the right flank man, face to the right as in marching, march forward until a 4-inch interval has been obtained, halt, and face to the left. They then obtain proper interval as in falling in at close interval.

7. TO OBTAIN NORMAL FROM CLOSE INTERVAL IN LINE.

The command is EXTEND, MARCH. All men, except the right flank man, face to the left as in marching, march forward until approximate normal interval is obtained, halt, and face to the right. Obtain proper interval as in falling in.

8. TO OBTAIN DOUBLE-ARM INTERVAL IN LINE.

a. The command is TAKE INTERVAL TO THE LEFT, MARCH. Movement is as in extending except that both arms are raised (right flank man raises only his left arm and the left flank man raises only his right arm).

b. To return to normal interval, the command is ASSEMBLE TO THE RIGHT, MARCH.

9. TO MARCH TO THE FLANK FROM IN LINE.

a. The commands are RIGHT (LEFT) FACE; FORWARD, MARCH.

b. Under arms, the commands are RIGHT, (LEFT) FACE; RIGHT SHOULDER, ARMS; FORWARD MARCH.

10. TO MARCH TO THE OBLIQUE.

a. The command is RIGHT (LEFT) OBLIQUE, MARCH. Each man faces half right (left) in marching and steps off at a 45° angle from the original direction of march.

b. To return to the original direction, the command is FORWARD, MARCH.

c. If marching in the oblique and given HALT, each man takes one more step in oblique, faces 45° in the original direction of march, and halts.

d. For a temporary halt in the oblique direction, the command is, IN PLACE, HALT. The only command that can be given after halting in place is, RESUME, MARCH.

11. **TO MARCH TO THE FLANK.**

a. To move a column a short distance to the right or left while marching the command is, BY THE RIGHT (LEFT) FLANK, MARCH.

b. Each man takes one more step and faces to the right (left) in marching and steps out in the new direction.

c. The command will not be given at the halt.

12. **TO CHANGE THE DIRECTION OF A COLUMN.**

a. The command is COLUMN RIGHT (COLUMN LEFT, COLUMN HALF RIGHT, COLUMN HALF LEFT), MARCH. The front man faces to the right (left) in marching and steps out with his right (left) foot in the new direction. Other men in the column continue the march to the point where the front man pivoted. At that point they face successively to the right (left) in marching and continue in the new direction.

b. When halted, at the command MARCH, the front man faces to the new direction in marching and steps out with his left foot. At the same time, all other men march forward and successively face in the new direction on the same pivot point used by the front man.

c. For slight changes of direction, the command is INCLINE TO THE RIGHT (LEFT). At the command, the front man changes direction as commanded. All other men do likewise when they come to the pivot point used by the front man. This is not a precise movement. It is executed when marching around a curve in a road or to bypass an obstacle such as a parked car.

13. TO FORM COLUMN OF TWOS FROM SINGLE FILE (fig 3-24).

a. When the squad is halted in column, the command is COLUMN OF TWOS TO THE LEFT (RIGHT), MARCH

b. On MARCH, the front man stands fast. Even numbered men (counting from front to rear) face half left in marching take two steps, face half right in marching, and move forward until next to and at normal interval from the odd-numbered men who were in front of them. Odd-numbered men, except the front man, march forward and halt as they reach normal distance from the odd-numbered men in front of them. All men required to move do so at the same time.

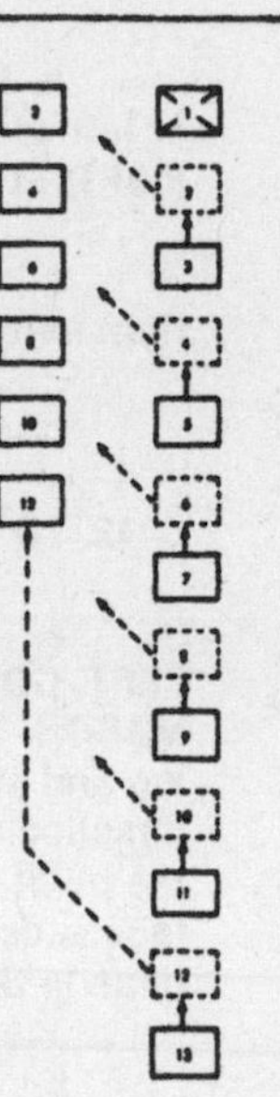

Fig 3-24. Forming column of twos from a single file.

14. TO SINGLE FILE FROM COLUMN OF TWOS (fig 3-25).

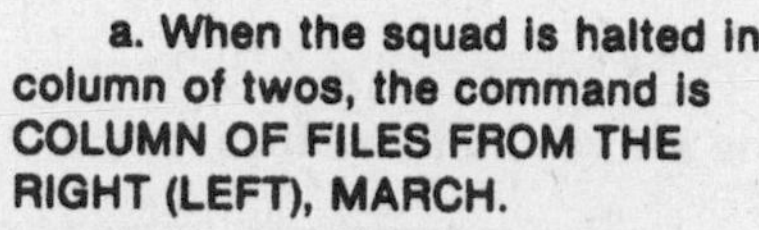

a. When the squad is halted in column of twos, the command is COLUMN OF FILES FROM THE RIGHT (LEFT), MARCH.

b. At the command MARCH, number one man and number two man step off at the same time. Number one man moves forward and the number two man faces to the half right, moves two steps and faces half left in marching, and follows the number one man at normal distance. Remaining odd and even-numbered men step off in pairs, execute the same movements as one and two, and follow in file at normal distance.

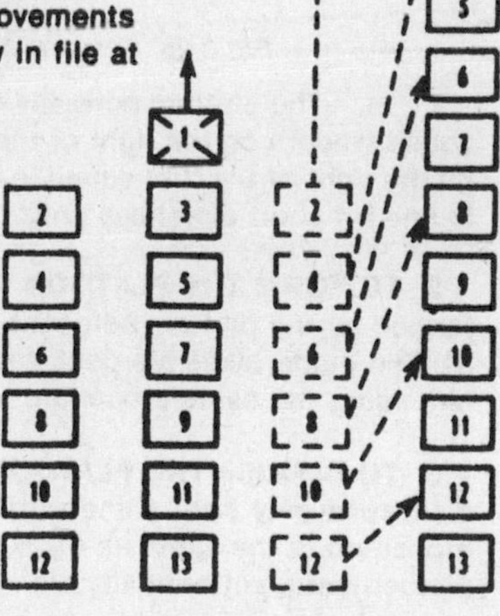

Fig 3-25. Forming single file from column of twos.

B. PLATOON DRILL

1. FORMATIONS.

a. Column and line are the two formations for a platoon (figs 3-26 and 3-27).

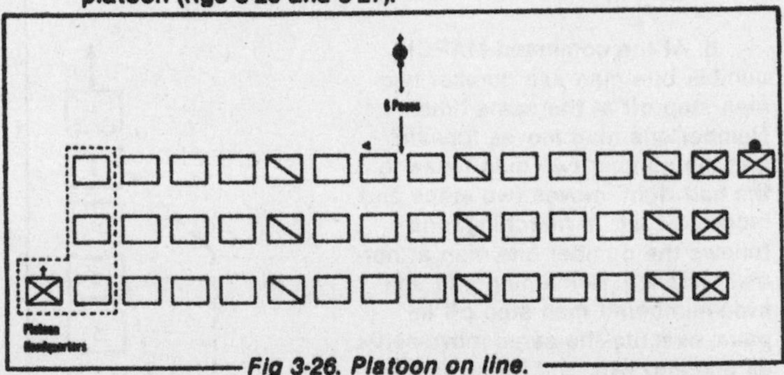

Fig 3-26. Platoon on line.

b. The platoon normally forms in line with the squad leaders on the right of their squads and the guide on the right of the first squad leader. The platoon marches in line for short distances only.

2. TO FORM THE PLATOON. The platoon is normally formed by the platoon sergeant with the command, FALL IN. The guide takes his post and the platoon alines on him using the same procedure as the squad drill.

3. TO DISMISS THE PLATOON. The platoon is dismissed only from a line with men at attention. The procedure is the same as for squad drill except that the platoon sergeant normally dismisses the platoon.

4. TO ALINE THE PLATOON. Procedure is the same as in squad drill except that the platoon commander will verify alinement of all three squads. Upon commanding READY, FRONT, he then commands, COVER.

5. TO MARCH TO THE RIGHT (LEFT). The platoon being in line, to march to the right (left), the commands are RIGHT (LEFT), FACE; FORWARD, MARCH.

6. SUPPLEMENTARY COMMANDS. When commands are given for movements in which all squads of the platoon do not move at the same time, the squad leaders give appropriate supplementary commands.

7. TO CHANGE THE DIRECTION OF A COLUMN (fig 3-28). The command is COLUMN RIGHT (COLUMN LEFT, COLUMN HALF RIGHT, COLUMN HALF LEFT), MARCH.

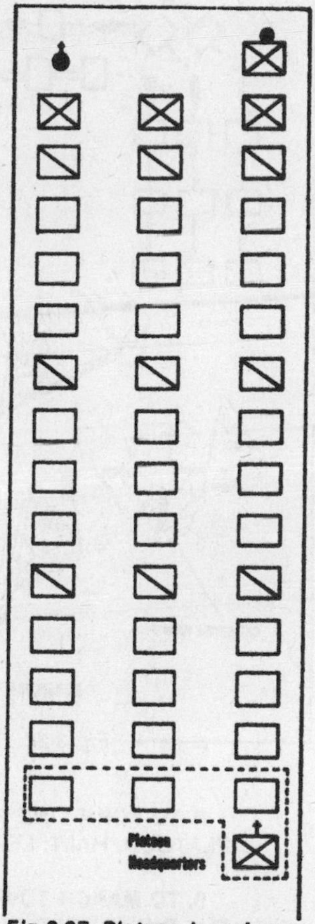

Platoon Headquarters

Fig 3-27. Platoon in column.

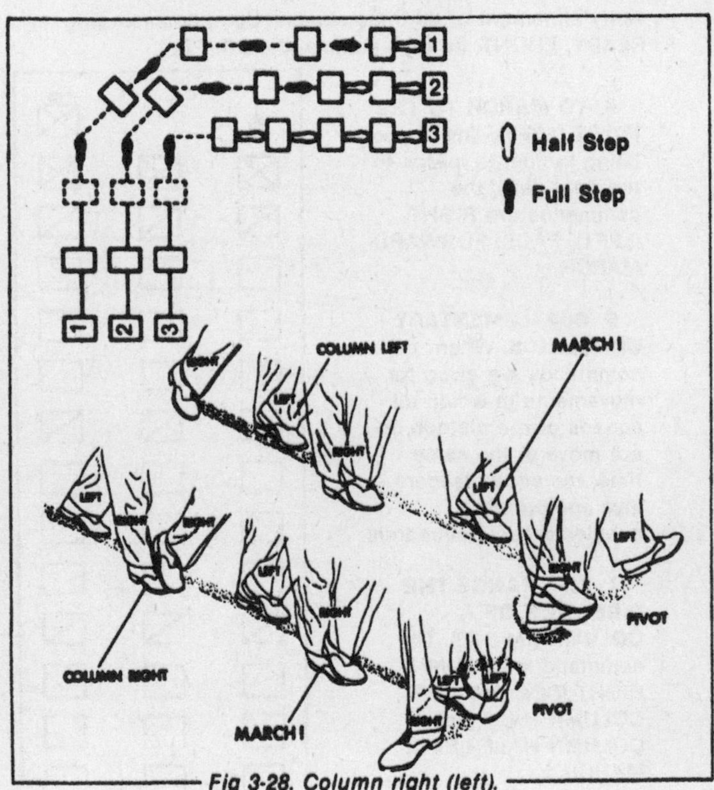

Fig 3-28. Column right (left).

8. **TO FORM LINE FORM COLUMN.** The commands are, PLATOON, HALT; LEFT, FACE.

9. **TO MARCH TOWARD A FLANK.** The command is BY THE RIGHT (LEFT) FLANK, MARCH.

10. **TO OPEN RANKS.** The commands are OPEN RANKS, MARCH; READY, FRONT. At the command MARCH, the front rank takes two paces forward, halts and executes dress right, dress. The second rank takes one pace forward, halts and executes dress right, dress. The third rank stands fast and executes dress right, dress. The platoon commander verifies alinement as for dress right, dress.

11. **TO CLOSE RANKS.** The command is CLOSE RANKS, MARCH. The front rank stands fast; the second rank takes one pace forward and halts; the third rank takes two paces forward and halts.

12. **TO FORM COLUMN OF TWOS AND SINGLE FILE AND REFORM.**

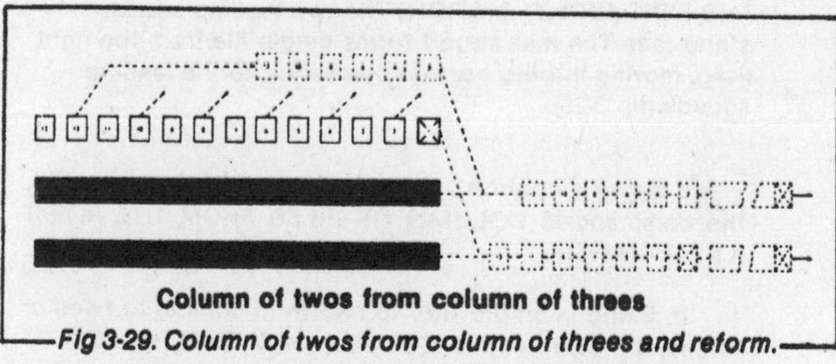

Column of twos from column of threes

Fig 3-29. Column of twos from column of threes and reform.

a. Being in a column of threes at a halt, to form a column of twos, the commands are COLUMN OF TWOS FROM THE RIGHT (LEFT), MARCH. The two right squads march forward; the left squad forms column of twos to the left and then executes column half right and column half left so as to follow the leading squads in column (fig 3-29).

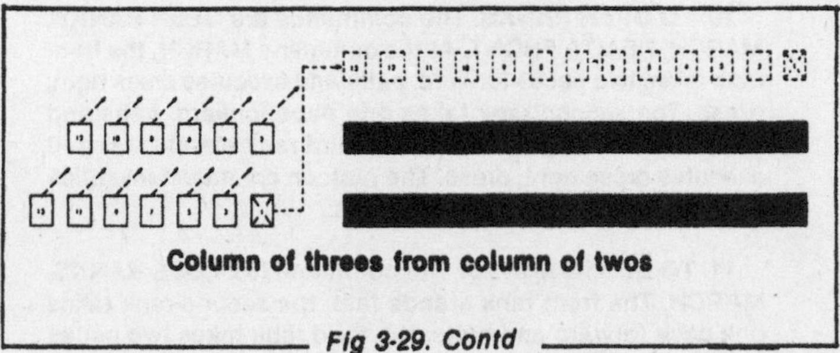

Column of threes from column of twos

Fig 3-29. Contd

b. Being in column of twos, to reform in column of threes, the commands are COLUMN OF THREES TO THE LEFT (RIGHT), MARCH. The two leading squads stand fast. The rear squad forms single file from the right (left), moving into its normal place next to the leading squads (fig 3-29).

c. Being in column of twos or threes, to form single file, the command is COLUMN OF FILES FROM THE RIGHT (LEFT), MARCH.

d. Being in single file, to reform in column of twos or threes, the command is COLUMN OF TWOS (THREES) TO THE LEFT (RIGHT), MARCH.

For additional training in this area, the following reference is provided:

1. NAVMC 2691 Drill and Ceremonies Manual

Chapter 4. Interior Guard

Section I. The Eleven General Orders

Objectives:

1. Explain the purpose of interior guard.

2. Recite the eleven General Orders and explain the meaning of each.

A MARINE ON DUTY HAS NO FRIENDS

A. PURPOSE: THE GUARD IS DETAILED BY A COMMANDER TO PRESERVE ORDER, PROTECT PROPERTY, AND ENFORCE REGULATIONS WITHIN THE JURISDICTION OF HIS COMMAND.

B. GENERAL ORDER 1

TO TAKE CHARGE OF THIS POST AND ALL GOVERNMENT PROPERTY IN VIEW.

1. TAKE CHARGE OF THIS POST—You are responsible for your post and everything that takes place on it.

2. ALL GOVERNMENT PROPERTY IN VIEW—Check your post thoroughly when posted—windows, doors, standing lights, everything. Watch for violations

and unusual activity on and off your post during your tour. Now you have "taken charge of your post!"

C. **GENERAL ORDER 2**

TO WALK MY POST IN A MILITARY MANNER, KEEPING ALWAYS ON THE ALERT AND OBSERVING EVERYTHING THAT TAKES PLACE WITHIN SIGHT OR HEARING.

1. TO WALK MY POST IN A MILITARY MANNER— Your attention to duty while a sentry on post is reflected in your general appearance, carriage, and alert attitude.

2. KEEPING ALWAYS ON THE ALERT AND OBSERVING EVERYTHING THAT TAKES PLACE WITHIN SIGHT OR HEARING— Don't let boredom get the better of you. Find ways to stay alert and DO observe everything that takes place on your post.

D. **GENERAL ORDER 3**

TO REPORT ALL VIOLATIONS OF ORDERS I AM INSTRUCTED TO ENFORCE.

1. Your actions will be guided while on post by the 11 General Orders, the special orders for your post, and any additional instruction given by officers and noncommissioned officers of the guard.

2. REPORT ALL VIOLATIONS of any of the orders that guide your actions while on post to the Corporal of the Guard.

E. GENERAL ORDER 4

TO REPEAT ALL CALLS FROM POSTS MORE DISTANT FROM THE GUARDHOUSE THAN MY OWN.

1. TO REPEAT ALL CALLS—If you hear any call, you will pass it on to the guardhouse.

2. FROM POSTS MORE DISTANT FROM THE GUARDHOUSE THAN MY OWN—You will often find that your post is equipped with a telephone. Sometimes the sentry on a post will not be able to get to his phone. You will have to use your own judgment to determine if you should use your phone or simply repeat the call.

F. GENERAL ORDER 5

TO QUIT MY POST ONLY WHEN PROPERLY RELIEVED.

1. **TO QUIT MY POST ONLY WHEN PROPERLY RELIEVED**—You may quit your post only if relieved by a member in the guard chain of command.
2. If you become sick or for some other reason need to be relieved, you must remain at your post until a proper relief arrives.

G. GENERAL ORDER 6

TO RECEIVE, OBEY, AND PASS ON TO THE SENTRY WHO RELIEVES ME ALL ORDERS FROM THE COMMANDING OFFICER, OFFICER OF THE DAY, AND OFFICERS AND NONCOMMISSIONED OFFICERS OF THE GUARD ONLY.

1. Upon being relieved, you must pass on all orders you were given prior to and during your tour on your post.
2. As a sentry, you will receive orders pertaining to the conduct of your post only from members of the guard.

H. GENERAL ORDER 7

TO TALK TO NO ONE EXCEPT IN THE LINE OF DUTY.

1. **TALK TO NO ONE EXCEPT—** you may be tempted to talk to people who are on or near your post. DON'T! Keep your mind on your duties.

2. **IN THE LINE OF DUTY—**Line of duty means government business pertaining to your job as sentry on your post. Conversations with all personnel will be short, concise, and official.

I. GENERAL ORDER 8

TO GIVE THE ALARM IN CASE OF FIRE OR DISORDER.

1. **TO GIVE THE ALARM—** This part of the order is the key to your action. Sound the proper alarm immediately by the fastest and most effective means available.

J. GENERAL ORDER 9

TO CALL THE CORPORAL OF THE GUARD IN ANY CASE NOT COVERED BY INSTRUCTIONS.

1. **TO CALL THE CORPORAL OF THE GUARD**—As a sentry on post you are to call the guardhouse for instructions or assistance when you are in doubt concerning the proper action to take.

2. **IN ANY CASE NOT COVERED BY INSTRUCTIONS**—You will usually have special orders and instructions pertaining to the conduct of your post. When an incident not covered occurs, you must call the Corporal of the Guard.

K. GENERAL ORDER 10

TO SALUTE ALL OFFICERS AND ALL COLORS AND STANDARDS NOT CASED.

1. TO SALUTE ALL OFFICERS—Which officers? All officers of the guard, U.S. armed forces, and U.S. allies are to be saluted by you while a sentry on post.

2. ALL COLORS AND STANDARDS NOT CASED—You must remain alert to the military courtesy required of a sentry. You will salute uncased colors and standards.

L. GENERAL ORDER 11

TO BE ESPECIALLY WATCHFUL AT NIGHT AND DURING THE TIME FOR CHALLENGING, TO CHALLENGE ALL PERSONS ON OR NEAR MY POST, AND TO ALLOW NO ONE TO PASS WITHOUT PROPER AUTHORITY.

1. BE ESPECIALLY WATCHFUL AT NIGHT—Be aware of the limits of your post and its problem areas and watch for intruders.

2. CHALLENGE PERSONS ON OR NEAR MY POST—Challenge and check all persons on or near your post to determine their business on your post.

3. ALLOW NO ONE TO PASS WITHOUT PROPER AUTHORITY—Detain anyone attempting to pass without authority. Allow no one to pass if you are in doubt about him.

M. GENERAL ORDER MEMORY KEY

1. TO TAKE
2. TO WALK
3. TO REPORT
4. TO REPEAT
5. TO QUIT
6. TO RECEIVE
7. TO TALK
8. TO GIVE
9. TO CALL
10. TO SALUTE
11. TO BE

For additional training in this area, the following reference is provided below:

NAVMC 2691A	U.S. Marine Corps Interior Guard Manual

Section II. Reporting a Sentry Post and the Procedure for Challenging and Reply with the Password.

Objectives:

1. When posted as a sentry, report a post properly.

2. When posted as a sentry, challenge properly to include the use of the challenge and password.

A. REPORTING A SENTRY POST

1. A sentry reports his post to a superior by saying: "Sir, Private—reports post number—all secure, sir." (or report anything that is out of the ordinary).

2. Following the above report, the sentry will add appropriate comments. Examples:

   a. "Nothing unusual has occurred during my tour."

   b. "There are several standing lights which are not working."

B. CHALLENGING ONE PERSON

ACTION OF THE MARINE SENTRY	ACTION OF THE PERSON CHALLENGED
To a person about to enter his post:	
"HALT, WHO IS (GOES) THERE?"	Person halts immediately and answers. "LT JONES, THE SUPPLY OFFICER."
Sentry will order person forward: **"ADVANCE,** LT JONES TO BE RECOGNIZED."	Person will advance without replying.

When person is close enough to identify, the sentry commands:

"HALT!" (LT JONES IS NOT RECOGNIZED.)

Person will halt on command and wait for further instructions.

Challenge—The sentry will challenge in a low voice:

The person challenged will reply with the password in a low voice:

The WATER in the river is low.

It's always low in the SUMMER.

When the sentry has identified the person, he will permit him to proceed:

"PASS, SIR!"

Person will proceed on his way when told to pass.

C. CHALLENGING A GROUP

ACTION OF THE MARINE SENTRY	ACTION OF THE GROUP CHALLENGED
To a group of persons about to enter his post:	
"HALT, WHO IS (GOES) THERE?"	Group will immediately halt, and senior will answer: **"CORPORAL OF THE GUARD WITH RELIEF."**
Sentry will order the senior (Cpl of the Guard) forward:	
"ADVANCE, CORPORAL OF THE GUARD TO BE RECOGNIZED."	Person will advance without replying.
When the Corporal of the Guard is close enough to identify, the sentry will command:	
"HALT!"	Corporal of the Guard will halt.
Upon recognizing the Corporal of the Guard, the sentry will command:	
"ADVANCE THE RELIEF TO BE RECOGNIZED."	The relief will come forward when directed to be identified by the Corporal of the Guard.

The sentry will halt, identify, and/or control the relief as the situation demands.

Relief will be effected by the Corporal of the Guard.

D. CHALLENGING TWO PEOPLE IN DIFFERENT DIRECTIONS

You are a sentry on a challenging post. It is night and you observe two people approaching from different directions. After you have challenged both, you determine that one is the sergeant of the guard and the other is the OOD. Which one do you deal with first?

"THE SENIOR IS DEALT WITH FIRST."

For additional training in this area, the following reference is provided below:

NAVMC 2691A — U.S. Marine Corps Interior Guard Manual

Section III. Use of Deadly Force

Objectives:

1. Define deadly force according to Marine Corps regulations.

2. Explain the occasions under which deadly force may be applied while posted as a sentry.

A. GENERAL

Deadly force is defined as that force which a person uses with the purpose of causing-or which he knows or should reasonably know, would create substantial risk of causing-death or serious bodily harm. Deadly force is justified under conditions of extreme necessity and only as a last resort when all lesser means have failed or cannot reasonably be employed. The firing of weapons at another person by a member of the guard is considered justified only under one or more of the circumstances listed below.

B. APPLICATION

1. **IN SELF-DEFENSE.** When deadly force reasonably appears to be necessary to protect military law enforcement or security personnel who reasonably believe themselves to be in imminent danger of death or serious bodily harm.

2. **IN DEFENSE OF PROPERTY INVOLVING NATIONAL SECURITY.** When deadly force reasonably appears necessary.

a. To prevent the threatened theft of, damage to, or espionage aimed at property or information specifically designated by the commanding officer or other competent authority as vital to the national security.

b. To prevent the actual theft, or damage to, or espionage aimed at property or information which—though not vital to the national security—is of substantial importance to the national security.

3. **IN DEFENSE OF PROPERTY NOT INVOLVING NATIONAL SECURITY, BUT INHERENTLY DANGEROUS TO OTHERS.** When deadly force reasonably appears to be necessary to prevent the actual theft or sabotage of property, such as operable weapons or ammunition, which is inherently dangerous to others; i.e., presents a substantial potential danger of death or serious bodily harm to others.

4. **TO PREVENT SERIOUS OFFENSES AGAINST PERSONS.** When deadly force reasonably appears to be necessary to prevent the commission of a serious offense involving violence and threatening death or serious bodily harm to other persons such as arson, armed robbery, aggravated assault, or rape.

5. **APPREHENSION AND ESCAPE.**

a. When deadly force reasonably appears to be necessary to apprehend or prevent the escape of a person reasonably believed to have committed an offense of the nature specified in paragraphs 2a, 2b and 3 above, or

b. When deadly force reasonably appears to be necessary to apprehend or prevent the escape of an individual whose unauthorized presence in the vicinity of property or information vital to the national security reasonably appears to present a threat of theft, damage, or espionage. Property shall be specifically designated as vital to the national security only when its loss, damage, or compromise would seriously prejudice the national security or jeopardize the fulfillment of an essential national defense mission, or

c. When deadly force has been specifically authorized by competent authority and reasonably appears to be necessary to prevent the escape of a prisoner.

6. **LAWFUL ORDER.** When the application of a deadly force has been directed by the lawful order of a superior authority.

C. ADDITIONAL INSTRUCTIONS INVOLVING FIREARMS

1. If in any of the circumstances set forth above, it becomes necessary to use a firearm, the following precautions will be observed, provided it is possible to do so consistent with the prevention of death or serious bodily harm:

a. An order to halt shall be given and a shot will not be fired unless it is reasonably apparent that the order is being disregarded.

b. Shots shall not be fired if they are likely to endanger the safety of innocent bystanders.

c. Shots shall be aimed to disable. However, if circumstances render it difficult to direct fire with sufficient precision to assure that the person will be disabled rather than killed, such circumstances will not preclude the use of a firearm provided such use is authorized by competent authority.

2. All military law enforcement and security personnel will be fully instructed in the use and safe handling of the weapons with which armed in accordance with the provisions of appropriate manuals and orders pertaining to the variety of other weapons associated with military law enforcement and security duties.

3. In view of the dangers inherent in automatic pistols, personnel so armed will not insert a loaded magazine in the weapon until the weapon has been cleared, the slide released, the trigger pulled, and the pistol placed in the holster. The pistol will not be drawn from the holster except when required in the performance of duty, i.e., when the use of the weapon is properly required, when effecting relief of military law enforcement or security personnel, or when returned to a place of storage.
Note: Warning shots shall not be fired.

D. SPECIFIC INSTRUCTIONS FOR ARMED SENTRIES

I am justified in using the weapon with which I am armed to apply deadly force only under conditions of absolute necessity and only as a last resort when all other means have failed or cannot be employed. If such is the case, I can use deadly force:

1. To protect myself, if I reasonably believe that I am in immediate danger of death or serious bodily harm.

2. To protect others, if I reasonably believe that they are in immediate danger of death or serious bodily harm.

3. To prevent acts which reasonably appear to threaten property or information designated by my commanding officer as vital to national security and to prevent the escape of someone who presents such a threat.

4. To prevent the actual theft or destruction of property designated by my commanding officer as having substantial importance to national security, when it appears reasonably necessary to do so.

5. To prevent the actual theft or destruction of property that is, of itself, dangerous to others, (e.g., explosives, weapons, ammunition, etc.), when it appears reasonably necessary to do so.

6. To affect the apprehension of someone I reasonably believe has committed a serious offense such as murder, rape, aggravated assault, armed robbery, or arson.

7. To prevent the escape of a particular prisoner when specifically authorized on an individual basis by my commanding officer.

8. On any other occasion, when directed by the lawful order of a superior in my chain of command.

For additional training in this area, the following reference is provided below:

NAVMC 2691A	U.S. Marine Corps Interior Guard Manual

Chapter 5. First Aid and Field Sanitation

Section I. First Aid

Objectives:

1. State the four lifesaving steps and explain the sequence in which they are administered.

2. Administer mouth-to-mouth resuscitation to an adult or mouth-to-nose resuscitation to a small child to restore breathing.

3. Demonstrate both the abdominal and chest thrust procedure to clear the airway of a choking victim.

> **NOTE:** *Placement of the hands must be below the rib cage to prevent injury.*

4. When provided with two pressure dressings, apply a pressure dressing to an arm or leg wound.

5. When provided with the appropriate materials, (web belt, strip of cloth, and a tent peg or a short stick), apply a tourniquet to stop a bleeding wound.

6. Describe the symptoms of shock and demonstrate the proper treatment.

7. When provided with appropriate splinting materials, (leg and arm splinting boards or rolled newspaper or rifle), apply a splint to an open or closed arm or leg fracture.

8. Explain the symptoms of heat stroke, heat exhaustion, and heat cramps and give the proper treatment and preventive measures for each condition.

9. Explain the symptoms of hypothermia, frostbite, and snow blindness and give the proper treatment and preventive measures for each condition.

10. Explain the symptoms of blisters, immersion foot, and fungal infection and give the proper treatment and preventive measures for

each condition.

11. With the assistance of another Marine and provided with the appropriate materials (blanket, utility jacket, a poncho and two poles of sufficient length), improvise a stretcher and move a casualty.

12. Move a casualty using a one-man carry.

13. With the assistance of another Marine, move a casualty using a two-man carry.

Everyone in the Marine Corps must know the principles of first aid and must be prepared to give competent assistance to persons injured in battle or accidents. It is essential that first aid techniques be practiced until all hands are prepared to act with calmness and precision despite of excitement, danger, and confusion which may be present.

A. LIFESAVING STEPS

1. GENERAL. The four lifesaving steps for victims are as follows:

RESTORE THE BREATHING
STOP THE BLEEDING
PROTECT THE WOUND
TREAT FOR SHOCK

All steps are closely related and the relative importance of each will depend on the existing situation. The person applying first aid should, in all cases, examine the injured person to determine the full extent of the injuries involved. He can then determine which of the lifesaving measures will be necessary in the treatment of a single casualty. In some cases, not all of the measures will be required.

2. ARTIFICIAL RESPIRATION

a. CLEAR THE AIRWAY.

(1) Clear the upper airway passages.

(a) Turn the casualty's head to one side.

(b) Run your fingers behind the casualty's lower teeth and over the back of his/her tongue to scrape out debris. If the casualty's tongue is blocking the airway (collapsed against the windpipe entrance), grasp it between the thumb and forefinger and extend it to its natural position by pulling it forward.

b. MOUTH-TO-MOUTH (NOSE) METHOD.

(1) Position the casualty on his back and position yourself near the casualty's head (see a, figure 5-1).

(2) Position the casualty's head face up and place a rolled blanket or similar object under the casualty's upper shoulders to extend the neck.

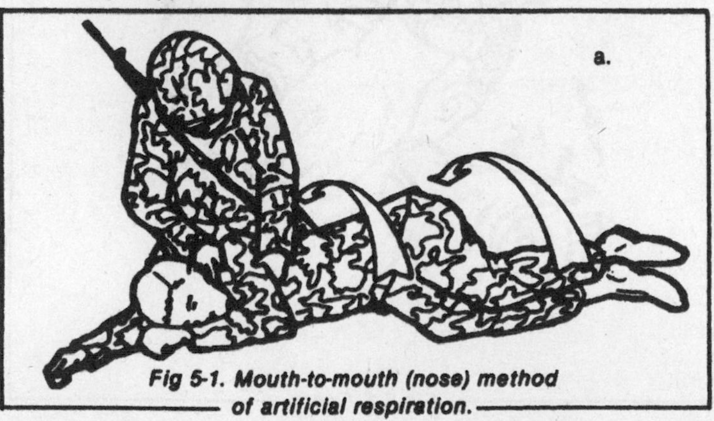

Fig 5-1. Mouth-to-mouth (nose) method of artificial respiration.

(3) Adjust the casualty's lower jaw to a jutting out position.

METHOD ONE—Using the two-hand jaw lift:

(a) Grasp the angles of the casualty's lower jaw with both hands (see b, figure 5-1)

(b) Lift it forcibly forward.

(c) Open the casualty's lips by pushing the lower lip toward the chin with the thumbs.

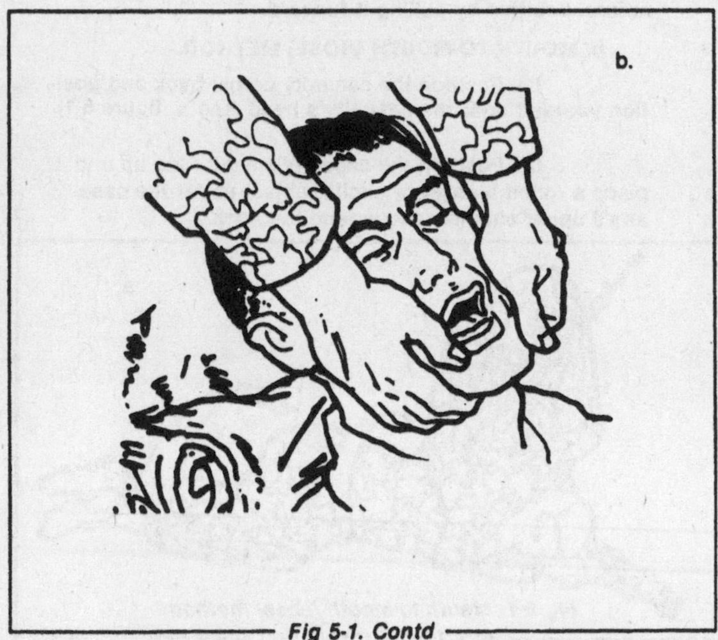

Fig 5-1. Contd

Fig 5-1. Contd

METHOD TWO—Using the thumb jaw lift:

(a) Place your thumb in the casualty's mouth by forcing it between the teeth (see c, figure 5-1).

(b) Grasp the casualty's lower jaw firmly.

(c) Lift the casualty's jaw forward.

(4) Seal the casualty's airway opening (mouth or nose) which is not to be used while inflating his lungs. If you use the mouth, pinch the nose shut or seal with your cheek while continuing to hold the jaw in a jutting out position. If you have to use the nose because of facial injuries which prevent using the mouth or you cannot get the mouth open, seal the lips by placing your fingers lengthwise across them.

(5) Take a deep breath and open your mouth wide.

(6) Place your mouth around the casualty's mouth (nose) and press down hard to make an airtight seal (see a, fig 5-2). For small children ensure both nose and mouth are covered making an airtight seal (see b, fig 5-2).

(7) Focus your eyes on the casualty's chest and blow forcefully into the casualty's mouth (nose). A rise in the chest will be observed if air is reaching the lungs. For a small child **DO NOT** blow forcefully.

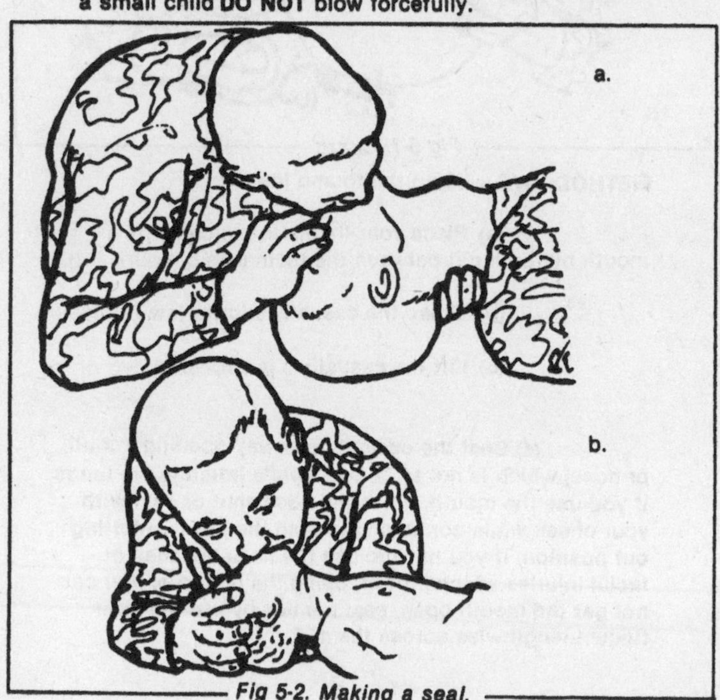

Fig 5-2. Making a seal.

(8) Remove your mouth, allowing the casualty to exhale. Listen for the return of air from the casualty's lungs (see c, fig 5-2). If the casualty's exhalation is noisy, widen the airway and continue to administer mouth-to-mouth (nose) resuscitation by carrying out the following steps:

Fig 5-2. Continued.

(9) Elevate the casualty's jaw more to widen the airway.

(10) Replace your mouth and again blow forcefully. For small children you should blow gently.

(11) Remove your mouth, allowing the casualty to exhale. Repeat the actions described in steps 7 and 8 at the rate of 12-20 cycles per minute until the casualty is able to breathe unassisted or until medical assistance arrives and you are relieved.

NOTE: If the casualty's stomach begins to bulge indicating that some air has entered the stomach, expel the air by gently pushing on his stomach.

c. **CHEST PRESSURE-ARMLIFT METHOD.**

It is not always possible to use the mouth-to-mouth or mouth-to-nose methods. For example, a casualty may have severe facial injuries. If you must use an alternate method the chest pressure-armlift method is preferred. This method is not recommended unless the mouth-to-mouth or mouth-to-nose method cannot be performed for some reason. This step also includes restoring breathing. This first procedure discussed may also be used in an NBC environment.

(1) Clear the casualty's upper airway. Clearing the airway is done by grasping the casualty's tongue and lower jaw between your thumb and fingers and pulling up. Insert the index finger of your other hand into the casualty's mouth along the inside of one cheek, deep into the throat to the base of the tongue. Using a hooking motion across the other cheek, loosen and remove the obstructing material.

(2) Position the casualty on his back.

(3) Position the casualty's head, vertically.

(4) Position yourself: Stand at the casualty's head and face his feet; then kneel on one knee and place your opposite foot to the other side of his head and against his shoulder to steady it. If you become uncomfortable after a period of time, quickly switch to the other knee.

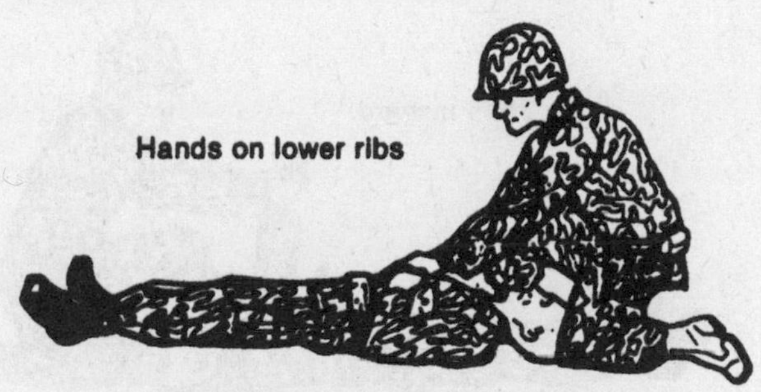

(5) Administer artificial respiration:

(a) Grasping the casualty's hands and holding them over his lower ribs, rock forward and exert steady, uniform pressure almost directly downward until you meet firm resistance. This pressure forces air out of the lungs.

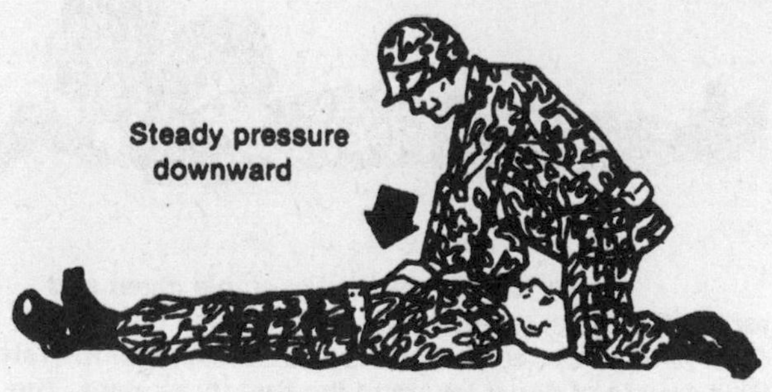

(b) Lift his arms vertically upward above his head; then stretch them backward as far as possible. This process of lifting and stretching the arms increases the size of the chest and draws air into the lungs.

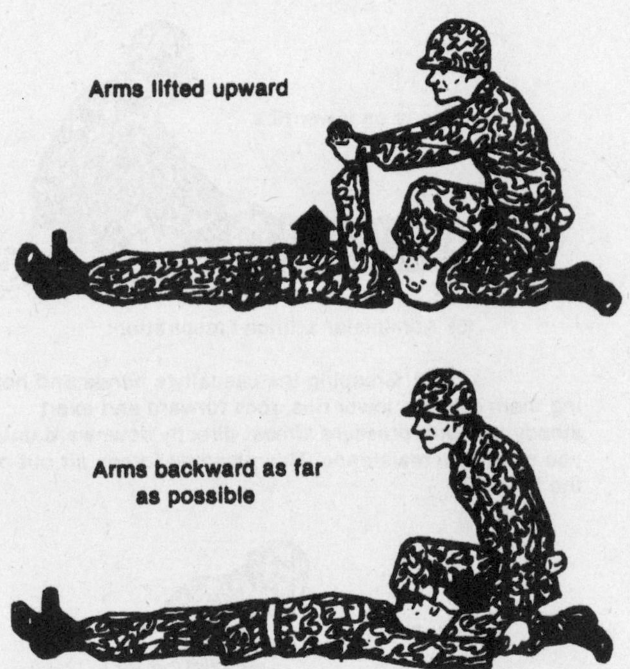

(c) Replace his hands on his chest and repeat the cycle: (1) Press (2) Lift (3) Stretch (4) Replace. Give 10 to 12 cycles per minute at a steady, uniform rate. Give counts of equal length to the first three steps. The fourth or "replace" step should be performed as quickly as possible.

(d) Continue artificial respiration until the casualty can breathe satisfactorily for himself or until you are positive life is gone. As the casualty attempts to breathe, adjust the timing of your efforts to assist him.

(e) When you become tired, have another Marine take your place without interrupting the rhythm of the cycle. Position your replacement next to you so he can grab the victim's hands and continue with the chest pressure-armlift method as you move out of the way.

NOTE: If this procedure must be done in an NBC environment and the casualty is already wearing a protective mask, lift the mask only enough to perform the clearing of the airway and return the protective mask to its proper position. If the casualty is not masked, check the airway and mask him.

3. CHOKING

a. **ABDOMINAL/CHEST THRUST METHOD.** This procedure may be administered to either conscious or unconscious victims.

(1) **PROCEDURE FOR ADMINISTERING ABDOMINAL THRUSTS TO A CONSCIOUS, CHOKING VICTIM.** Abdominal thrusts are in given in the middle of the abdomen, between the waist and the bottom edge of the rib cage (fig 5-3).

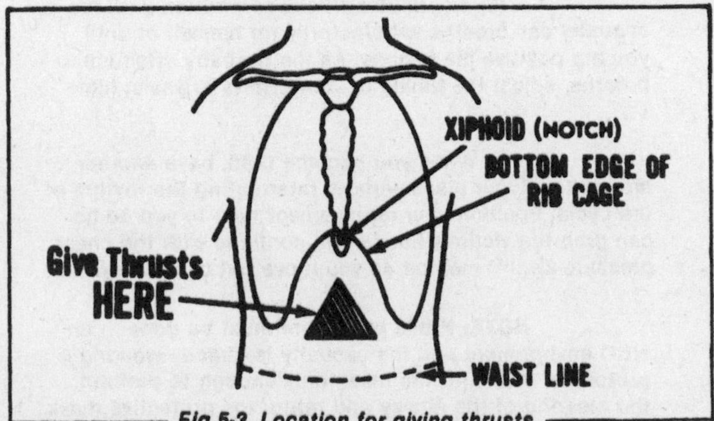

Fig 5-3. Location for giving thrusts.

STEP 1: Put the thumb side of your fist (fig 5-4) against midline of the abdomen between the rib cage and the waist (fig 5-5). Your thumbnail should be over the second joint of the forefinger as shown.

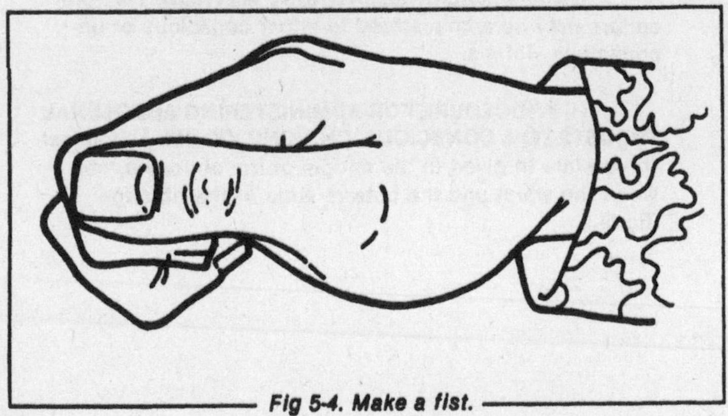

Fig 5-4. Make a fist.

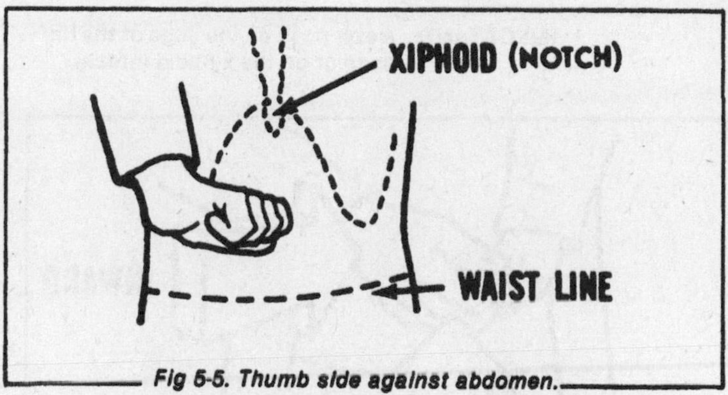

Fig 5-5. Thumb side against abdomen.

STEP 2: Reaching around from behind the victim, grasp your fist with your other hand and press it into the victim's abdomen (fig 5-6).

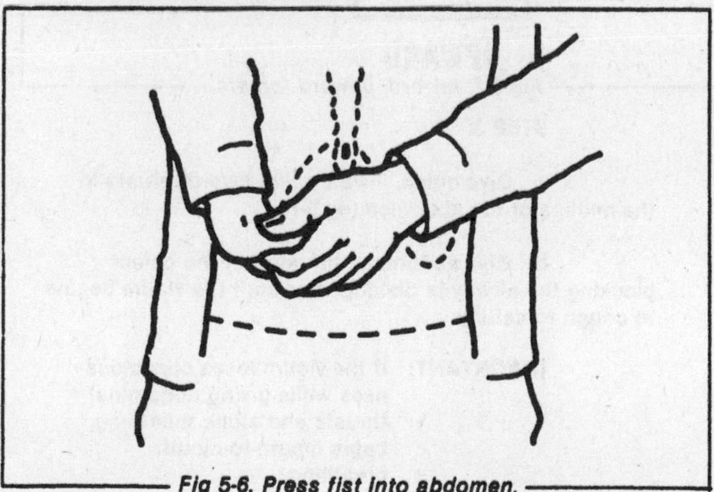

Fig 5-6. Press fist into abdomen.

IMPORTANT: Never push on the edge of the rib cage or on the xiphoid (notch).

Fig 5-7. Inward, upward thrusts.

STEP 3:

a. Give quick, inward and upward thrusts in the midline of the abdomen (fig 5-7).

b. Give abdominal thrust until the object blocking the airway is dislodged or until the victim begins to cough forcefully.

IMPORTANT: If the victim loses consciousness while giving abdominal thrusts and stops breathing, begin mouth-to-mouth breathing.

(2) **PROCEDURE FOR ADMINISTERING CHEST THRUST TO A CONSCIOUS, CHOKING VICTIM.**

STEP 1: Reach around the victim's chest from behind, with your arms directly under the victims armpits.

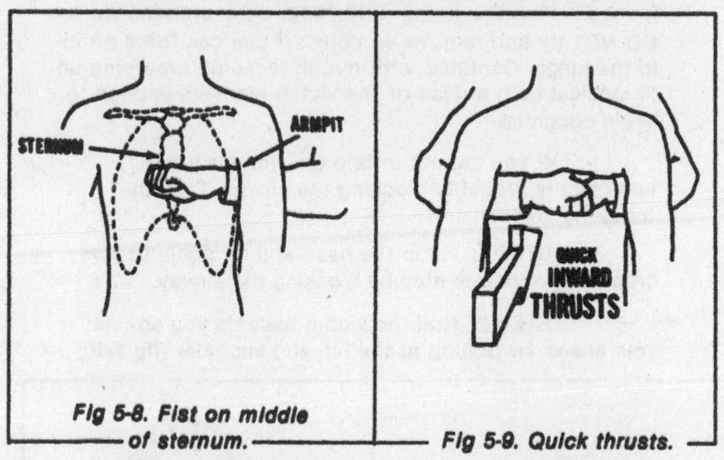

Fig 5-8. Fist on middle of sternum.

Fig 5-9. Quick thrusts.

STEP 2: Place the thumb side of your fist on the middle of the sternum at about the level of the armpit (fig 5-8).

STEP 3: Grasp your fist with your other hand, and pull straight back with quick thrusts (fig 5-9).

IMPORTANT: If the victim is pregnant, give chest thrusts, not abdominal thrusts. If the victim loses consciousness while giving chest thrusts and stops breathing, begin mouth-to-mouth breathing.

(3) **PROCEDURES FOR ADMINISTERING ABDOMINAL THRUSTS TO AN UNCONSCIOUS CHOKING VICTIM.** Lay the victim on a hard surface, tip the head and check for breathing. If the victim is not breathing normally, try to restore breathing. If the airway is partly blocked, but you can force air into the lungs with long, slow breaths, do so. **DO NOT** try and remove an object if you can force air into the lungs. Continue with mouth-to-mouth breathing until medical help arrives or the victim recovers enough to begin coughing.

If you cannot inflate the victim's lungs, an object is probably blocking the airway. Take the following steps:

STEP 1: Retip the head and try again to give breaths, the tongue may be blocking the airway.

STEP 2: Roll the victim towards you against your knees, by pulling at the hip and shoulder (fig 5-10)

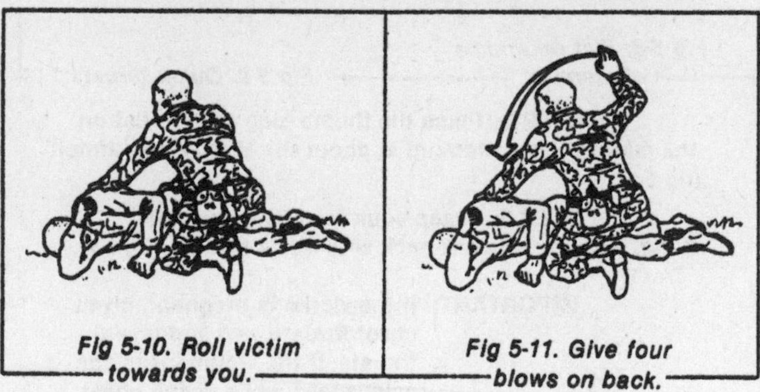

Fig 5-10. Roll victim towards you.

Fig 5-11. Give four blows on back.

STEP 3: Hit the victim with the heel of your hand, 4 times, over the spine, between the shoulder blades (fig 5-11).

NOTE: Give the blows as rapidly as possible, hitting hard enough to dislodge the airway obstruction. If the obstruction is dislodged, roll the victim onto his back and attempt to administer mouth-to-mouth resuscitation.

STEP 4: If the back blows do not dislodge the obstruction, roll the victim onto his back and place the heel of one hand on the victim's abdomen, between the rib cage and waist (fig 5-12).

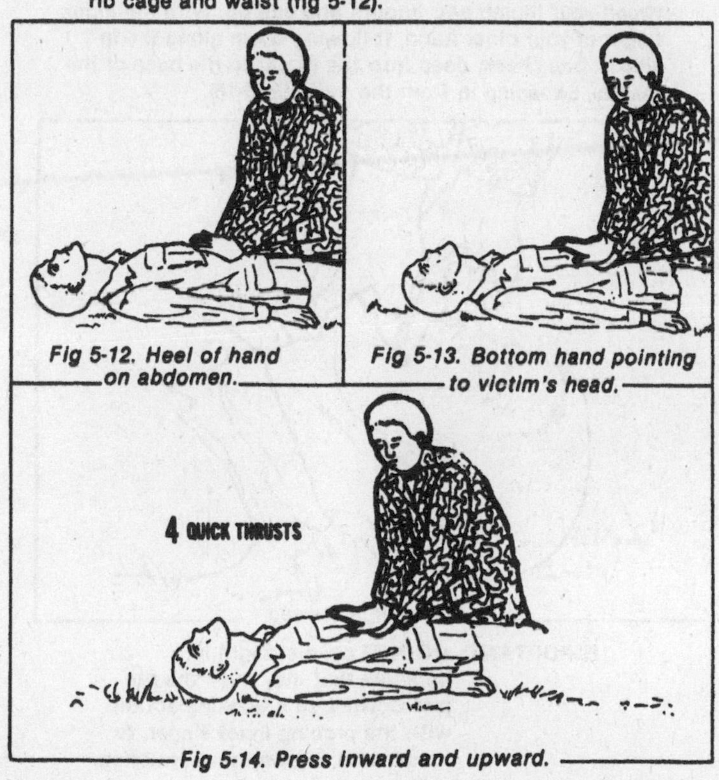

Fig 5-12. Heel of hand on abdomen.

Fig 5-13. Bottom hand pointing to victim's head.

Fig 5-14. Press inward and upward.

STEP 5: Put your other hand on top of the first with the fingers of the bottom hand pointing toward the victim's head (fig 5-13).

STEP 6: With your shoulders directly over the victim's abdomen, press inward and upward with four quick thrusts (fig 5-14).

STEP 7: Grasp the tongue and lower jaw between your thumb and fingers and pull up. With the index finger of your other hand, following down along the inside of one cheek, deep into the throat to the base of the tongue, sweeping in from the side (fig 5-15).

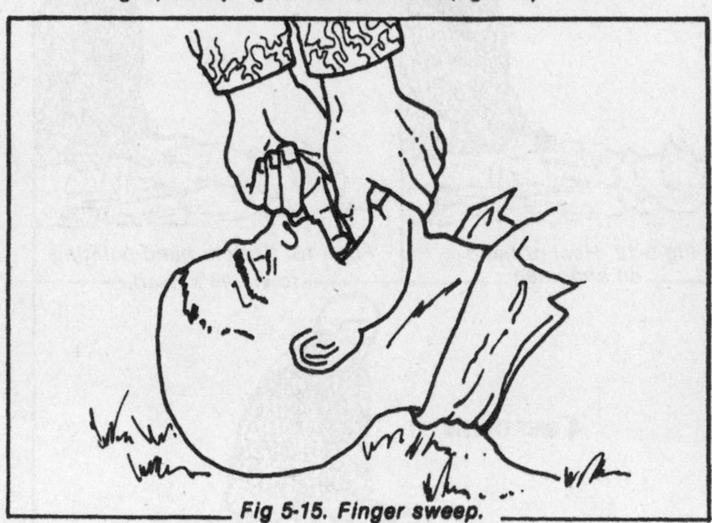

Fig 5-15. Finger sweep.

IMPORTANT: DO NOT poke straight in, because that may push the object down. Use a hooking action with the probing index finger, to loosen and remove the obstruction.

STEP 8: Attempt again to restore breathing by using mouth-to-mouth resuscitation. If the victim's lungs fail to inflate, repeat steps 2 through 7 until breathing is restored or medical authorities arrive.

4. STOP THE BLEEDING/PROTECT THE WOUND.

a. GENERAL. Uncontrolled bleeding causes shock and, finally, death. The use of a pressure dressing is the best method for the control of bleeding in an emergency situation. The application of a tourniquet is another method to control bleeding, but it should not be used unless the pressure dressing fails to stop the bleeding.

b. APPLICATION OF A PRESSURE DRESSING (fig 5-16). The application of a sterile dressing with pressure to a bleeding wound helps clot formation, compresses the open blood vessels, and protects the wound from further invasion of germs.

STEP 1:
Look for more than one wound.

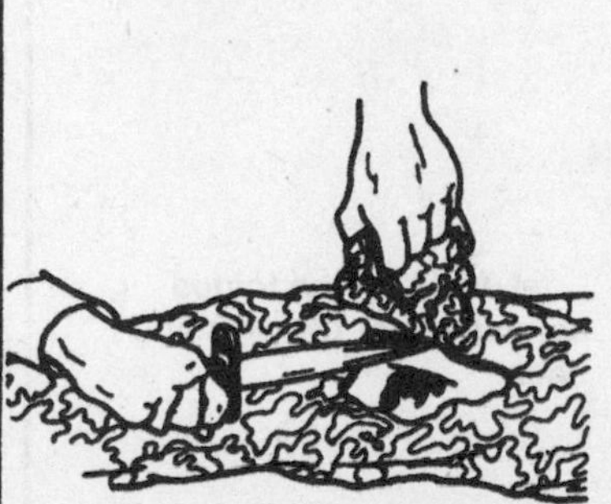

STEP 2:
Cut the clothing around the wound and lift it away from the wound.

NOTE: **DO NOT** touch the wound or attempt to clean it.

Fig 5-16. Application of a pressure dressing.

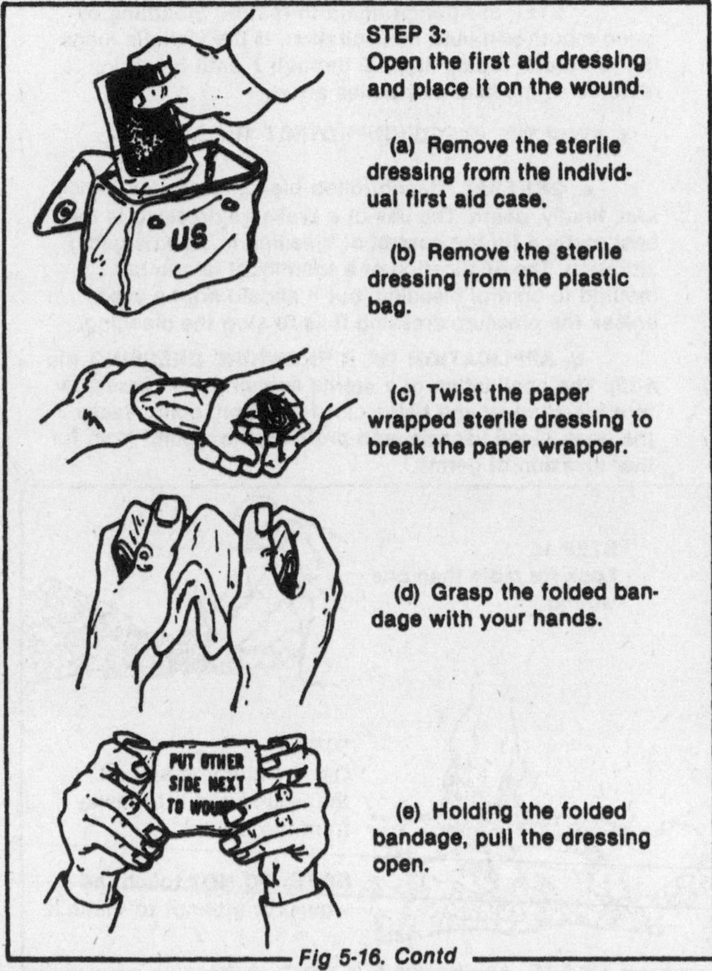

STEP 3:
Open the first aid dressing and place it on the wound.

(a) Remove the sterile dressing from the individual first aid case.

(b) Remove the sterile dressing from the plastic bag.

(c) Twist the paper wrapped sterile dressing to break the paper wrapper.

(d) Grasp the folded bandage with your hands.

(e) Holding the folded bandage, pull the dressing open.

Fig 5-16. Contd

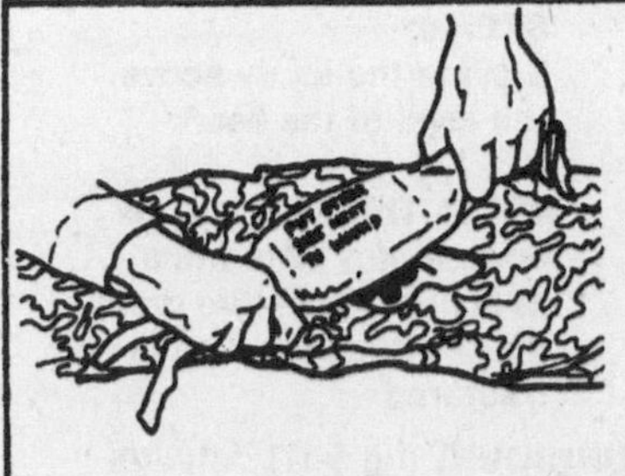

(f) Place dressing on wound without allowing it to touch anything else.

STEP 4:
Wrap the bandage tails tightly around the limb and over the dressing. Apply firm pressure to stop the bleeding, and tie the ends of the bandage securely.

NOTE: The knots should be on top of the dressing, if possible.

Fig 5-16. Contd

If additional pressure is required to stop the bleeding, apply another pressure dressing on top of the first dressing.

STEP 5:
Open a second first aid dressing and place it on top of the first dressing.

STEP 6:
Wrap the bandage tails tightly around the limb and over the dressing, apply more pressure to the second dressing, and tie the ends of the bandage securely.

STEP 7:
If additional pressure is required, place your hand over the dressing and apply pressure.

STEP 8:
Elevate the injury above the level of the heart.

NOTE: This step may be done at any time while applying a pressure dressing provided the limb is not fractured.

c. **APPLICATION OF TOURNIQUET** (fig 5-17). A tourniquet is a constricting band placed around a limb to stop severe bleeding. If the first aid dressing under hard hand pressure becomes soaked with blood and wound continues to bleed, you should apply a tourniquet.

(1) Place the tourniquet around the limb and between the wound and the heart. Never place it directly over a wound or fracture.

(a) For amputation or partial amputation of the foot, leg, hand or arm and for bleeding from the upper arm or thigh, place the tourniquet just above the wound or amputation.

(b) For bleeding from the hand or forearm with no associated amputation, place the tourniquet 2 to 4 inches above the wound.

(c) For bleeding from the foot or lower leg with no associated amputation, place the tourniquet 2 to 4 inches above the wound.

(2) When possible, place the tourniquet over the smoothed sleeve or trouser leg to prevent skin from being pinched or twisted.

(3) Once a tourniquet has been applied, inspect it and the dressing frequently to see if the tourniquet has slipped and if any sign of further bleeding is present. If necessary, tighten the tourniquet but under no circumstances loosen it. It should only be loosened by medical personnel.

NOTE: Tourniquets are applied as a last resort to stop bleeding.

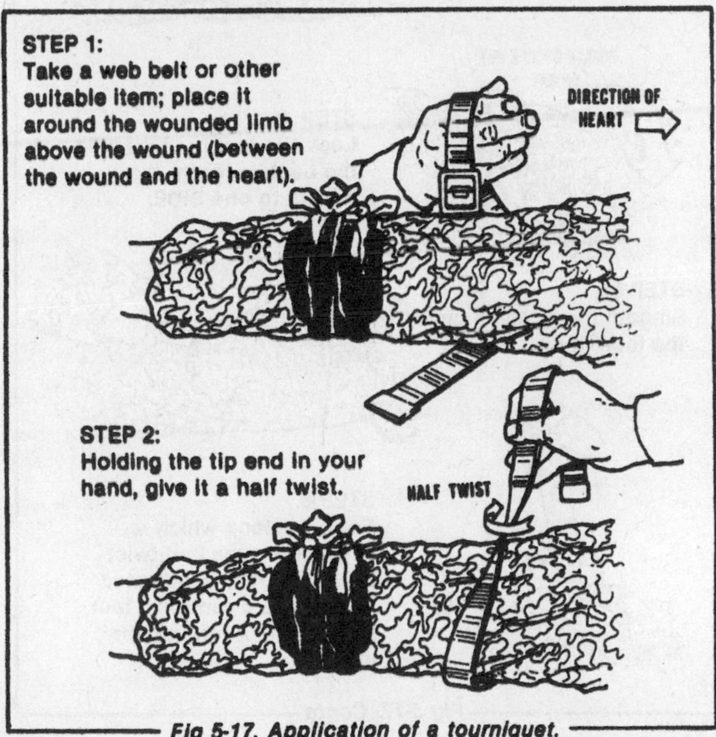

Fig 5-17. Application of a tourniquet.

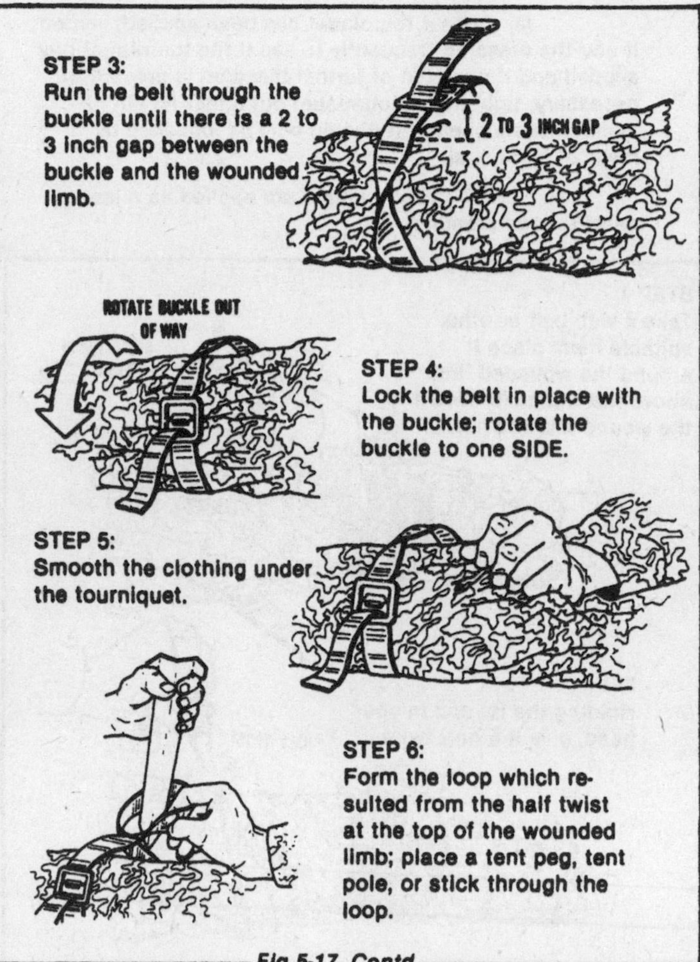

Fig 5-17. Contd

STEP 7:
Tighten the tourniquet by twisting the stick in one direction until the blood flow from the wound is decreased.

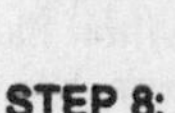

STEP 8:
Secure the tourniquet in place by wrapping the free (tip) end of the belt around the free end of the stick and under itself.

NOTE: Tourniquets must be inspected frequently to ensure that they have not loosened.

Tourniquets are to be loosened by medical personnel only.

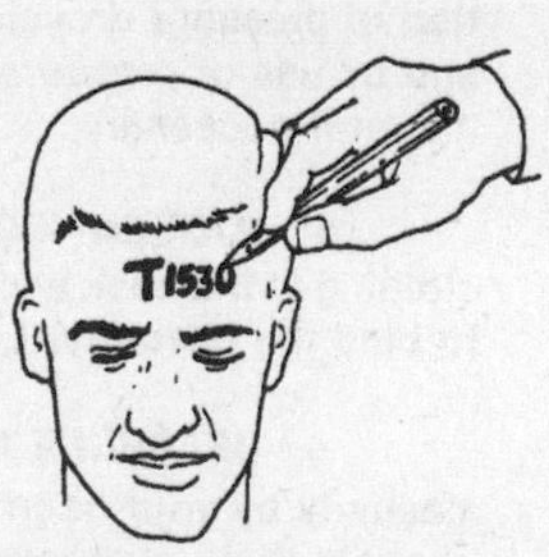

STEP 9:
Mark the casualty:

a. Leave the tourniquet uncovered and mark a "T" on the casualty's forehead.
b. Indicate the time and date the tourniquet was applied.

Fig 5-17. Contd

5. TREAT FOR SHOCK.

a. **GENERAL.** Shock may result from any type of injury. The more severe the injury, the more likely shock will develop. The early signs of shock are restlessness, thirst, paleness of the skin, and a rapid heartbeat. A casualty in shock may be excited or he may be calm and appear very tired. He may be sweating even though his skin feels cool and clammy. As shock becomes worse, the casualty breathes in small, fast breaths or gasps even when his airway is clear. He may stare vacantly into space. His skin may have a blotchy or bluish appearance, especially around the lips.

b. **MAINTAIN ADEQUATE RESPIRATION.** To maintain adequate respiration, you may need to do nothing more than clear the casualty's upper airway, position him to ensure adequate drainage of any fluid obstructing his airway, and observe him to ensure that his airway remains unobstructed. If you need to administer artificial respiration, follow instructions in paragraph 2.

c. **CONTROL BLEEDING.** Control bleeding by application of pressure dressing, by elevation of specific limbs, and by use of pressure points as appropriate. Apply tourniquet if necessary.

d. **LOOSEN CONSTRICTIVE CLOTHING.** Loosen clothing at the neck and waist and at other areas which tend to bind the casualty. Loosen, but do not remove shoes.

e. **REASSURE THE CASUALTY.** Take charge. Show the casualty by your calm self-confidence and gentle yet firm manner that you know what you are doing. Initiate conversation and reassure him. Avoid talking to the casualty about his injuries.

Remember, ill-timed or erroneous information can increase the casualty's anxiety.

f. **SPLINT FRACTURES.** If the casualty has a fracture, apply a splint.

g. **POSITION THE CASUALTY.** The position in which the casualty should be placed varies, depending upon the type of wound or injury and whether the casualty is conscious or unconscious. Unless the casualty has an injury for which a special position is prescribed, gently place him on a blanket or another suitable protective item in one of the following positions:

> If the casualty is conscious, place him on his back on a level surface with his lower extremities elevated 6 to 8 inches to increase the flow of blood to his heart. This may be accomplished by placing his pack or another suitable object under his feet. Remember, however, do not move a casualty who has a fracture until it has been properly splinted.
>
> If the casualty is unconscious, place him on his side or on his abdomen with his head turned to one side to prevent his choking on vomitus, blood, or other fluid.

h. **KEEP THE CASUALTY COMFORTABLY WARM WITHOUT OVERHEATING.** If possible, place a blanket, a poncho, a shelter half, or other suitable material under him. He may not need a blanket over him, depending upon the weather. Weather will dictate whether the victim should be covered.

B. SPLINTING FRACTURES

1. **IMMOBILIZATION.** A body part that contains a fracture must be immobilized to prevent the razor-sharp edges of the bone from moving and cutting tissue, muscles, blood vessels and nerves. Immobilization is accomplished by splinting. (See figures 5-18 through 5-24 for examples.)

2. **RULES FOR SPLINTING.** If the fracture is an open one, first stop the bleeding, apply a dressing, and bandage as you would for any other wound.

a. Apply the proven principle, "Splint them where they lie." This means to splint the fractured part before any movement of the casualty is attempted and without any change in the position of the fractured part. If a bone is in an unnatural position or a joint is bent, do not try to straighten it. If a joint is not bent, do not try to bend it. After a fractured part has been splinted, place the casualty on a litter before transporting him. If circumstances make it necessary to move a casualty with a fractured leg before a splint can be applied, use the uninjured leg as a splint. Tie the fractured leg to the leg which serves as a splint. Then grasp the casualty beneath his armpits and pull him in a straight line, ensuring that the victim does not roll or move sideways.

b. Apply splints so that the joint above the fracture and joint below the fracture are immobilized. Place a splint on each side of the wound.

c. Use padding between the injured part and the splint to prevent undue pressure and further injury to tissue, blood vessels, and nerves. This is especially important at the crotch, in the armpit, and on places where the splints come in contact with bony parts such as the elbow, wrist, knee and ankle joint.

d. Bind splints securely with bandages at several points above and below the fracture but do not bind tightly enough to interfere with the flow of blood. Tie bandages with a square knot and put the knot on the outer splint.

e. Support a splinted arm which is bent at the elbow with a sling. A sling is also used to support a sprained arm or an arm with a painful wound.

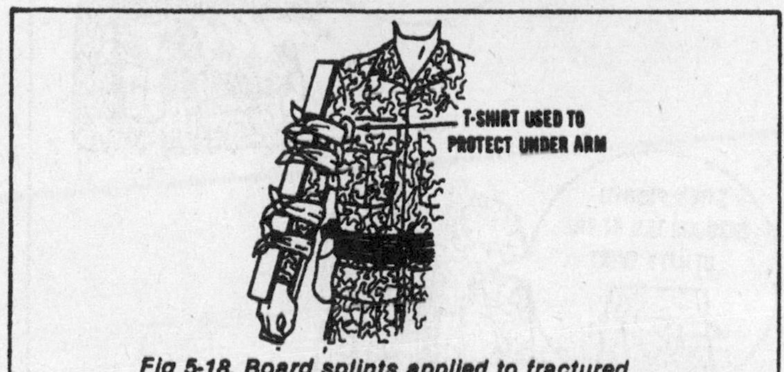

Fig 5-18. Board splints applied to fractured arm or elbow when elbow is not bent.

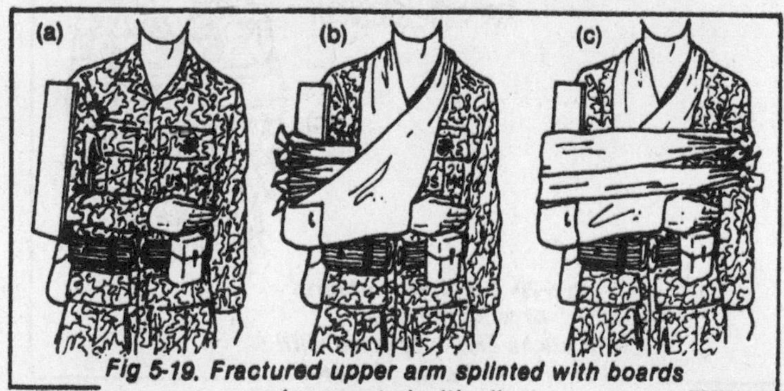

Fig 5-19. Fractured upper arm splinted with boards and supported with slings.

Fig 5-20. Fractured forearm or wrist splinted with sticks and supported with tail of shirt and strip of material.

Fig 5-21. Chest wall used as splint when no splint is available.

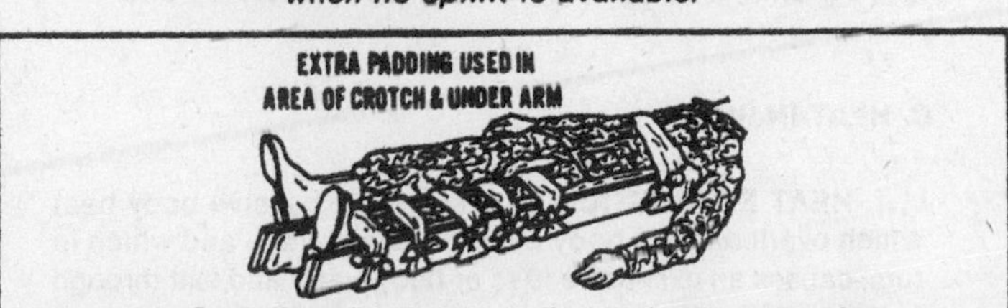

Fig 5-22. Board splints applied to lower extremity.

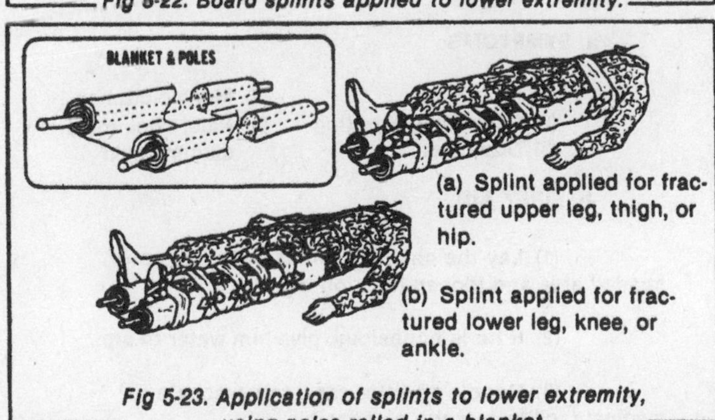

(a) Splint applied for fractured upper leg, thigh, or hip.

(b) Splint applied for fractured lower leg, knee, or ankle.

Fig 5-23. Application of splints to lower extremity, using poles rolled in a blanket.

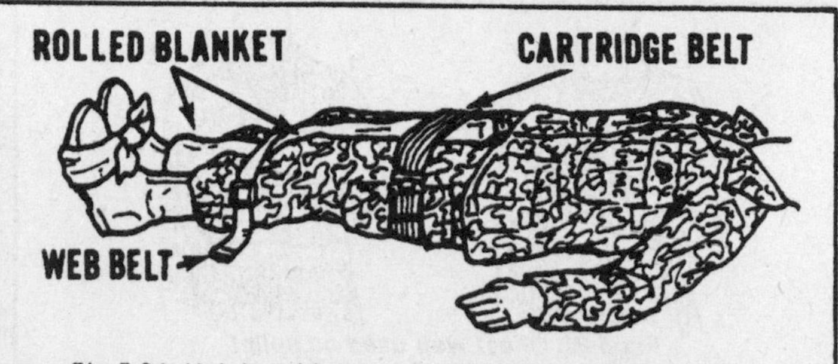

Fig 5-24. Uninjured leg used as splint for fractured one.

C. HEAT INJURIES

1. **HEAT EXHAUSTION.** Caused by excessive body heat which overloads the body control mechanism, and which in turn, causes an excessive loss of body water and salt through prolonged sweating.

a. **SYMPTOMS.**

(1) Headache
(2) Excessive sweating
(3) Dizziness
(4) Muscle cramps
(5) Pale, cool, moist clammy skin

b. **FIRST AID.**

(1) Lay the casualty on his back in a cool, shaded area and loosen his clothing.

(2) If he is conscious, give him water to sip.

(3) Handle as litter case and evacuate to medical facility as soon as possible.

2. HEATSTROKE. Caused by a failure of the body's heat regulating mechanisms which causes the body to become overheated. Sometimes called "sunstroke."

a. SYMPTOMS.

(1) Lack of sweating
(2) Hot, dry, skin
(3) Headache
(4) Dizziness
(5) Rapid pulse
(6) Mental confusion
(7) Collapse and unconsciousness
(8) Face may appear flushed or red

b. FIRST AID.

(1) Immerse casualty in coldest water available.

(2) If a cold water bath is not possible, get the casualty into the shade, remove his clothing, and keep his entire body wet by pouring water over him. Cool him further by fanning his wet body.

(3) Transport him to the nearest medical facility at once and continue to cool his body on the way. Handle as a litter case.

3. HEATCRAMPS.

a. SYMPTOMS. Painful spasms of muscles (legs arms, abdomen).

b. FIRST AID.

(1) Give casualty salt water to drink. Dissolve two crushed salt tablets (1/4 teaspoon of table salt) in a canteen (quart) of cool water. The casualty should drink 3 to 5 canteens during a period of 12 hours.

(2) If cramps are severe, take casualty to a medical facility.

D. COLD INJURIES

1. **HYPOTHERMIA** (severe chilling). Hypothermia is an unanticipated and deceiving injury resulting in a dangerous lowering of the entire body temperature. Hypothermia occurs when the individual loses body heat at a rate faster than it is produced.

a. **SYMPTOMS.** Nonspecific and are often disregarded by Marines.

(1) Abnormal fatigue
(2) Weakness
(3) Weariness
(4) Mental confusion
(5) Stopping of shivering

b. **FIRST AID.**

(1) Forestall further heat loss.

(2) Warm the body by any means available (preferred treatment is warming in a hot bath).

(3) Treat for shock and seek aid.

c. **PREVENTIVE MEASURES.**

(1) Use multiple layers of dry clothing.

(2) Avoid sweating.

2. **FROSTBITE.** Frostbite is the freezing of some part of the body by exposure to freezing temperature. Frostbite can cause the loss of limbs or other serious, permanent injury. It is the most common cold injury.

CAUTION: If a frostbitten area of the body is thawed and then refrozen, the effects are more severe.

a. **SYMPTOMS.**

(1) Uncomfortable sensation of coldness followed by numbness.

(2) Tingling, stinging, or aching sensation, even cramping pain.

(3) Numbness may be a first sign of frostbite. The skin may also have a pale, waxy appearance. The affected area may be firmer to the touch than the skin of the surrounding areas.

(4) White spots form on the skin before they can be felt.

b. **FIRST AID.**

(1) Get the casualty into a heated shelter if possible. Remove all items which constrict circulation without further injury to the frostbitten area.

(2) The only safe way to warm a frostbite victim in the field is by body heat. Place frostbitten hands in the armpits and frostbitten feet on the stomach or between the thighs. Warm frostbitten ears and face with the hands.

(3) A casualty with frostbitten feet should be treated as a litter case and should avoid walking if possible.

(4) Dry the casualty carefully being sure NOT to rub the frostbitten part or area. Drying of frostbitten areas can be accomplished by gently patting the area being sure not to rub the frostbitten area. Cover the victim, but do not let the covers come in contact with the frostbitten limb or skin area.

(5) Keep the frostbitten limbs or skin area dry. Sterile gauze or cloth pads should be used to protect the injured area.

(6) If possible, keep the frostbitten limbs or skin area slightly elevated.

(7) Never rub or massage a frostbitten area. This may tear the frozen skin tissues and cause infection or gangrene.

(8) Never rub any part of the body with ice or snow. Do not apply cold water to the affected part.

(9) Never forcibly remove frozen shoes, mittens, or clothing. Thaw them first.

(10) Do not walk on frostbitten feet if it can be avoided.

(11) Never rewarm frostbitten areas by exposure to an open fire. Overheating can cause additional pain or injury.

(12) Be prepared for pain when thawing occurs.

c. **PREVENTIVE MEASURES.**

(1) Dress to protect yourself; wear sufficient clothing for protection against cold and wind. In high winds, take special precautions to protect your face.

(2) Make every effort to keep your clothing and body dry. Avoid overdressing which causes excessive perspiration. Change your socks whenever your feet become moist either from perspiration or other sources.

(3) In extremely low temperatures, be careful not to touch metal with your bare skin.

(4) Exercise exposed parts of your body frequently. Exercise your fingers and toes from time to time to keep them warm and to detect numb or hard areas. Warm your face and ears from time to time with your hands for the same purpose.

(5) Always use the buddy system. Watch your buddy's face to see if any frozen spots show, and have him watch yours. Thaw any frozen spots immediately, using bare hands or other sources of body heat.

(6) Any interference with the circulation of your blood reduces the amount of heat delivered to your extremities. Wear properly fitted clothing and equipment. Tight-fitting socks, boots, and gloves are especially dangerous in very cold climates.

3. **SNOW BLINDNESS.** Snow blindness is caused by glare on unprotected eyes from an icefield or a snowfield. It is more dangerous on cloudy or hazy days when Marines are less wary. Once you have had snow blindness you are more susceptible to further attacks.

a. **SYMPTOMS.**

(1) Sensation of grit in eyes.

(2) Pain in and over eyes made worse by eye movement

(3) Redness

(4) Headache

(5) Increased pain on exposure to light

b. **FIRST AID.** Cover the victim's eyes with a dark cloth to shut out all light. The victim should then be taken to a medical treatment facility.

c. **PREVENTIVE MEASURES.**

(1) Wear dark glasses when conditions warrant.

(2) Carry an extra pair of sun glasses in case of damage.

(3) Improvise eye coverings by cutting narrow slits in a small piece of cardboard, wood, leather or cloth and tying it over the eyes (fig 5-25).

Fig 5-25. Improvised glasses.

E. FOOT CARE

1. **GENERAL.** Special attention should be paid by each individual to the proper care of his feet. Several things can go wrong that will take you out of action almost as effectively as a bullet. Blisters, immersion foot, and fungal infection (athletes's foot) will be discussed in the following paragraphs.

2. **BLISTERS.** Blisters are caused by ill-fitting footwear, heat, moisture, and friction. Rubbing of the foot against the shoe over a period of time results in the conditions shown in fig 26.

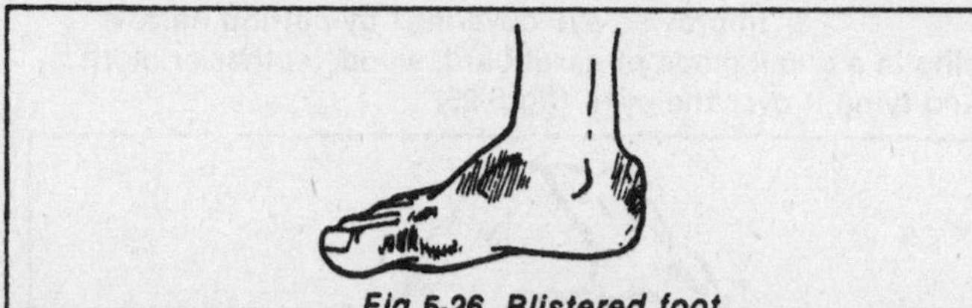

Fig 5-26. Blistered foot.

a. **SYMPTOMS.**

(1) Redness and soreness of the skin

(2) Puffiness in the sore area

(3) Fluid buildup under the skin

(4) Broken skin

b. **FIRST AID.** If blisters develop and medical personnel are not available, you should follow the steps listed below:

(1) Wash the blister area.

(2) Blisters should be dressed with an antiseptic, gauze pad and tape. Puncturing blisters is discouraged since infection can easily become a very real and disabling factor.

c. **PREVENTIVE MEASURES.**

(1) Wear properly fitting boots and shoes.

(2) Wear properly fitting clean socks.

(3) Keep feet clean and dry.

(4) Use foot powder.

3. **IMMERSION FOOT.** Immersion foot is caused by standing in water for a prolonged period of time (usually more than 12 hours). Although immersion foot is usually caused by lowering the temperature of the feet, exposure even in warm water for period exceeding 24 hours can cause this injury. Tight clothing and footwear can also be factors in the severity of the condition.

a. **SYMPTOMS.**

(1) Numbness

(2) Stiffness

(3) Painful

(4) Swelling

(5) White and wrinkled skin

b. **FIRST AID.**

(1) Dry the feet.

(2) Elevate and expose to air (if not too cold).

(3) Seek medical aid (victim should be carried, if possible).

c. **PREVENTIVE MEASURES.**

(1) Socks and boots should be cleaned and dried at every opportunity.

(2) The feet should be dried as soon as possible after getting them wet. They may be warmed with the hands. Foot powder should be applied and dry socks put on.

(3) If it becomes necessary to wear wet boots and socks, the feet should be exercised continually by wiggling the toes and bending the ankles. Tight boots should never be worn.

4. **FUNGAL INFECTION** (athlete's foot). Fungal infection usually occurs between the toes and on the sole of the foot.

a. **SYMPTOMS.**

(1) Itchy feet

(2) Cracks in the skin between the toes

(3) Flaky patches of skin

b. **FIRST AID.**

(1) Apply foot powder daily.

(2) Apply fungicidal ointment.

(3) Seek medical aid if (1) and (2) fail to clear up the infection.

c. **PREVENTIVE MEASURES.**

(1) Clean and dry feet daily.

(2) Apply foot powder daily.

(3) Wear clean socks.

F. TRANSPORTATION OF SICK OR WOUNDED

Knowing how to transport a seriously injured person is one of the most important parts of first aid. Careless or rough handling may increase the seriousness of his injury and increase the likelihood of death. Unless there is good reason for transporting a casualty, do not do so until some means of medical evacuation is provided. In the event that no medevac facilities are available, you will have to transport the casualty yourself. The casualty should receive appropriate first aid before moving him. If he has a broken bone, do not transport him until you splint or immobilize the part. A litter should be used whenever possible. If he has a fractured back or neck, don't move him with a litter.

1. IMPROVISED LITTERS. Figures 5-27 through 5-29 show several methods of improvising litters.

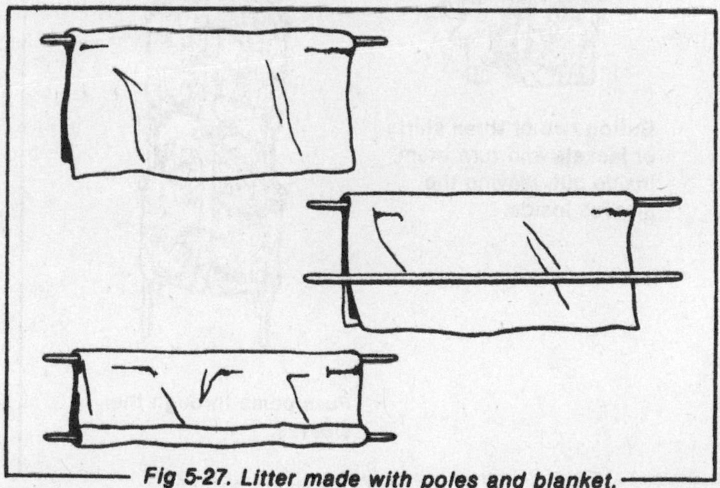

Fig 5-27. Litter made with poles and blanket.

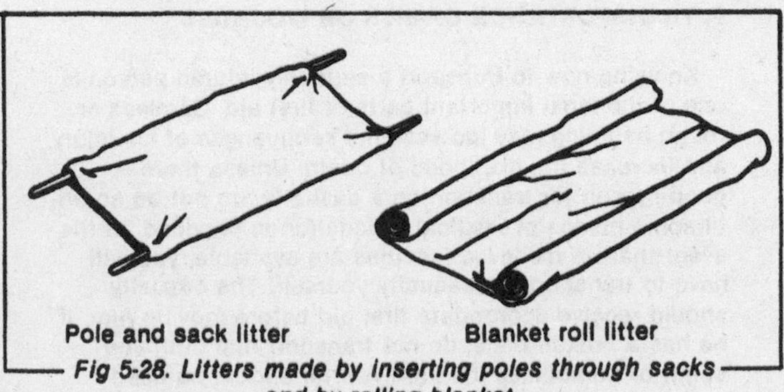

Fig 5-28. Litters made by inserting poles through sacks and by rolling blanket.

Button two or three shirts or jackets and turn them inside out, leaving the sleeves inside.

Pass poles through the sleeves.

Fig 5-29. Litter made with poles and jackets.

2. **ONE-MAN CARRY.** Whenever possible, use a two-man carry, but be prepared to transport a casualty by yourself. Figures 5-30 through 5-36 illustrate various one-man carries. Use the carry that is least likely to aggravate the injury.

Fig 5-30. Arms carry. *Fig 5-31. Supporting carry.* *Fig 5-32. Saddleback carry.*

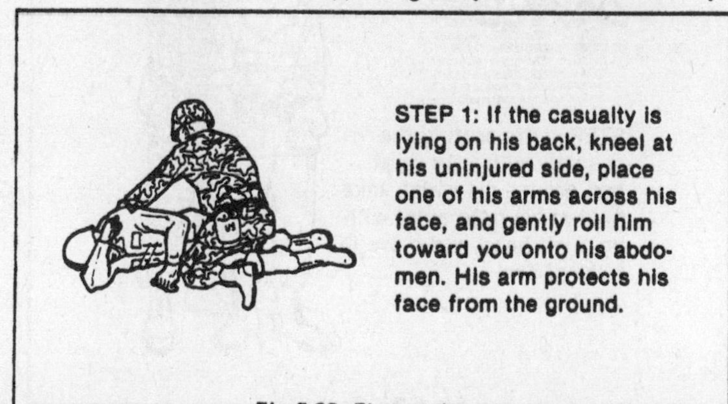

STEP 1: If the casualty is lying on his back, kneel at his uninjured side, place one of his arms across his face, and gently roll him toward you onto his abdomen. His arm protects his face from the ground.

Fig 5-33. Fireman's carry.

STEP 2: Straddle the casualty and grasp him by extending your hands under his armpits and against his chest.

STEP 3: Lift the casualty to his knees; then secure your hold and raise him to a standing position until his knees lock.

STEP 4: Supporting the casualty with your right arm around his waist, take hold of his right wrist with your left hand and move in front of him.

Fig 5-33. Contd.

STEP 5: Raise the casualty's right arm over your head.

STEP 6: Bend at the waist and knees; then pull the casualty's arm over and down your left shoulder, thus bringing his body across your shoulders. At the same time pass your right arm between his legs and grasp his right knee with your hand.

NOTE: While bent in this position, pick up both rifles.

STEP 7: Stand with the casualty on your shoulders.

Fig 5-33. Contd

STEP 8: Grasp the casualty's right wrist with your right hand, leaving your left hand free to carry your rifle and the casualty's.

You can carry another person some distance in this manner.

Fig 5-33. Contd

STEP 2: Kneel on one knee at the casualty's head facing his feet; then grasp him by extending your hands under his armpits, down his sides, and across his back.

STEP 3: As you rise, lift the casualty to his knees; then secure your hold and raise him to a standing position until his knees lock.

STEP 4: Supporting the casualty with your right arm around his waist, take hold of his right wrist with your left hand.

Fig 5-34. Fireman's carry (alternate steps 2, 3, and 4)

Fig 5-35. Pack-strap carry.

STEP 1: Link together two pistol belts to form a sling. Place the sling under the casualty's thighs and lower back so that a loop extends from each side.

STEP 2: Lie between the casualty's outstretched legs. Thrust your arms through the loops. Grasp casualty's hand and trouser leg on his injured side.

STEP 3: Roll toward the casualty's uninjured side onto your abdomen, bringing the casualty onto your back. Adjust sling as necessary.

Fig 5-36. Pistol-belt carry.

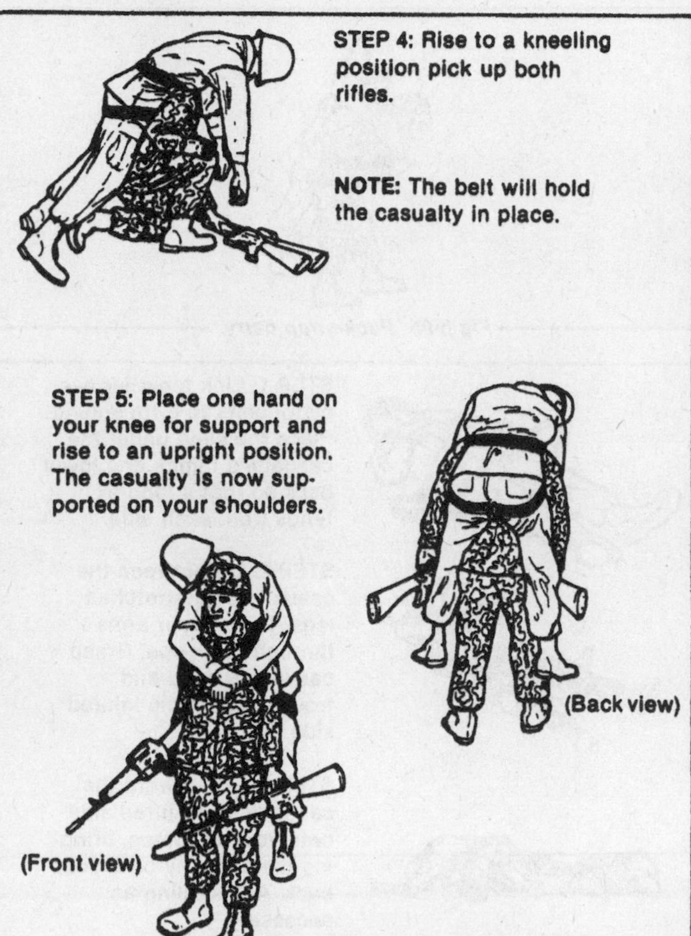

Fig 5-36. Contd

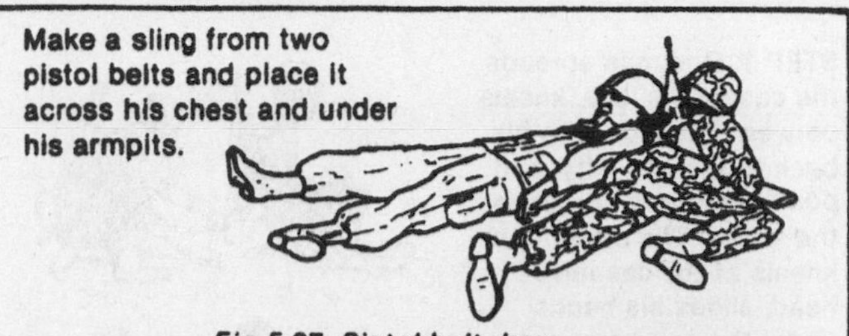

Fig 5-37. Pistol-belt drag.

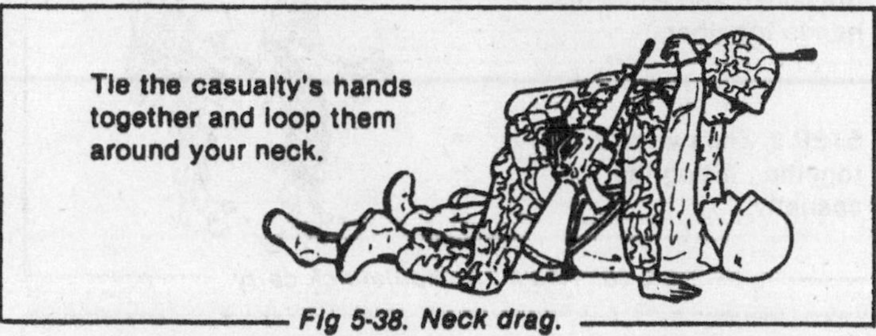

Fig 5-38. Neck drag.

3. TWO-MAN CARRY. Two-man carries are shown in figures 5-39 through 5-42.

Fig 5-39. Two-man supporting carry.

STEP 1: One man spreads the casualty's legs, kneels between the legs with his back to the casualty, and positions his hands under the knees. The other man kneels at the casualty's head, slides his hands under the arms and across the chest, and locks his hands together.

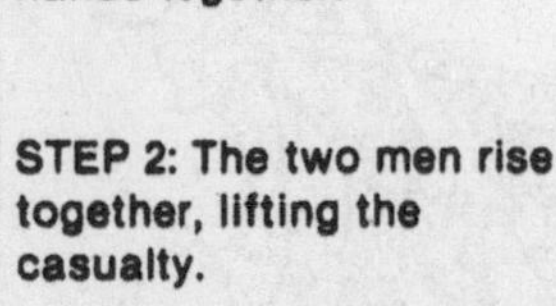

STEP 2: The two men rise together, lifting the casualty.

Fig 5-40. Two-man saddleback carry.

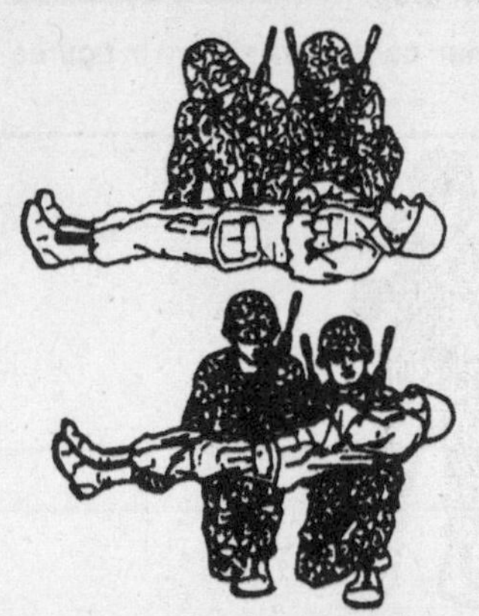

STEP 1: Two men kneel at one side of the casualty and place their arms beneath the casualty's shoulders, back, hips, and knees.

STEP 2: The men then lift the casualty as they rise to their knees.

Fig 5-41. Two-man arms carry.

STEP 3: As the men rise to their feet, they turn the casualty toward their chests.

NOTE: The casualty is carried high to lessen the carrier's fatigue.

Fig 5-41. Contd

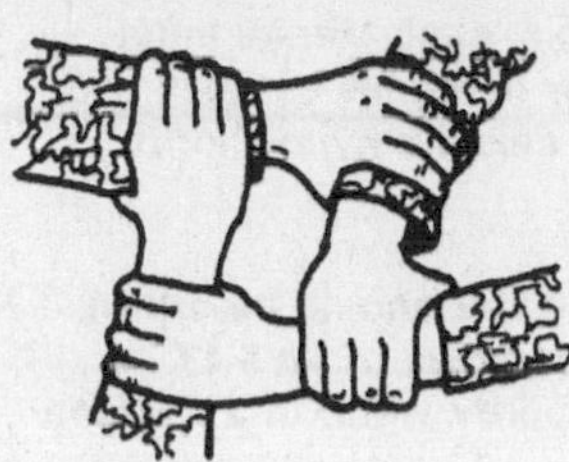

STEP 1: Each man grasps one of his wrists and one of the other man's wrists, thus forming a packsaddle.

STEP 2: The two men lower themselves sufficiently for the casualty to sit on the packsaddle; then they have the casualty place his arms around their shoulders for support before they rise to an upright position.

Fig 5-42. Four-hand (packsaddle) carry.

Section II. Field Sanitation

Objective: Apply the techniques of field sanitation and personal hygiene which affect individual health and comfort and the unit's mission.

A. INDIVIDUAL WATER TREATMENT

When safe water is not available, each Marine must produce his own potable water by using his canteen and iodine purification tablets or the calcium hypochlorite supplied in ampules.

1. **IODINE TABLETS.** Drinking water should be drawn upstream from other activities as shown in fig 5-43. Iodine tables should be used to purify water in a canteen as shown in fig 5-44.

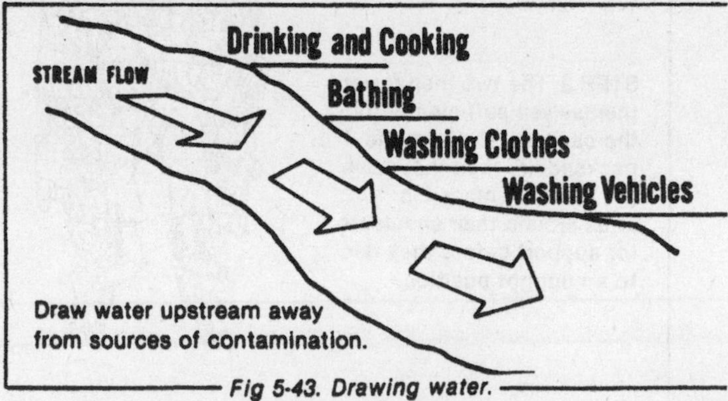

Fig 5-43. Drawing water.

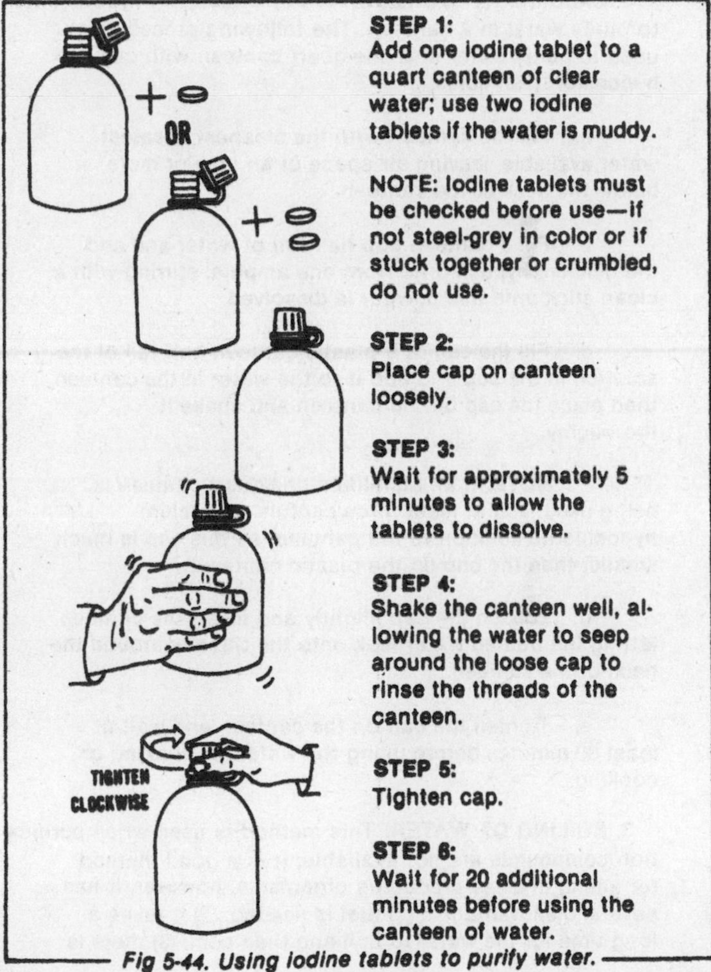

Fig 5-44. Using iodine tablets to purify water.

2. **CALCIUM HYPOCHLORITE.** Use of calcium hypochlorite to purify water in a canteen. The following procedure is used to purify water in a one-quart canteen with calcium hypochlorite ampules.

a. Fill the canteen with the cleanest, clearest water available, leaving air space of an inch or more below the neck of the canteen.

b. Fill a canteen cup half full of water and add the calcium hypochlorite from one ampule, stirring with a clean stick until this powder is dissolved.

c. Fill the cap of a plastic canteen half full of the solution in the cup and add it to the water in the canteen, then place the cap on the canteen and shake it thoroughly.

NOTE: If an aluminum one-quart canteen is being used, add at least three capfuls of calcium hypochlorite solution to the canteen, as this cap is much smaller than the one on the plastic canteen.

d. Loosen the cap slightly and invert the canteen, letting the treated water leak onto the threads around the neck of the canteen.

e. Tighten the cap on the canteen and wait at least 30 minutes before using the water for drinking or cooking.

3. **BOILING OF WATER.** This method is used when purification compounds are not available. It is a good method for killing disease producing organisms, however, it has several disadvantages: (1) fuel is needed; (2) it takes a long time for the water to boil and then cool: (3) there is

no residual protection against recontamination. Water must be held at a rolling boil for at least 15 seconds to make it safe for drinking.

B. CLEANING INDIVIDUAL MESS GEAR

In the field, each Marine cares for his own mess gear. Proper washing is important, otherwise food particles will create a breeding ground for germs.

1. **EQUIPMENT REQUIRED.** Four corrugated cans or other similar containers placed in a row are required for washing mess gear (fig 5-45). The first can contains hot soapy water and is used as a prewash; the second can contains hot soapy water (150°F) for a second wash; and the third and fourth cans contain clear water which is kept boiling (rolling boil) throughout the work period. Long-handled wash brushes and a garbage can or pit are also needed. Additional cans may be used for garbage and waste.

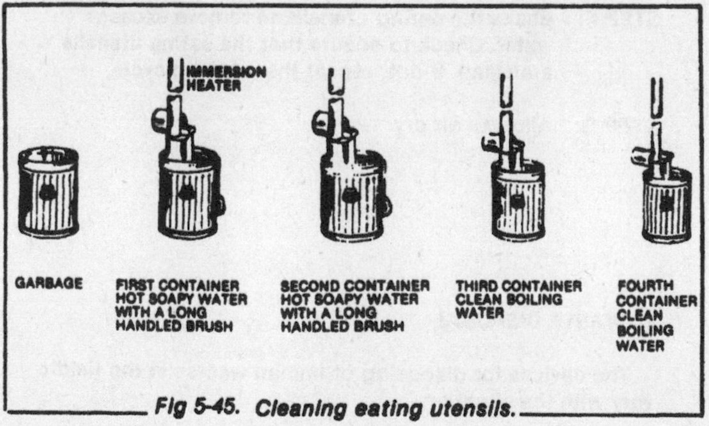

Fig 5-45. Cleaning eating utensils.

2. PROCEDURES FOR CLEANING MESS GEAR.

STEP A: Scrape the food particles from eating utensils into a garbage can.

STEP B: Using the long handled brush provided, wash the eating utensils in the first container of hot soapy water.

STEP C: Using the long handled brush provided, wash the eating utensils in the second container of hot soapy water.

STEP D: Immerse the eating utensils in the first container of clear boiling water for approximately 30 seconds.

STEP E: Immerse the eating utensils in the second container of clear boiling water for approximately 30 seconds.

STEP F: Shake the eating utensils to remove excess water. Check to ensure that the eating utensils are clean. If not, repeat the washing cycle.

STEP G: Allow to air dry.

C. WASTE DISPOSAL

The devices for disposing of human wastes in the field vary with the situation.

1. **CAT HOLE** (fig 5-46). When troops are on the march, each person uses a "cat hole" latrine during short halts. It is dug approximately 1 foot deep and is completely covered and packed down after use.

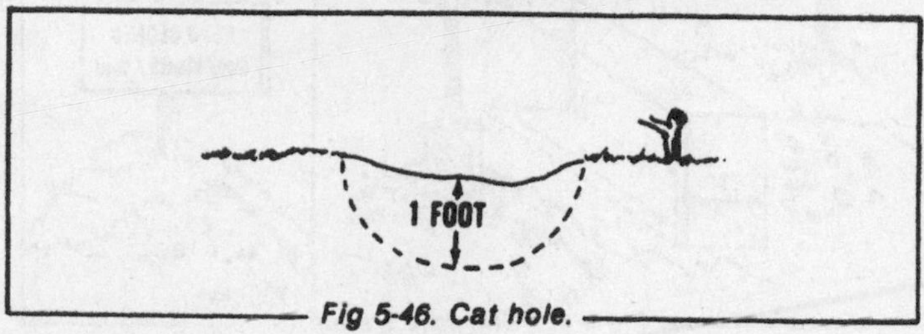

Fig 5-46. Cat hole.

2. **STRADDLE TRENCH** (fig 5-47). In a temporary bivouac of 1 to 3 days, the straddle trench is most likely to be used unless more permanent facilities are provided for a unit. A straddle trench is dug 1 foot wide, 2 1/2 feet deep, and 4 feet long. The straddle trench should be located on the leeward side of the camp well away from the galley and 50 to 100 yards away from the bivouac area. The number of trenches provided should be sufficient to serve at least 8 percent of the unit strength at one time. The earth removed in digging is piled at the end of the trench with a can or shovel so that each man can cover his waste after using the trench. This is continued until the unit leaves or the straddle trenches are filled to within one foot of the surface. Before breaking camp, all straddle trenches must be filled, mounded over, and marked with the date they were closed.

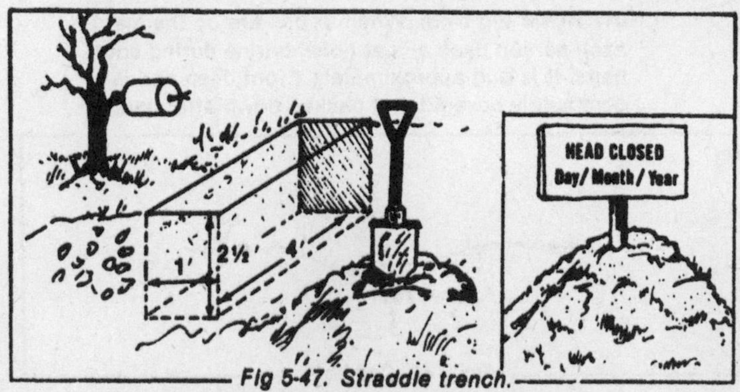

Fig 5-47. Straddle trench.

3. GARBAGE AND RUBBISH DISPOSAL (fig 5-48). Dispose of all garbage and rubbish in a temporary bivouac by burial.

Fig 5-48. Burial of garbage and rubbish.

For additional training in this area, references are provided: below:

1. FM 21-20	Military Sanitation
2. FM 21-10	Field Hygiene and Sanitation
3. MCI Course 03.15m	Individual Protective Measures
4. FM 21-11	First Aid for Soldiers
5. TEC Lesson Series #300-	First Aid

Chapter 6. Uniform Clothing and Equipment

The U.S. Marines have been admired by people worldwide for their outstanding appearance. Marines have gained a high level of recognition by wearing their distinctive uniforms with personal pride.

Proper maintenance of individual equipment and clothing is essential to each Marine's ability to perform his mission.

All Marines are required to have in their possession, in serviceable condition, a minimum allowance of clothing and a specific quantity of equipment in custody to them.

Section I. Marking of Clothing

Objective: Demonstrate how each article of uniform clothing is to be marked.

A. MARKING PROCEDURES

1. **GENERAL.** Every article of uniform clothing in the possession of enlisted personnel, except those issued by the parent organization on a temporary memorandum receipt, will be marked plainly and indelibly with the owner's name. Marks will be of a size appropriate to the article of clothing and the space available for marking, and shall consist of block letters not more than one half inch in size. Name tape or stamps, as appropriate, may

be used. The use of sewn-on name tapes or embroidered nametags on the utility jacket is prohibited. Names will be marked in black on light-colored material and utilities and in white on dark-colored materials. Marks will be placed so that they do not show when clothing is worn. In order to standardize throughout the Marine Corps, and prevent variation from station to station, no elaboration of the following guide for marking items shall be made, nor shall any greater preciseness of location be prescribed.

Articles of uniform clothing obtained from sources other than through the supply system which are marked with another individual's name will have the first owner's name obliterated by blocking out the name or by using a commercial eradicator. The new owner's name should be re-marked in accordance with instructions contained herein. All re-marked clothing in the possession of an individual must be substantiated with an appropriate entry on the administrative remarks page of the service record book.

2. **LOCATION OF NAME ON ARTICLES** (enlisted personnel).

a. Bag, duffel. On the outside of the bottom of the bag.

b. Belts (except trouser belts). On the underside, near the buckle end.

c. Belts, web, trouser. On one side only, as near the buckle end as possible.

d. Caps, frame, garrison, service and utility. Inside on the sweatband.

e. Coats, all-weather, overcoats, raincoats, service/dress coats and utility coats. Inside the neckband.

f. Cover, cap. Inside the band.

g. Drawers, boxer. Immediately below the stretch waistband, near the front.

h. Drawers, brief. On the plain waistband, near the front.

i. Gloves. Inside at the wrist.

j. Handbag. Stenciled on space provided.

k. Havelock, plastic. On underside of sweatband.

l. Hood, raincoat. Along edge of inside neck seam.

m. Neckties/Necktabs (Women Marines). On the inside of the neckloop.

n. Raincoats. Inside the neckband.

o. Shirts, khaki. Inside the neckband.

p. Skirts, slacks. Inside the waistband, near the center of the back.

q. Shoes and boots. Inside near the top.

r. Socks. Near the top.

s. Trousers. Inside the waistband.

t. Undershirts. Near the neckband.

Section II. Displaying Clothing and Equipment

Objective: Properly prepare and display Marine Corps clothing and equipment for inspection.

A. CLOTHING AND EQUIPMENT DISPLAYS

Clothing and equipment displays are the usual method of inspecting the number, marking, and condition of required items. Depending on the location of the unit and the types of facilities available, the commanding officer may have to prescribe displays that will vary from the suggested ones illustrated below. To promote uniformity throughout the Marine Corps, however, the illustrations should be used as the model displays whenever possible. A commander may require any combination of bunk and wall locker/wardrobe displays that is necessary to achieve his inspection purposes. (See figures 6-1 through 6-12.)

Fig 6-1. Field equipment and service rifle-bunk display.
See footnotes 1. and 2. on page 6-17.

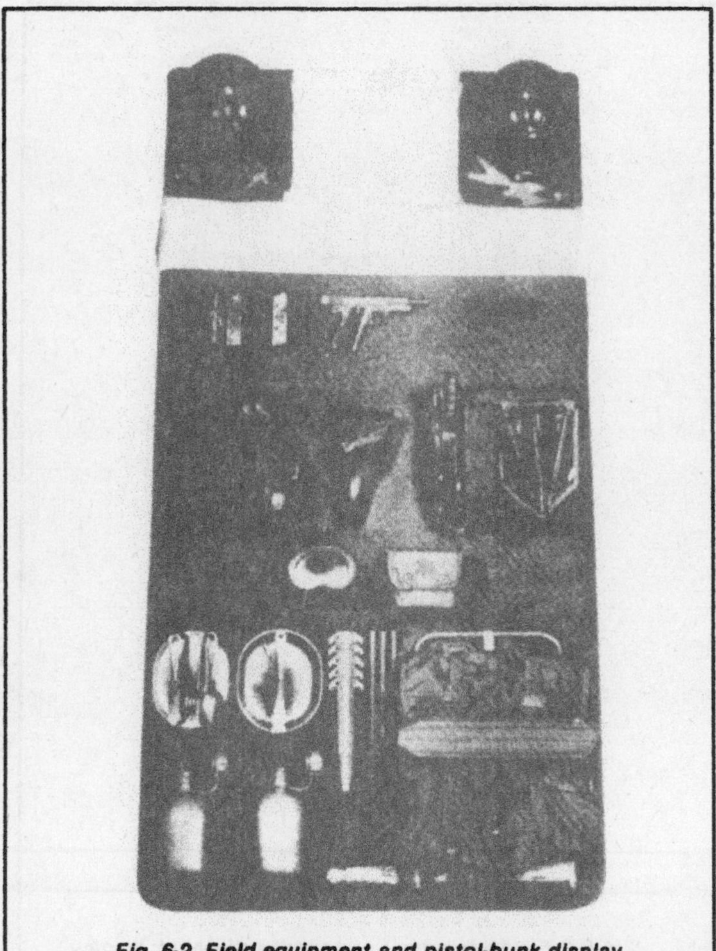

Fig 6-2. Field equipment and pistol-bunk display.
See footnote 1. on page 6-17.

Fig 6-3. Garrison equipment and service rifle-bunk display. (Generally used in combination with wall locker/ wardrobe display.) See footnotes 1., 2., 3., 4., and 5. on page 6-17.

Fig 6-4. Garrison equipment and pistol-bunk display. (Generally used in combination with wall locker/ wardrobe display. See footnotes 1., 3., 4., and 5. on page 6-17.

Fig 6-5. Field equipment, partial uniform clothing, and service rifle-bunk display. (Generally used in combination with wall locker/wardrobe display.) See footnotes 1., 2., 3., 4., and 5. on page 6-17.

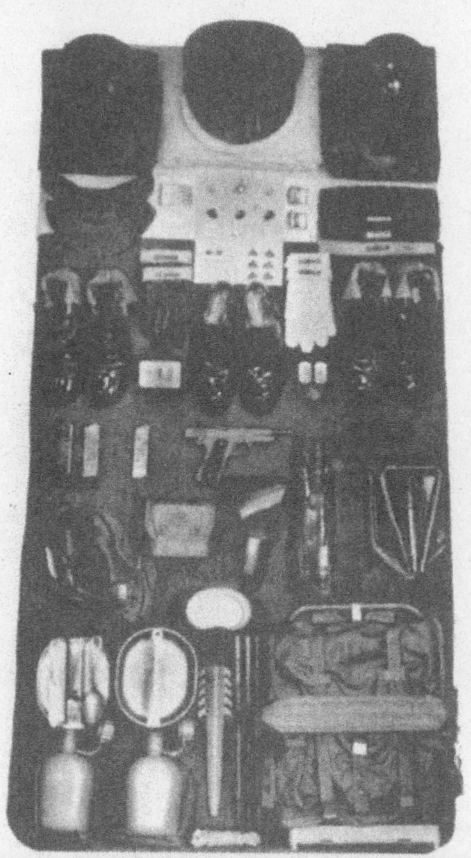

Fig 6-6. Field equipment, partial uniform clothing and pistol-bunk display. (Generally used in combination with wall locker/wardrobe display.) See footnotes 1., 3., 4., and 5. on page 6-17.

Fig 6-7. Uniform clothing-wall locker display.
See footnotes 3., 6., and 7. on page 6-17.

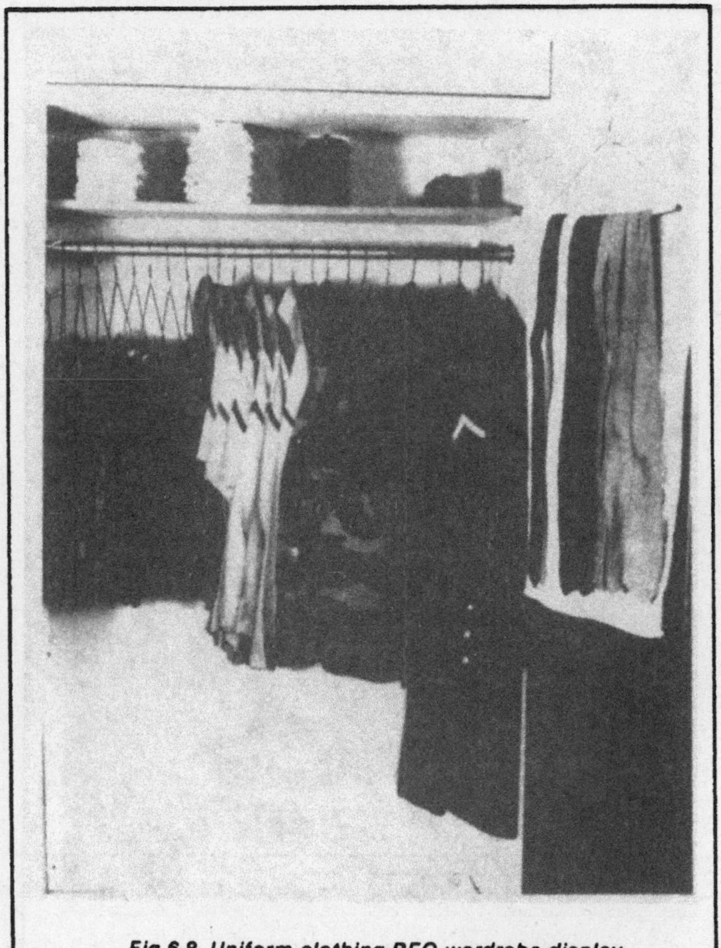

Fig 6-8. Uniform clothing-BEQ wardrobe display.
See footnotes 3. and 6. on page 6-17.

Fig 6-9. Field equipment and service rifle-field display. (Contents of pack are at the discretion of unit commander.) See footnotes 1., 2., and 8. on page 6-17.

Fig 6-10. Field equipment and pistol-field display. (Contents of pack are at the discretion of unit commander.) See footnotes 1., 8., and 9. on page 6-17.

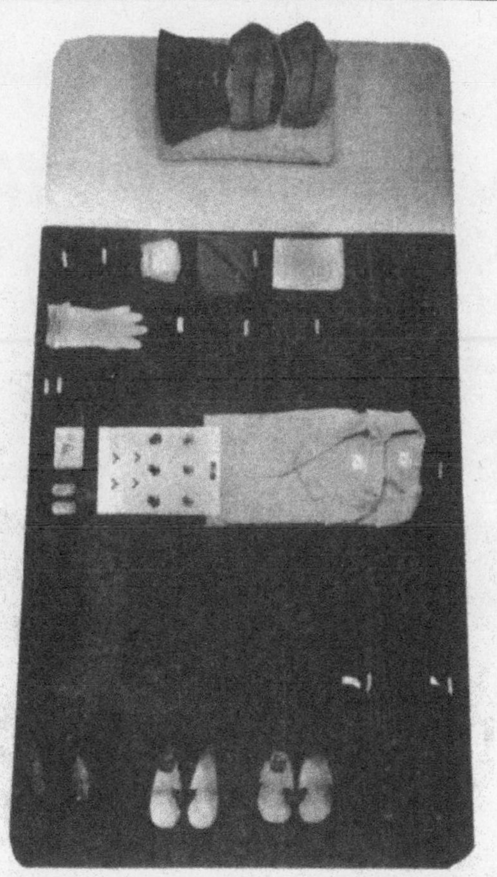

Fig 6-11. Women Marine uniform clothing display-bunk display. See footnotes 3., 4., 10., and 11. on page 6-17.

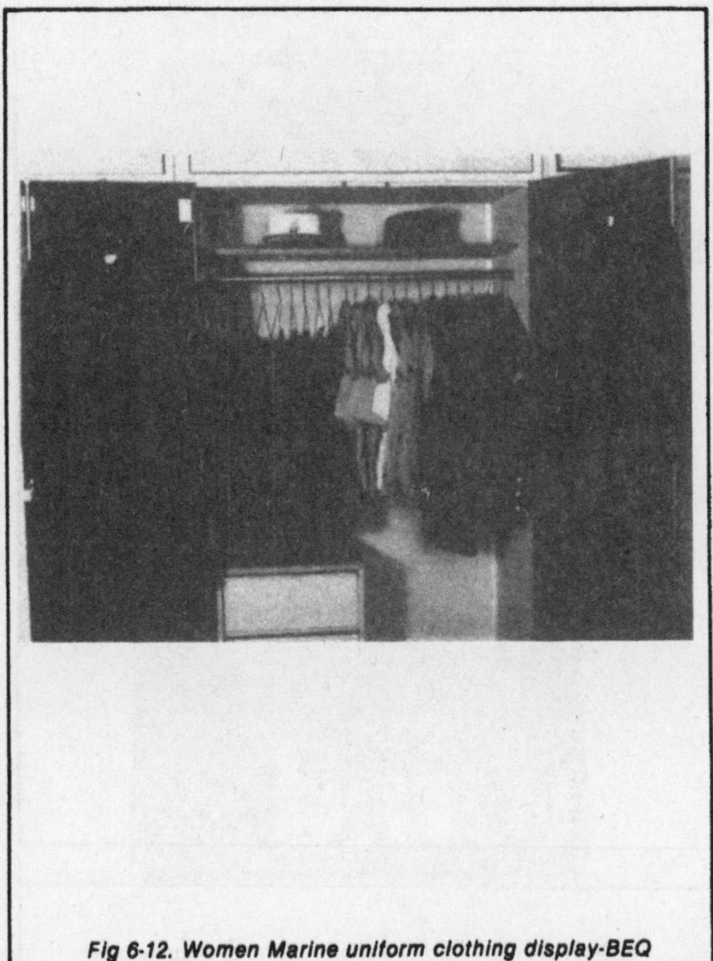

Fig 6-12. Women Marine uniform clothing display-BEQ wardrobe display. See footnotes 3. and 12. on page 6-17.

FOOTNOTES

1. Substitute or older items of equipment will be displayed in the approximate position of similar items shown.

2. When extra rifle magazines are issued they will be placed between magazine pouches and the distance between pouches will be adjusted accordingly.

3. All articles of uniform clothing possessed by an individual will be displayed regardless of current allowances. Items not displayed will be those worn by the individual at the time of the inspection and those accounted for by an itemized laundry, dry cleaning, tailor, or cobbler slip. Marking of uniform clothing is to be accomplished in accordance with the current edition of MCO P1020.34.

4. Individuals required to wear a Medical Warning tag in accordance with the current edition of BUMED Instruction 6150.29 will display this tag next to their identification tags.

5. This display is normally used in combination with either the display in figure 6-7 or 6-8.

6. Trousers will be positioned together in the same right to left sequence as matching coats and shirts (i.e., all blue trousers, then all green service trousers, etc., right to left as the viewer faces the wall locker or wardrobe).

7. Raincoat is placed behind overcoat on locker door.

8. The contents of the pack which are displayed are representative only. Commanders will designate specific contents and vary display accordingly.

9. Organizational equipment such as those representative items shown (compass and binoculars) are to be positioned in the center of the display.

10. Two pairs of oxfords may be displayed in accordance with the current edition of MCO P10120.28, if replacement of either pair in the initial issue has not been necessary.

11. The display is normally used in combination with the display in figure 6-12.

12. Skirts will be positioned immediately to the right of matching coats e.g., all green service coats, then all green service skirts, etc., left to right as the viewer faces the wardrobe.

B. ALL-PURPOSE LIGHTWEIGHT INDIVIDUAL CARRYING EQUIPMENT (ALICE) PACK

The recently adopted load carrying system has many advantages over the packs that Marines have been carrying since 1941. The features include a water-resistant, lightweight nylon material for quick drying, wide padded shoulder straps, and a lightweight metal pack frame. There are three easy access pockets on the outside of the pack for gear that is needed more frequently. Inside the pack is a pocket that will carry and conceal the field radio.

The pack also has quick release straps that enable it to be separated from the normal fighting load which is suspended from the belt.

The pack may be worn with or without the pack frame (See figures 6-13 through 6-16).

Fig 6-13. All-purpose Lightweight Individual Carrying Equipment (ALICE).

Fig 6-14. Components of ALICE.

a. Back

b. Side

Fig 6-15. ALICE without frame (back and side).

a. Front

b. Back

c. Side

Fig 6-16. ALICE with frame (front, back, and side).

For additional training in this area, the following reference is provided:

1. MCO P10120.28___ Individual Clothing Regulations

Section III. Minimum Requirements List-Issue

Objective: When provided with a list of uniform clothing items, properly identify those articles of clothing that are contained in the basic allowance.

A. MINIMUM REQUIREMENTS LIST-ISSUE

Each Marine enlisting into the regular component receives a basic issue of uniform clothing under "Clothing Monetary Allowance System." This system provides the initial issue made to you, and a cash allowance that you receive in your pay. Each fiscal year, the maximum amount of money that can be spent for each individual's initial issue and payment to the individual for maintenance each month are prescribed by the Secretary of Defense. As a result, you are required to maintain, at a minimum, each article contained in your basic allowance; properly altered, serviceable, and ready for inspection at all times.

In order to properly maintain your clothing ready for inspection, make necessary repairs, and purchase replacement articles, you must know each item and its quantity contained in your basic allowance. Tables 6-1 and 6-2 list those items and quantities contained in the minimum requirements list-issue.

Quantity	Article
1	BAG, DUFFEL: w/carrying strap
2	BELT, TROUSERS: web, khaki
2	BOOT, COMBAT: leather, black, pair
2	BUCKLE: f/belt, web, khaki
1	BUCKLE: f/belt (coat)
1	CAP, GARRISON: wool, serge, green
2	CAP, GARRISON: polyester/wool, green
3	CAP, UTILITY: cotton, camouflage
1	CLASP, NECKTIE
1	COAT, MAN'S: wool, serge, green, w/belt
1	COAT, MAN'S: polyester/wool, green, w/belt
4	COAT, MAN'S: camouflage, tropical
6	DRAWERS, MAN'S: cotton, white, pair
1	GLOVES, LEATHER: black, pair
1	INSIGNIA, BRANCH OF SERVICE: black (collar), pair
1	INSIGNIA, BRANCH OF SERVICE: black (collar, left)
2	NECKTIE: khaki
1	OVERCOAT, MAN'S: wool, green
1	RAINCOAT, MAN'S: nylon, rubber-coated
2	DECAL, "USMC"; SET: (3 decals per set)
3	SHIRT, MAN'S: polyester/cotton, khaki, long-sleeve
3	SHIRT, MAN'S: polyester/cotton, khaki, w/quarter-length sleeve
1	SHOE, DRESS: black, pair
4	SOCKS, MAN'S: black, pair
4	SOCKS, MAN'S: w/cushion sole, pair
2	TROUSERS, MAN'S: wool, serge, green, pair
2	TROUSERS, MAN'S: polyester/wool, green, pair
4	TROUSERS, MAN'S: camouflage, tropical, pair
6	UNDERSHIRT, MAN'S: cotton, white

Table 6-1. Minimum Requirements List, Men's

Quantity	Article
1	BAG, DUFFEL: w/carryng strap
2	BELT, TROUSERS: web, khaki
1	BOOT, COMBAT: leather, black, pair
1	BUCKLE: f/belt, web
1	CAP, SERVICE: wool, serge, green
2	CAP, UTILITY: cotton, camouflage
3	COAT, MAN'S: camouflage, tropical
1	COAT, WOMAN'S: polyester/wool, green
1	COAT, WOMAN'S: wool, serge, green
1	GLOVES, CLOTH: black, pair
1	HANDBAG, WOMAN'S: black
1	HAVELOCK: plastic
1	HOOD, RAIN: green
1	INSIGNIA, BRANCH OF SERVICE: black (cap, screwpost)
1	INSIGNIA, BRANCH OF SERVICE: collar, black, pair
2	NECKTIE (COLLAR TAB): green
1	OVERCOAT, WOMAN'S: wool, serge, green
1	RAINCOAT, WOMAN'S: green
1	DECAL, "USMC"; SET: (3 decals per set)
3	SHIRT, WOMAN'S: polyester/cotton, khaki (long sleeve)
3	SHIRT, WOMAN'S: polyester/cotton, khaki (short sleeve)
1	SHOE, DRESS: oxford, black, pair
1	SHOE, DRESS: pump, black, pair
2	SKIRT, WOMAN'S: polyester/wool, green
1	SKIRT, WOMAN'S: wool, serge, green
2	SLACKS, WOMAN'S: polyester/wool, green
4	SOCKS, MAN'S: w/cushion sole, pair
6	STOCKINGS, WOMAN'S: nylon pair
3	TROUSERS, MAN'S: camouflage, tropical, pair
3	UNDERSHIRT, MAN'S: cotton, white
$45	PERSONAL ITEMS CASH ALLOWANCE

Table 6-2. Minimum Requirements List, Women's

B. DESIGNATION OF UNIFORM (MALE AND FEMALE)

1. GENERAL.

a. Authorized uniforms for male enlisted personnel are designated as blue dress "A," blue dress "B," blue dress "C," blue dress "D," blue-white dress "A," blue-white dress "B," winter service "A," winter service "B," winter service "C," summer service, "A," summer service "B," summer service "C," and utility.

b. Except for those commands authorized the blue uniform, the uniform of the day will be the service uniform appropriate to the season. For those commands authorized the blue uniform supplementary allowance, the uniform fo the day will be the service of blue dress "B," "C," or "D" at the discretion of the commander. The service uniform and the blue dress "B" uniform may be prescribed for leave or liberty within the United States.

c. Except for personnel on duty with the Department of State, commanders will prescribe the duty, liberty, and leave uniform for Marines stationed outside the United States. All uniforms so prescribed will conform with uniform regulations. Uniform regulations applicable to personnel on duty with the Department of State are prescribed by Headquarters Marine Corps.

d. The wearing of blue uniforms of mixed materials by enlisted personnel is authorized. Gabardine coats and kersey trousers or vice versa may be worn on all occasions including formations.

2. DRESS "A" UNIFORMS.

a. The blue dress "A" uniform shall be prescribed for parades, ceremonies, reviews, and official social functions when the commander considers it desirable to pay social honors to the occasion.

b. The blue dress "A" uniform includes medals.

c. The blue-white dress "A" may be prescribed for parades, ceremonies, and reviews on or off base, and will not be worn on leave, liberty, or social functions either on or off base.

d. The blue-white dress "A" uniform shall consist of the same items as blue dress "A" except that the trousers shall be standard white trousers as issued by the Marine Corps supply system.

3. DRESS "B" UNIFORMS.

a. The blue dress "B" shall be prescribed for enlisted personnel when reporting for sea duty, and for parades, ceremonies, reviews, and other such functions as determined by the commander.

b. The blue-white dress "B" may be prescribed for parades, ceremonies, and reviews only, and will not be worn on leave, liberty, or at social functions either on or off base.

c. The blue dress "B" uniform is authorized for leave or liberty.

d. The blue dress "B" uniforms shall consist of the same items as the corresponding dress "A" uniforms, except that ribbons and badges shall be worn in lieu of medals.

e. The blue dress uniform with long-sleeve shirt is designated as blue dress "C." The khaki shirt, insignia of grade, ribbons, and service necktie clasp may be prescribed in lieu of the blue coat. In those commands authorized the blue uniform, commanders may prescribe blue dress "C" as the uniform of the day; however, this uniform will not be worn in ceremonies, parades, on liberty, leave or other functions for which the coat would appropriate.

f. The blue dress uniform with quarter-length sleeve snirt is designated as blue dress "D." In commands authorized the blue uniform, commanders may prescribe blue dress "D" as the uniform of the day; however, this uniform will not be worn on leave or liberty. Commanders may prescribe the wearing of this uniform for honors and ceremonies where climatic conditions preclude the comfortable wearing of blue dress "A" or "B" uniforms.

4. **SERVICE UNIFORMS.**

a. The service "A" uniform appropriate to the season shall be prescribed for the following official military occasions:

(1) When reporting for duty on shore.

(2) When assigned duty as a member of a court martial.

The service "A" uniform shall include the green coat with ribbons. Badges are optional unless prescribed by the commanding officer. Black gloves may be worn or carried at the individual's option. All personnel shall wear or carry black gloves at all times with the topcoat, overcoat, raincoat, or the all-weather coat when the winter service uniform is prescribed.

b. The service "B" uniform shall consist of the same items of uniform as the service "A" uniform except that the service coat is not worn. When the service "A" is worn, enlisted personnel may dispense with the wearing of the coat at the discretion of the commander within the confines of the installation. Commanders may, at their discretion, authorize enlisted personnel to wear service "B" when commuting to and from work by private conveyance, with necessary stops en route. This uniform will not be authorized for leave or liberty.

c. The quarter-length sleeve shirt with appropriate service trousers is designated as the service "C" uniform. The service "C" uniform may be worn as a uniform of the day and for leave or liberty unless otherwise prescribed by the commander. During the period when the winter service uniform is prescribed, commanders may, at their discretion, when the weather requires, authorize the wearing of winter service "C." It may be prescribed for wear in formation, at ceremonies and parades on and off military bases.

d. When the coat is not worn, the standard gold-colored necktie clasp will be worn with the service uniforms except that staff NCO's may elect to wear the optional cuff link and tie clasp set.

e. The uniform may be worn for most occasions, such as: work, liberty, leave and religious services. The wearing of the uniform is not authorized to solicit public funds outside of a military base, to endorse a commercial product, or to participate in any type of protest march.

5. **UTILITY UNIFORM.** The utility uniform shall be worn only in the field, for field type exercises, and for work under conditions where it is not practical to wear the service uniform.

6. For dress uniform designations that are specific to women Marines, see table 6-3.

DESIGNATION	CONSIST OF THESE ARTICLES
Blue dress "A" or "B"	Blue coat and skirt/slacks, White shirt Black neck tab White dress cap Black leather handbag* White gloves
Blue dress "C"	Blue skirt/slacks, wool gabardine Shirt, Khaki (long sleeve) White dress cap Black leather handbag
Blue dress "D"	Blue skirt/slacks *or* Shirt, Khaki (short sleeve), without necktab White dress cap Black leather handbag

*Clutch purse with black cover may be worn by staff non-commissioned officers in accordance with the reference.

Table 6-3. Designated Dress Uniform Combinations (Women).

DESIGNATION	CAP AND NECK TAB	COAT	SKIRT	SHIRT	GLOVES	HANDBAG	SHOES	HOSE	OUTER COAT	INSIGNIA	RIBBONS
WINTER SERVICE "A" (h)	Green	Green (Serge) (h)	Green (Serge) (f)	Khaki (LS) (SS)	(a)	Black	Black Pumps (b)	(c)	All-Weather Overcoat Raincoat (d)	Service	Yes
WINTER SERVICE "B" (i)	Green		Green (Serge) (f)	Khaki (LS) (h)	(a)	Black	Black Pumps (b)	(c)	All-Weather Overcoat Raincoat (d)		(d) (d)
WINTER SERVICE "C" (i)	Green (e)		Green (Serge) (f)	Khaki (SS) (g)	(a)	Black	Black Pumps (b)	(c) (d)	All-Weather Raincoat		(f)
SUMMER SERVICE "A" (h)	Green	Green (Poly/ Wool) (h)	Green (Poly/ Wool) (f)	Khaki (LS) (SS)		Black	Black Pumps (b)	(c)	All-Weather Raincoat (d)	Service	Yes
SUMMER SERVICE "B" (i)	Green		Green (Poly/ Wool) (f)	Khaki (LS) (g)		Black	Black Pumps (b)	(c)	All-Weather Raincoat (d)		(d)
SUMMER SERVICE "C" (i)	Green (e)		Green (Poly/ Wool) (f)	Khaki (SS) (g)		Black	Black Pumps (b)	(c)	All-Weather Raincoat (d)		(d)

Note: letters contained in ( ) are footnotes presented on page 6-33.

Table 6-4. Designated Service Uniform Combinations.

Footnotes for Table 6-4

a. Black gloves worn with outer coat.

b. Oxfords are not authorized except when deemed appropriate by the commander.

c. Hose should harmonize with the natural skin tone, except that dark hose of the gray/smoky shades shall be worn with blue dress.

d. Optional, but may be prescribed.

e. No neck tab will be worn.

f. Slacks may be authorized by commanders. See local uniform orders.

g. Green service sweater may be worn at option of individual. This uniform is not authorized for ceremonial formations, parades, and ceremonies.

h. Authorized for leave and liberty.

i. Authorized for leave and liberty at the discretion of local commanders.

For additional training in this area references are provided below:

1.	MCO P10120.28___	Individual Clothing Regulations
2.	MCBul 1020 (dtd 16 Jan 81)	Wearing of Khaki Shirts by Women Marines
3.	MCBul 1020 (dtd 18 Nov 81)	Adoption of New Dress Blue Uniform for Wear of Enlisted Women Marines
4.	MCO P1020.34	Marine Corps Uniform Regulations

Section IV. Regulations Governing Personal Appearance

Objectives:

1. Demonstrate personal appearance standards prescribed by the Marine Corps.

2. Explain the meaning of the term "appropriate civilian attire."

A. GROOMING (MALES)

1. The face will be clean shaven, except that a mustache may be worn. When worn, a mustache will be neatly and closely trimmed and must be contained within the lines of B, and the margin area of the upper lip as shown in figures 6-17 and 6-18. The length of a mustache hair fully extended must not exceed ½-inch.

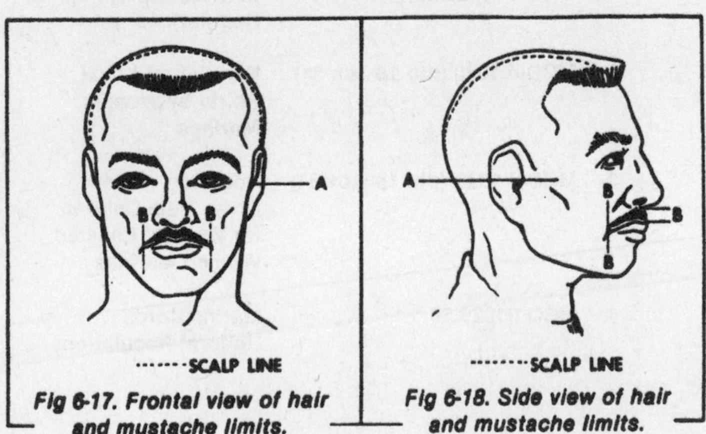

Fig 6-17. Frontal view of hair and mustache limits.

Fig 6-18. Side view of hair and mustache limits.

2. Hair shall be worn neatly and closely trimmed. It may be clipped at the edges of the side and back and will be evenly graduated from zero length at the hairline on the lower portion of the head up to a maximum of 3 inches on the top of the head. Hair will be worn in such a manner so as not to interfere with the proper wearing of uniform headgear.

3. Sideburns will not extend below the top of the orifice of the ear, as indicated by line A in figures 6-17 and 6-18. The length of hair on the sideburn will not exceed 1/8 inch when fully extended.

4. No articles such as pencils, pens, watch chains, fobs, pins, jewelry, handkerchiefs, combs, cigars, cigarettes, pipes, or similar items shall be worn or carried exposed upon the uniform.

5. Inconspicuous wrist watches, watch bands, and rings are permitted while in uniform. Sun glasses may be worn on leave, liberty, and in garrison, but not in formation with troops. Eye glasses/sun glasses shall be conservative in appearance. Eccentric or conspicuous eyepieces are prohibited.

B. GROOMING (FEMALES)

1. The hair shall be neatly shaped and arranged in an attractive, feminine style. Elaborate hairstyles that do not allow for the proper wearing of the cap are prohibited. Hair may touch the collar but may not fall below the collar's lower edge. Conspicuous barrettes, pins, and combs shall not be worn in the hair when the uniform is worn. Hairnets shall not be worn unless authorized for a specific type of duty. If dyes, tints, or bleaches are used on the hair, the artificial color must harmonize with the per-

son's complexion tone and eye color. Conspicuous artificial color changes are prohibited. Wigs, if worn in uniform, must look natural and conform to all of the above listed regulations.

2. Cosmetics shall be applied conservatively. Exaggerated or faddish cosmetic styles are inappropriate with the uniform and shall not be worn. Lipstick and colored nail polish worn with the green service blue, or officer's evening dress or mess dress uniforms shall harmonize with the scarlet trim of these uniforms. When the summer uniform is prescribed, extreme shades of lipstick, such as lavender, purple, white or flesh color shall not be worn. Nail polish, if used, shall either harmonize with the lipstick or be colorless.

3. No pencils, pens, pins, handkerchiefs, or jewelry shall be worn or be carried exposed upon the uniform. Earrings, hair ribbons, and other hair ornaments shall not be worn.

4. Wrist watches and inconspicuous rings are permitted while in uniform. Sun glasses may be worn on leave, liberty, and in garrison, but not in formation with troops. Sunglasses, when worn, shall be conservative in appearance. Chains or ribbons will not be attached to eyeglasses.

C. WEIGHT

1. **GENERAL.** Any Marine who exceeds the weight standards or displays poor military appearance due to improper weight distribution will be placed in the unit's weight/personal appearance program. Weigh-ins will be utilized to monitor individual progress. If you do not satisfactorily lose excess body fat and/or improve your personal appearance, you may be discharged from the Marine Corps due to unsuitability.

2. **MALE WEIGHT STANDARDS.** Weight standards for male Marines, regardless of age, are shown in table 6-5 below.

Table 6-5. Male Weight Standards

HEIGHT (inches)	64	65	66	67	68	69	70	71
WEIGHT (pounds)								
Minimum	105	106	107	111	115	119	123	127
Maximum	160	165	170	175	181	186	192	197
HEIGHT (inches)		72	73	74	75	76	77	78
WEIGHT (pounds)								
Minimum		131	135	139	143	147	151	153
Maximum		203	209	214	219	225	230	235

3. FEMALE WEIGHT STANDARDS. Weight standards for women Marines, regardless of age, are shown in table 6-6 below:

Table 6-6. Female Weight Standards

HEIGHT (inches)	58	59	60	61	62	63	64	65
WEIGHT (pounds)								
Minimum	90	92	94	96	98	100	102	104
Maximum	121	123	125	127	130	134	138	142
HEIGHT (inches)	66	67	68	69	70	71	72	73
WEIGHT (pounds)								
Minimum	106	109	112	115	118	122	125	128
Maximum	147	151	156	160	165	170	175	180

4. ALTERNATIVE MAXIMUM WEIGHT LIMITS FOR MALE MARINES. Table 6-7 indicates the percentage of body fat by anthropometric measurements. It is closely associated with a sophisticated and expensive system called hydrostatic weighing. Hydrostatic weighing is weighing a person under water to determine his specific gravity which is then converted to percentage of body fat. The Marine Corps has established 18 percent and below as maximum allowable percent of body fat for the alternative weight limits for male Marines.

ABDOMEN (IN.)	13.00	13.25	13.50	13.75	14.00	14.25	14.50	14.75	15.00	15.25	15.50	15.75	16.00	16.25
25.0	6.3	5.5	4.7	3.9	3.1	2.3	1.5	.7						
25.5	7.2	6.4	5.6	4.8	4.0	3.3	2.5	1.7	.9	.1				
26.0	8.2	7.4	6.6	5.8	5.0	4.2	3.4	2.6	1.8	1.0	.2			
26.5	9.1	8.3	7.5	6.7	5.9	5.1	4.3	3.5	2.8	2.0	1.2	.4		
27.0	10.0	9.2	8.4	7.7	6.9	6.1	5.3	4.5	3.7	2.9	2.1	1.3	.5	
27.5	11.0	10.2	9.4	8.6	7.8	7.0	6.2	5.4	4.6	3.8	3.0	2.3	1.5	.7
28.0	11.9	11.1	10.3	9.5	8.7	7.9	7.2	6.4	5.5	4.8	4.0	3.2	2.4	1.6
28.5	12.9	12.1	11.3	10.5	9.7	8.9	8.1	7.3	6.5	5.7	4.9	4.1	3.3	2.5
29.0	13.8	13.0	12.2	11.4	10.6	9.8	9.0	8.2	7.4	6.7	5.9	5.1	4.3	3.5
29.5	14.7	13.9	13.1	12.4	11.6	10.8	10.0	9.2	8.4	7.6	6.8	6.0	5.2	4.4
30.0	15.7	14.9	14.1	13.3	12.5	11.7	10.9	10.1	9.3	8.5	7.7	6.9	6.2	5.4
30.5	16.6	15.8	15.0	14.2	13.4	12.6	11.9	11.1	10.3	9.5	8.7	7.9	7.1	6.3
31.0	17.6	16.8	16.0	15.2	14.4	13.6	12.8	12.0	11.2	10.4	9.6	8.8	8.0	7.2
31.5	18.5	17.7	16.9	16.1	15.3	14.5	13.7	12.9	12.1	11.4	10.6	9.8	9.0	8.2
32.0	19.4	18.6	17.8	17.1	16.3	15.5	14.7	13.9	13.1	12.3	11.5	10.7	9.9	9.1
32.5	20.4	19.6	18.8	18.0	17.2	16.4	15.6	14.8	14.0	13.2	12.4	11.6	10.9	10.1
33.0	21.3	20.5	19.7	18.9	18.1	17.3	16.6	15.8	15.0	14.2	13.4	12.6	11.8	11.0
33.5	22.3	21.5	20.7	19.9	19.1	18.3	17.5	16.7	15.9	15.1	14.3	13.5	12.7	11.9
34.0	23.2	22.4	21.6	20.8	20.0	19.2	18.4	17.6	16.8	16.1	15.3	14.5	13.7	12.9
34.5	24.1	23.3	22.5	21.8	21.0	20.2	19.4	18.6	17.8	17.0	16.2	15.4	14.6	13.8
35.0	25.1	24.3	23.5	22.7	21.9	21.1	20.3	19.5	18.7	17.9	17.1	16.3	15.6	14.8
35.5	26.0	25.2	24.4	23.6	22.8	22.0	21.3	20.5	19.7	18.9	18.1	17.3	16.5	15.7
36.0	27.0	26.2	25.4	24.6	23.8	23.0	22.2	21.4	20.6	19.8	19.0	18.2	17.4	16.6
36.5	27.9	27.1	26.3	25.5	24.7	23.9	23.1	22.3	21.5	20.8	20.0	19.2	18.4	17.6
37.0	28.8	28.0	27.2	26.5	25.7	24.9	24.1	23.3	22.5	21.7	20.9	20.1	19.3	18.5
37.5	29.8	29.0	28.2	27.4	26.6	25.8	25.0	24.2	23.4	22.6	21.8	21.0	20.3	19.5
38.0	30.7	29.9	29.1	28.3	27.5	26.7	26.0	25.2	24.4	23.6	22.8	22.0	21.2	20.4
38.5	31.7	30.9	30.1	29.3	28.5	27.7	26.9	26.1	25.3	24.5	23.7	22.9	22.1	21.3
39.0	32.6	31.8	31.0	30.2	29.4	28.6	27.8	27.0	26.2	25.5	24.7	23.9	23.1	22.3
39.5	33.5	32.7	31.9	31.2	30.4	29.6	28.8	28.0	27.2	26.4	25.6	24.8	24.0	23.2
40.0	34.5	33.7	32.9	32.1	31.3	30.5	29.7	28.9	28.1	27.3	26.5	25.7	25.0	24.2
40.5	35.4	34.6	33.8	33.0	32.2	31.4	30.7	29.9	29.1	28.3	27.5	26.7	25.9	25.1
41.0	36.3	35.6	34.8	34.0	33.2	32.4	31.6	30.8	30.0	29.2	28.4	27.6	26.8	26.0
41.5	37.3	36.5	35.7	34.9	34.1	33.3	32.5	31.7	30.9	30.2	29.4	28.6	27.8	27.0
42.0	38.2	37.4	36.6	35.8	35.1	34.3	33.5	32.7	31.9	31.1	30.3	29.5	28.7	27.9
42.5	39.2	38.4	37.6	36.8	36.0	35.2	34.4	33.6	32.8	32.0	31.2	30.4	29.7	28.9
43.0	40.1	39.3	38.5	37.7	36.9	36.1	35.4	34.6	33.8	33.0	32.2	31.4	30.6	29.8
43.5	41.0	40.3	39.5	38.7	37.9	37.1	36.3	35.5	34.7	33.9	33.1	32.3	31.5	30.7
44.0	42.0	41.2	40.4	39.6	38.8	38.0	37.2	36.4	35.6	34.9	34.1	33.3	32.5	31.7
44.5	42.9	42.1	41.3	40.5	39.8	39.0	38.2	37.4	36.6	35.8	35.0	34.2	33.4	32.6
45.0	43.9	43.1	42.3	41.5	40.7	39.9	39.1	38.3	37.5	36.7	35.9	35.1	34.4	33.6
45.5	44.8	44.0	43.2	42.4	41.6	40.8	40.0	39.3	38.5	37.7	36.9	36.1	35.3	34.5
46.0	45.7	45.0	44.2	43.4	42.6	41.8	41.0	40.2	39.4	38.6	37.8	37.0	36.2	35.4
46.5	46.7	45.9	45.1	44.3	43.5	42.7	41.9	41.1	40.3	39.5	38.8	38.0	37.2	36.4
47.0	47.6	46.8	46.0	45.2	44.5	43.7	42.9	42.1	41.3	40.5	39.7	38.9	38.1	37.3
47.5	48.6	47.8	47.0	46.2	45.4	44.6	43.8	43.0	42.2	41.4	40.6	39.8	39.0	38.3
48.0	49.5	48.7	47.9	47.1	46.3	45.5	44.7	44.0	43.2	42.4	41.6	40.8	40.0	39.2
48.5	50.4	49.7	48.9	48.1	47.3	46.5	45.7	44.9	44.1	43.3	42.5	41.7	40.9	40.1
49.0	51.4	50.6	49.8	49.0	48.2	47.4	46.6	45.8	45.0	44.2	43.5	42.7	41.9	41.1
49.5	52.3	51.5	50.7	49.9	49.2	48.4	47.6	46.8	46.0	45.2	44.4	43.6	42.8	42.0
50.0	53.3	52.5	51.7	50.9	50.1	49.3	48.5	47.7	46.9	46.1	45.3	44.5	43.7	43.0

Table 6-7. Percent Fat Prediction in Males from Abdomen and Neck Circumference

NECK (IN.)

ABDOMEN (IN.)	16.50	16.75	17.00	17.25	17.50	17.75	18.00	18.25	18.50	18.75	19.00	19.25	19.50	19.75
25.0														
25.5														
26.0														
26.5														
27.0														
27.5														
28.0	.8	.0												
28.5	1.8	1.0	.2											
29.0	2.7	1.9	1.1	.3										
29.5	3.6	2.8	2.0	1.3	.5									
30.0	4.6	3.8	3.0	2.2	1.4	.6								
30.5	5.5	4.7	3.9	3.1	2.3	1.5	.8							
31.0	6.5	5.7	4.9	4.1	3.3	2.5	1.7	9	.1					
31.5	7.4	6.6	5.8	5.0	4.2	3.4	2.6	1.8	1.0	.3				
32.0	8.3	7.5	6.7	6.0	5.2	4.4	3.6	2.8	2.0	1.2	.4			
32.5	9.3	8.5	7.7	6.9	6.1	5.3	4.5	3.7	2.9	2.1	1.3	.5		
33.0	10.2	9.4	8.6	7.8	7.0	6.2	5.5	4.7	3.9	3.1	2.3	1.5	.7	
33.5	11.1	10.4	9.6	8.8	8.0	7.2	6.4	5.6	4.8	4.0	3.2	2.4	1.6	.8
34.0	12.1	11.3	10.5	9.7	8.9	8.1	7.3	6.5	5.7	5.0	4.2	3.4	2.6	1.8
34.5	13.0	12.2	11.4	10.6	9.9	9.1	8.3	7.5	6.7	5.9	5.1	4.3	3.5	2.7
35.0	14.0	13.2	12.4	11.6	10.8	10.0	9.2	8.4	7.6	6.8	6.0	5.2	4.5	3.7
35.5	14.9	14.1	13.3	12.5	11.7	10.9	10.1	9.4	8.6	7.8	7.0	6.2	5.4	4.6
36.0	15.8	15.1	14.3	13.5	12.7	11.9	11.1	10.3	9.5	8.7	7.9	7.1	6.3	5.5
36.5	16.8	16.0	15.2	14.4	13.6	12.8	12.0	11.2	10.4	9.6	8.9	8.1	7.3	6.5
37.0	17.7	16.9	16.1	15.3	14.6	13.8	13.0	12.2	11.4	10.6	9.8	9.0	8.2	7.4
37.5	18.7	17.9	17.1	16.3	15.5	14.7	13.9	13.1	12.3	11.5	10.7	9.9	9.2	8.4
38.0	19.6	18.8	18.0	17.2	16.4	15.6	14.8	14.1	13.3	12.5	11.7	10.9	10.1	9.3
38.5	20.5	19.8	19.0	18.2	17.4	16.6	15.8	15.0	14.2	13.4	12.6	11.8	11.0	10.2
39.0	21.5	20.7	19.9	19.1	18.3	17.5	16.7	15.9	15.1	14.3	13.6	12.8	12.0	11.2
39.5	22.4	21.6	20.8	20.0	19.3	18.5	17.7	16.9	16.1	15.3	14.5	13.7	12.9	12.1
40.0	23.4	22.6	21.8	21.0	20.2	19.4	18.6	17.8	17.0	16.2	15.4	14.5	13.8	13.1
40.5	24.3	23.5	22.7	21.9	21.1	20.3	19.5	18.8	18.0	17.2	16.4	15.6	14.8	14.0
41.0	25.2	24.5	23.7	22.9	22.1	21.3	20.5	19.7	18.9	18.1	17.3	16.5	15.7	14.9
41.5	26.2	25.4	24.6	23.8	23.0	22.2	21.4	20.6	19.8	19.0	18.3	17.5	16.7	15.9
42.0	27.1	26.3	25.5	24.7	24.0	23.2	22.4	21.6	20.8	20.0	19.2	18.4	17.6	16.8
42.5	28.1	27.3	26.5	25.7	24.9	24.1	23.3	22.5	21.7	20.9	20.1	19.3	18.5	17.8
43.0	29.0	28.2	27.4	26.6	25.8	25.0	24.2	23.5	22.7	21.9	21.1	20.3	19.5	18.7
43.5	29.9	29.2	28.4	27.6	26.8	26.0	25.2	24.4	23.6	22.8	22.0	21.2	20.4	19.6
44.0	30.9	30.1	29.3	28.5	27.7	26.9	26.1	25.3	24.5	23.7	23.0	22.2	21.4	20.6
44.5	31.8	31.0	30.2	29.4	28.7	27.9	27.1	26.3	25.5	24.7	23.9	23.1	22.3	21.5
45.0	32.8	32.0	31.2	30.4	29.6	28.8	28.0	27.2	26.4	25.6	24.8	24.0	23.2	22.5
45.5	33.7	32.9	32.1	31.3	30.5	29.7	28.9	28.2	27.4	26.6	25.8	25.0	24.2	23.4
46.0	34.6	33.9	33.1	32.3	31.5	30.7	29.9	29.1	28.3	27.5	26.7	25.9	25.1	24.3
46.5	35.6	34.8	34.0	33.2	32.4	31.6	30.8	30.0	29.2	28.4	27.7	26.9	26.1	25.3
47.0	36.5	35.7	34.9	34.1	33.4	32.6	31.8	31.0	30.2	29.4	28.6	27.8	27.0	26.2
47.5	37.5	36.7	35.9	35.1	34.3	33.5	32.7	31.9	31.1	30.3	29.5	28.7	27.9	27.2
48.0	38.4	37.6	36.8	36.0	35.2	34.4	33.6	32.9	32.1	31.3	30.5	29.7	28.9	28.1
48.5	39.3	38.5	37.8	37.0	36.2	35.4	34.6	33.8	33.0	32.2	31.4	30.6	29.8	29.0
49.0	40.3	39.5	38.7	37.9	37.1	36.3	35.5	34.7	33.9	33.1	32.4	31.6	30.8	30.0
49.5	41.2	40.4	39.6	38.8	38.1	37.3	36.5	35.7	34.9	34.1	33.3	32.5	31.7	30.9
50.0	42.2	41.4	40.6	39.8	39.0	38.2	37.4	36.6	35.8	35.0	34.2	33.4	32.6	31.9

Table 6-7. Contd

NECK (IN.)

5. **ALTERNATIVE MAXIMUM WEIGHT LIMITS FOR FEMALE MARINES.** The maximum allowable percent of body fat for the establishment of an alternate weight standard for women Marines is established at 26 percent and below. The following charts are provided as a field measurement for the estimation of percent body fat for female Marines. A Marine need only find her specific measurement in each of the 5 girth columns. The point columns to the left of each girth measurement represent fat percentage points. Add the points representing each girth measurement, subtract from that the constant correction factor (54.598) and the resulting figure represents the total percent body fat. (See tables 6-8 through 6-12.)

NECK	10 0/8 inches =	12.7	pts.
ABDOMEN	28 0/8 inches =	8.7	pts.
BICEP	12 4/8 inches =	17.8	pts.
FOREARM	11 0/8 inches =	25.7	pts.
THIGH	19 0/8 inches =	11.0	pts.
TOTAL GIRTH MEASUREMENT POINTS =		75.800	pts.
MINUS CORRECTION FACTOR =		54.598	
BODY FAT PERCENTAGE =		21.202	

Table 6-8. Girth Measurement/Points (Example)

Neck. **The neck is measured at a point just below the larynx (adam's apple).**

PTS	NECK	PTS	NECK	PTS	NECK	PTS	NECK	PTS	NECK
.1	15.5/8	4.1	13 7/8	8.0	12 1/8	11.9	10 3/8	15.8	8 5/8
.4	15 4/8	4.3	13 6/8	8.2	12 0/8	12.1	10 2/8	16.1	8 4/8
.7	15 3/8	4.6	13 5/8	8.5	11 7/8	12.4	10 1/8	16.3	8 3/8
1.0	15 2/8	4.9	13 4/8	8.8	11 6/8	12.7	10 0/8	16.7	8 2/8
1.3	15 1/8	5.2	13 3/8	9.1	11 5/8	13.0	9 7/8	16.9	8 1/8
1.5	15 0/8	5.4	13 2/8	9.4	11 4/8	13.3	9 6/8	17.2	8 0/8
1.8	14 7/8	5.7	13 1/8	9.6	11 3/8	13.5	9 5/8	17.4	7 7/8
2.1	14 6/8	6.0	13 0/8	9.9	11 2/8	13.8	9 4/8	17.7	7 6/8
2.4	14 5/8	6.3	12 7/8	10.2	11 1/8	14.1	9 3/8	18.0	7 5/8
2.7	14 4/8	6.6	12 6/8	10.6	11 0/8	14.4	9 2/8	18.3	7 4/8
2.9	14 3/8	6.8	12 5/8	10.8	10 7/8	14.7	9 1/8	18.6	7 3/8
3.2	14 2/8	7.1	12 4/8	11.0	10 6/8	14.9	9 0/8		
3.5	14 1/8	7.4	12 3/8	11.3	10 5/8	15.2	8 7/8		
3.8	14 0/8	7.7	12 2/8	11.6	10 4/8	15.5	8 6/8		

Table 6-9. Neck Measurement/Points

Measure waist at top of hip bones.

PTS	ABDOMEN	PTS	ABDOMEN	PTS	ABDOMEN	PTS	ABDOMEN	PTS	ABDOMEN	PTS	ABDOMEN
.0	17 5/8	3.0	21 2/8	6.0	24 7/8	9.0	28 4/8	12.0	32 1/8	15.0	35 6/8
.1	17 6/8	3.1	21 3/8	6.1	25 0/8	9.1	28 5/8	12.1	32 2/8	15.1	35 7/8
.2	17 7/8	3.2	21 4/8	6.2	25 1/8	9.2	28 6/8	12.2	32 3/8	15.2	36 0/8
.3	18 0/8	3.3	21 5/8	6.3	25 2/8	9.3	28 7/8	12.3	32 4/8	15.3	36 1/8
.4	18 1/8	3.4	21 6/8	6.4	25 3/8	9.4	29 0/8	12.4	32 5/8	15.4	36 2/8
.5	18 2/8	3.5	21 7/8	6.5	25 4/8	9.5	29 1/8	12.5	32 6/8	15.5	36 3/8
.6	18 3/8	3.6	22 0/8	6.6	25 5/8	9.6	29 2/8	12.6	32 7/8	15.6	36 4/8
.7	18 4/8	3.7	22 1/8	6.7	25 6/8	9.7	29 3/8	12.7	33 0/8	15.7	36 5/8
.8	18 5/8	3.8	22 2/8	6.8	25 7/8	9.8	29 4/8	12.8	33 1/8	15.8	36 6/8
.9	18 6/8	3.9	22 3/8	6.9	26 0/8	9.9	29 5/8	12.9	33 2/8	15.9	36 7/8
1.0	18 7/8	4.0	22 4/8	7.0	26 1/8	10.0	29 6/8	13.0	33 3/8	16.0	37 0/8
1.1	19 0/8	4.1	22 5/8	7.1	26 2/8	10.1	29 7/8	13.1	33 4/8	16.1	37 1/8
1.2	19 1/8	4.2	22 6/8	7.2	26 3/8	10.2	30 0/8	13.2	33 5/8	16.2	37 2/8
1.3	19 2/8	4.3	22 7/8	7.3	26 4/8	10.3	30 1/8	13.3	33 6/8	16.3	37 3/8
1.4	19 3/8	4.4	23 0/8	7.4	26 5/8	10.4	30 2/8	13.4	33 7/8	16.4	37 4/8
1.5	19 4/8	4.5	23 1/8	7.5	26 6/8	10.5	30 3/8	13.5	34 0/8	16.5	37 5/8
1.6	19 5/8	4.6	23 2/8	7.6	26 7/8	10.6	30 4/8	13.6	34 1/8	16.6	37 6/8
1.7	19 6/8	4.7	23 3/8	7.7	27 0/8	10.7	30 5/8	13.7	34 2/8	16.7	37 7/8
1.8	19 7/8	4.8	23 4/8	7.8	27 1/8	10.8	30 6/8	13.8	34 3/8	16.8	38 0/8
1.9	20 0/8	4.9	23 5/8	7.9	27 2/8	10.9	30 7/8	14.0	34 4/8	17.0	38 1/8
2.0	20 1/8	5.0	23 6/8	8.1	27 3/8	11.1	31 0/8	14.1	34 5/8	17.1	38 2/8
2.2	20 2/8	5.2	23 7/8	8.2	27 4/8	11.2	31 1/8	14.2	34 6/8	17.2	38 3/8
2.3	20 3/8	5.3	24 0/8	8.3	27 5/8	11.3	31 2/8	14.3	34 7/8	17.3	38 4/8
2.4	20 4/8	5.4	24 1/8	8.4	27 6/8	11.4	31 3/8	14.4	35 0/8	17.4	38 5/8
2.5	20 5/8	5.5	24 2/8	8.5	27 7/8	11.5	31 4/8	14.5	35 1/8	17.5	38 6/8
2.6	20 6/8	5.6	24 3/8	8.6	28 0/8	11.6	31 5/8	14.6	35 2/8	17.6	38 7/8
2.7	20 7/8	5.7	24 4/8	8.7	28 1/8	11.7	31 6/8	14.7	35 3/8	17.7	39 0/8
2.8	21 0/8	5.8	24 5/8	8.8	28 2/8	11.8	31 7/8	14.8	35 4/8	17.8	39 1/8
2.9	21 1/8	5.9	24 6/8	8.9	28 3/8	11.9	32 0/8	14.9	35 5/8	17.9	39 2/8
18.0	39 3/8	19.4	41 1/8	20.8	42 7/8	22.3	44 5/8	23.8	46 3/8	25.2	48 1/8
18.1	39 4/8	19.5	41 2/8	21.0	43 0/8	22.4	44 6/8	23.9	46 4/8	25.3	48 2/8
18.2	39 5/8	19.6	41 3/8	21.1	43 1/8	22.5	44 7/8	24.0	46 5/8	25.4	48 3/8
18.3	39 6/8	19.7	41 4/8	21.2	43 2/8	22.6	45 0/8	24.1	46 6/8	25.5	48 4/8
18.4	39 7/8	19.9	41 5/8	21.3	43 3/8	22.7	45 1/8	24.2	46 7/8	25.6	48 5/8
18.5	40 0/8	20.0	41 6/8	21.4	43 4/8	22.9	45 2/8	24.3	47 0/8	25.8	48 6/8
18.6	40 1/8	20.1	41 7/8	21.5	43 5/8	23.0	45 3/8	24.4	47 1/8	25.9	48 7/8
18.7	40 2/8	20.2	42 0/8	21.6	43 6/8	23.1	45 4/8	24.5	47 2/8	26.0	49 0/8
18.8	40 3/8	20.3	42 1/8	21.7	43 7/8	23.2	45 5/8	24.6	47 3/8	26.1	49 1/8
18.9	40 4/8	20.4	42 2/8	21.8	44 0/8	23.3	45 6/8	24.7	47 4/8		
19.0	40 5/8	20.5	42 3/8	21.9	44 1/8	23.4	45 7/8	24.8	47 5/8		
19.1	40 6/8	20.6	42 4/8	22.0	44 2/8	23.5	46 0/8	34.9	47 6/8		
19.2	40 7/8	20.7	42 5/8	22.1	44 3/8	23.6	46 1/8	25.0	47 7/8		
19.3	41 0/8	20.8	42 6/8	22.2	44 4/8	23.7	46 2/8	25.1	48 0/8		

Table 6-10. Abdomen Measurement/Points

Table 6-11. Biceps and Forearm Measurement/Points

Biceps Extended. **The biceps are measured in the extended position with the arm raised to 90° with the palm upward. The tape is placed over the largest part of the bicep/tricep group.**

PTS	BICEPS	PTS	BICEPS	PTS	BICEPS	PTS	BICEPS	PTS	BICEPS
.1	5 7/8	4.8	7 5/8	9.4	9 3/8	14.1	11 1/8	18.8	12 7/8
.4	6 0/8	5.1	7 6/8	9.8	9 4/8	14.5	11 2/8	19.1	13 0/8
.8	6 1/8	5.4	7 7/8	10.1	9 5/8	14.8	11 3/8	19.5	13 1/8
1.1	6 2/8	5.8	8 0/8	10.4	9 6/8	15.1	11 4/8	19.8	13 2/8
1.4	6 3/8	6.1	8 1/8	10.8	9 7/8	15.5	11 5/8	20.1	13 3/8
1.8	6 4/8	6.4	8 2/8	11.1	10 0/8	15.8	11 6/8	20.5	13 4/8
2.1	6 5/8	6.8	8 3/8	11.4	10 1/8	16.1	11 7/8	20.8	13 5/8
2.4	6 6/8	7.1	8 4/8	11.8	10 2/8	16.5	12 0/8	21.1	13 6/8
2.8	6 7/8	7.4	8 5/8	12.1	10 3/8	16.8	12 1/8		
3.1	7 0/8	7.8	8 6/8	12.4	10 4/8	17.1	12 2/8		
3.4	7 1/8	8.1	8 7/8	12.8	10 5/8	17.5	12 3/8		
3.8	7 2/8	8.4	9 0/8	13.1	10 6/8	17.8	12 4/8		
4.1	7 3/8	8.8	9 1/8	13.5	10 7/8	18.1	12 5/8		
4.4	7 4/8	9.1	9 2/8	13.8	11 0/8	18.5	12 6/8		

Forearm. **The forearm is measured over the largest part of the forearm while the arm is raised to 90° elbow extended and with the palm upward.**

PTS	FOREARM	PTS	FOREARM	PTS	FOREARM	PTS	FOREARM	PTS	FOREARM
.2	17 5/8	9.3	15 2/8	18.5	12 7/8	27.7	10 4/8	36.8	8 1/8
.6	17 4/8	9.8	15 1/8	19.0	12 6/8	28.1	10 3/8	37.3	8 0/8
1.1	17 3/8	10.3	15 0/8	19.5	12 5/8	28.5	10 2/8	37.8	7 7/8
1.6	17 2/8	10.8	14 7/8	19.9	12 4/8	29.1	10 1/8	38.3	7 6/8
2.1	17 1/8	11.2	14 6/8	20.4	12 3/8	29.6	10 0/8	38.8	7 5/8
2.5	17 0/8	11.7	14 5/8	20.9	12 2/8	30.1	9 7/8	39.3	7 4/8
3.0	16 7/8	12.2	14 4/8	21.4	12 1/8	30.6	9 6/8	39.7	7 3/8
3.5	16 6/8	12.7	14 3/8	21.9	12 0/8	31.0	9 5/8	40.2	7 2/8
4.0	16 5/8	13.2	14 2/8	22.3	11 7/8	31.5	9 4/8	40.7	7 1/8
4.5	16 4/8	13.7	14 1/8	22.8	11 6/8	32.0	9 3/8	41.2	7 0/8
5.0	16 3/8	14.1	14 0/8	23.3	11 5/8	32.5	9 2/8	41.7	6 7/8
5.4	16 2/8	14.6	13 7/8	23.8	11 4/8	33.0	9 1/8	42.2	6 6/8
5.9	16 1/8	15.1	13 6/8	24.3	11 3/8	33.5	9 0/8	42.5	6 5/8
6.4	16 0/8	15.6	13 5/8	24.9	11 2/8	33.9	8 7/8	.0	0 0/8
6.9	15 7/8	16.1	13 4/8	25.2	11 1/8	34.4	8 6/8		
7.4	15 6/8	16.6	13 3/8	25.7	11 0/8	34.9	8 5/8		
7.9	15 5/8	17.0	13 2/8	26.2	10 7/8	35.4	8 4/8		
8.3	15 4/8	17.5	13 1/8	26.7	10 6/8	36.0	8 3/8		
8.8	15 3/8	18.0	13 0/8	27.2	10 5/8	36.4	8 2/8		

Table 6-11 (Cont'd)

Thigh. **The thigh measurement is taken with the subject's feet slightly apart. The tape is placed below the buttocks fold with the subject standing evenly on both legs.**

PTS	THIGH	PTS	THIGH	PTS	THIGH	PTS	THIGH	PTS	THIGH
.0	11 6/8	5.4	15 2/8	10.7	18 6/8	16.0	22 2/8	21.3	25 6/8
.2	11 7/8	5.5	15 3/8	10.9	18 7/8	16.2	22 3/8	21.5	25 7/8
.4	12 0/8	5.7	15 4/8	11.0	19 0/8	16.3	22 4/8	21.7	26 0/8
.6	12 1/8	5.9	15 5/8	11.2	19 1/8	16.5	22 5/8	21.8	26 1/8
.8	12 2/8	6.1	15 6/8	11.4	19 2/8	16.7	22 6/8	22.0	26 2/8
1.0	12 3/8	6.3	15 7/8	11.6	19 3/8	16.9	22 7/8	22.2	26 3/8
1.2	12 4/8	6.5	16 0/8	11.8	19 4/8	17.1	23 0/8	22.4	26 4/8
1.4	12 5/8	6.7	16 1/8	12.0	19 5/8	17.3	23 1/8	22.6	26 5/8
1.6	12 6/8	7.0	16 2/8	12.2	19 6/8	17.5	23 2/8	22.8	26 6/8
1.8	12 7/8	7.1	16 3/8	12.4	19 7/8	17.7	23 3/8	23.0	26 7/8
1.9	13 0/8	7.3	16 4/8	12.6	20 0/8	17.9	23 4/8	23.2	27 0/8
2.1	13 1/8	7.5	16 5/8	12.7	20 1/8	18.1	23 5/8	23.4	27 1/8
2.3	13 2/8	7.6	16 6/8	12.9	20 1/8	18.2	23 6/8	23.6	27 2/8
2.5	13 3/8	7.8	16 7/8	13.1	20 3/8	18.4	23 7/8	23.7	27 3/8
2.7	13 4/8	8.0	17 0/8	13.3	20 4/8	18.6	24 0/8	23.9	27 4/8
2.9	13 5/8	8.2	17 1/8	13.5	20 5/8	18.8	24 1/8	24.1	27 5/8
3.1	13 6/8	8.4	17 2/8	13.7	20 6/8	19.0	24 2/8	24.3	27 6/8
3.3	13 7/8	8.6	17 3/8	13.9	20 7/8	19.2	24 3/8	24.5	27 7/8
3.5	14 0/8	8.8	17 4/8	14.1	21 0/8	19.4	24 4/8	24.7	28 0/8
3.6	14 1/8	9.0	17 5/8	14.3	21 1/8	19.6	24 5/8	24.9	28 1/8
3.8	14 2/8	9.1	17 6/8	14.5	21 2/8	19.8	24 6/8	25.1	28 2/8
4.0	14 3/8	9.3	17 7/8	14.6	21 3/8	20.0	24 7/8	25.3	28 3/8
4.2	14 4/8	9.5	18 0/8	14.8	21 4/8	20.1	25 0/8	25.4	28 4/8
4.4	14 5/8	9.7	18 1/8	15.0	21 5/8	20.3	25 1/8	25.6	28 5/8
4.6	14 6/8	9.9	18 2/8	15.2	21 6/8	20.5	25 2/8	25.8	28 6/8
4.8	14 7/8	10.1	18 3/8	15.4	21 7/8	20.7	25 3/8	26.0	28 7/8
5.0	15 0/8	10.3	18 4/8	15.6	22 0/8	20.9	25 4/8	26.2	29 0/8
5.2	15 1/8	10.5	18 5/8	15.8	22 1/8	21.1	25 5/8	26.4	29 1/8
26.6	29 2/8	28.1	30 2/8	29.8	31 3/8	31.3	32 3/8	32.8	33 3/8
26.8	29 3/8	28.3	30 3/8	30.0	31 4/8	31.5	32 4/8	32.9	33 4/8
27.0	29 4/8	28.5	30 4/8	30.2	31 5/8	31.7	32 5/8		
27.2	29 5/8	28.9	30 6/8	30.4	31 6/8	31.9	32 6/8		
27.3	29 6/8	29.0	30 7/8	30.6	31 7/8	32.1	32 7/8		
27.5	29 7/8	29.2	31 0/8	30.8	32 0/8	32.3	33 0/8		
27.7	30 0/8	29.4	31 1/8	30.9	32 1/8	32.5	33 1/8		
27.9	30 1/8	29.6	31 2/8	31.1	32 2/8	32.7	33 2/8		

Table 6-12. Thigh Measurement/Points

D. APPROPRIATE CIVILIAN ATTIRE

Appropriate civilian attire is that type of clothing which, when worn by the individual Marine, presents a conservative personal appearance and is commensurate with the high standards traditionally associated with Marine Corps personnel. When civilian attire is authorized for wear in lieu of a uniform in a duty status, the appropriate civilian attire will be that which is comparable to the degree of formality as the uniform prescribed for such duty. No eccentricities of dress shall be permitted at any time.

The Commandant of the Marine Corps has extended the privilege of wearing civilian clothing to enlisted personnel of the Marine Corps within set limitations. When conditions require or permit the wearing of civilian clothing, only appropriate civilian attire will be worn.

When civilian clothing is worn on base, Marine Corps personnel shall ensure that their dress and personal appearance meet the same high standards established for personnel in uniform. No part of a prescribed uniform, except those items which are not exclusively military in character, shall be worn with civilian clothing, except as follows:

Men are restricted to gold cuff links, studs, and tie bar, mourning band, foot wear, socks, gloves, underwear, black bow ties, service sweater, and the raincoat and all-weather coat without insignia of grade.

Women are restricted to the white shirt without insignia, footwear, anklets, gloves, handbag, mourning band, service sweater, raincoat and all-weather coat without insignia.

For additional training in this area, references are provided below:

1. MCO 1020.34____ Marine Corps Uniform Regulations
2. MCO 6100.10 Weight Control and Military Appearance

Section V. Wearing and Maintaining Uniforms and Equipment

***Objective:** Correctly wear and maintain all Marine Corps uniforms and equipment prescribed by the unit to which assigned.*

A. WEARING THE UNIFORM (MEN)

1. **LONG SLEEVE SHIRT CUFF** (fig 6-19). The long sleeve shirt shall cover the wrist bone and extend to a point 2 inches above the second joint from the end of the thumb. A tolerance of 1/2 inch, plus or minus is acceptable.

Fig 6-19. Long sleeve cuff.

2. Trouser length (rear) (fig 6-20). The trousers shall be of sufficient length to reach the top of the heel of the shoe in the rear. A variation of 1/4-inch above or below the top of the heel is acceptable.

Fig 6-20. Trouser length.

3. **TROUSER LENGTH AND HEM** (fig 6-21). When the legs of the trousers have been hemmed, they will be 7/8 inch shorter in the front than in the back in order to present a slight "break" at the lower front above the shoe top. The sharpness of the "break" will vary, depending on the size of the shoe being worn, the height of the individual's instep, and the width of the legs of the trousers. Trousers should be finished with a 3-inch hem, but in all cases no less than 2 inches.

4. **TROUSER FIT** (fig 6-22). Trousers shall be of sufficient looseness around the hips and buttocks to prevent gapping of the pockets and visible horizontal wrinkles across the front.

The fly of the trousers shall hang in a vertical line without gapping when unzipped.

NOTE: The tip end of the web belt will pass through the buckle to the wearer's left and will extend not less than 2 inches nor more than 4 inches beyond the buckle. The right edge of the buckle is centered on line with the edge of the fly front or coat flap.

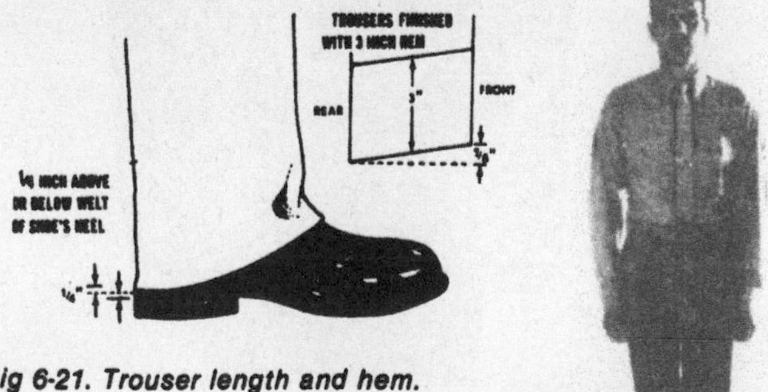

Fig 6-21. Trouser length and hem.

Fig 6-22. Trouser fit.

5. **GREEN SERVICE COAT** (fig 6-23). The left side of the front closure should overlap the right side by not less than 3-inches or more than 4-inches. When body conformation precludes obtaining the minimum, less than 3-inches is permissible provided the front does not gap open and is parallel to the pocket edges. The front closure of the coat will not form a vertical line with the crotch but only offset it by 3/4-inch to the wearer's right. The horizontal edges of the front panels shall be even, plus or minus 1/4-inch. The coat sleeve shall extend to a point 1-inch above the second joint from the end of the thumb, plus or minus 1/4-inch. The tip end of the green belt shall extend no less than 2 3/4 inches and no more than 3 3/4 inches past the buckle.

Fig 6-23. Green service coat.

6. GREEN SERVICE SWEATER (fig 6-24).

a. The service sweater is NOT authorized for wear with any blue dress uniform.

b. The green service sweater may be worn in lieu of the service coat when the service uniform is prescribed. This combination is NOT authorized for leave and liberty.

c. The sweater may be worn with either the long or quarter-length sleeve shirt (whichever is prescribed/ authorized as the seasonal uniform shirt). When the sweater is worn with the quarter-length sleeve shirt, the collar will be worn outside the sweater. When the sweater is worn with the long sleeve shirt, the necktie will not be worn. The top button of the shirt will be unbuttoned and the collar will be worn outside the sweater. The sleeves of the sweater may be turned up; however, the sleeves should be of sufficient length to conceal the shirt cuff. The waistband of the sweater may be turned under; however, the length of the sweater should be sufficient to cover the belt.

d. When the sweater is worn with the camouflage utility uniform, it will be worn underneath the camouflage utility coat.

e. The sweater is **NOT** authorized for wear in formal formations and during inspections, ceremonies, or parades on or off the installation.

f. The sweater is authorized for wear with civilian clothing and it may also be worn underneath the overcoat, raincoat, field coat, and all-weather coat.

Fig 6-24. Green service sweater.

7. **SERVICE STRIPES** (Fig 6-25). Each service stripe represents 4-years service. They are worn on the blue coat, the service coats, and the overcoat.

Fig 6-25. Service Stripes.

8. **GARRISON CAP** (Fig 6-26). The fit around the head shall be adequate to place the garrison cap on the head but will not cause the top or rear contour of the cap to "break."

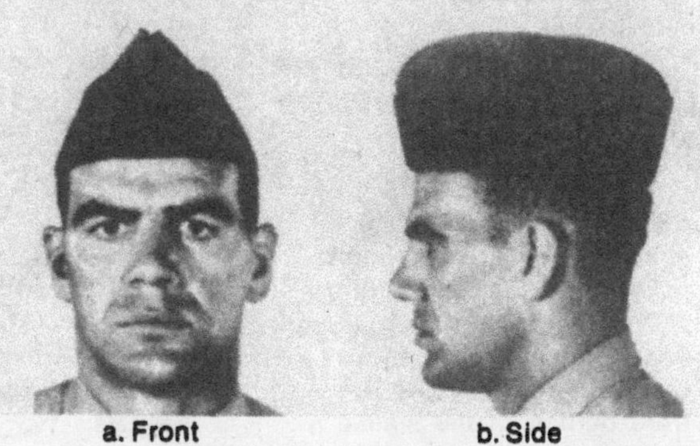

a. Front b. Side

Fig 6-26. Garrison cap.

9. **SERVICE CAP** (Fig 6-27). The service cap shall fit snugly and comfortably around the largest part of the head. The lower band of the frame shall rest high enough on the head to preclude the top of the head forcing the cover above its natural tautness. The front view of the frame shows the bottom of the visor to be slightly (approximately 1/2-inch) above the eye level of the wearer.

a. Front

b. Side

Fig 6-27. Service cap.

B. WEARING THE UNIFORM (WOMEN)

1. **SLACKS, GREEN SERVICE** (Fig 6-28). The slacks shall be of sufficient length to reach the junction of the welt of the shoe in the rear. A variation of ½ inch above the welt is acceptable. The front portion of the slacks should rest on the top of the shoe with a slight break. The

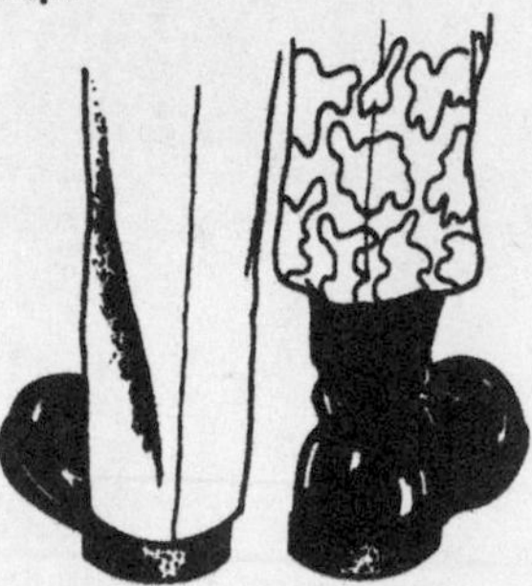
Fig 6-28. Service slacks and utility trousers.

front length should finish ¾ inch to 1 inch shorter than the back. The hem on the slacks will not be less than 2 inches or more than 3 inches.

2. **SERVICE CAP** (fig 6-29). Service and dress caps shall be centered and worn straight with the tip of the visor in line with the eyebrows.

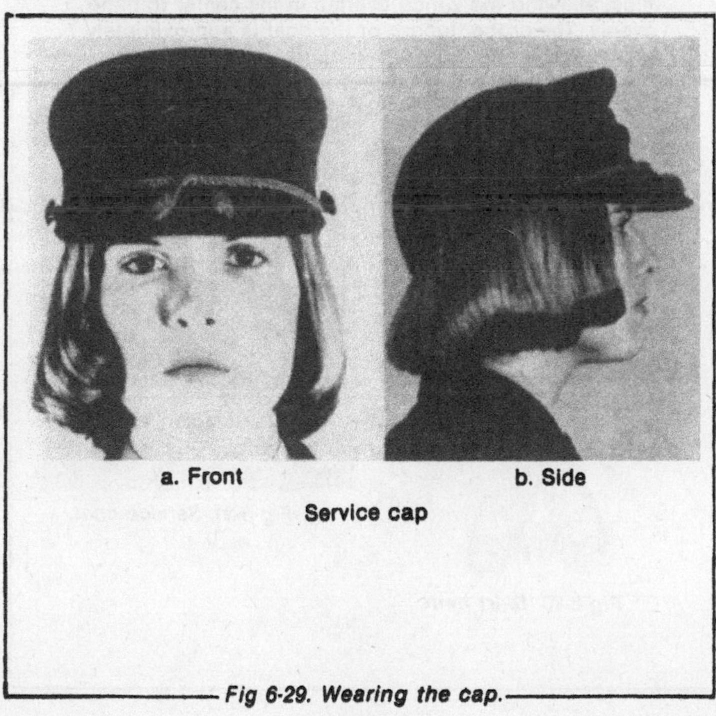

a. Front

b. Side

Service cap

Fig 6-29. Wearing the cap.

3. **SKIRT HEMS** (fig 6-30). Skirts shall have a hem or facing of not less than 2 inches nor more than 3 inches. They shall be of conventional length and sweep which is appropriate for the appearance of the uniform and the appearance of the individual. Skirts shall be knee length (not more than 1 inch above the top of the kneecap or more than 1 inch below the bottom of the kneecap).

4. **SERVICE COAT** (Fig 6-31). The coat should fit easily through the waist, extending to a smooth flare over the hips, allowing the 2-inch overlap in the center to hang evenly. The proper length of the coat is approximately 7 inches below the natural waistline.

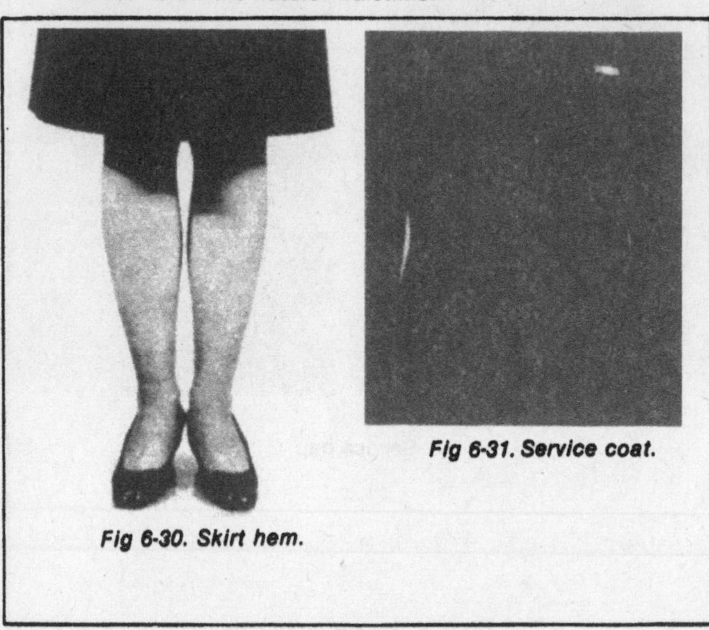

Fig 6-31. Service coat.

Fig 6-30. Skirt hem.

5. **KHAKI SHIRTS** (fig 6-32).

a. The long sleeve shirt may be worn as part of the winter/summer green service "A" and "B" uniforms.

b. The short sleeve shirt may be worn with the appropriate green service skirts/slacks when the winter/summer service "C" uniform is prescribed for wear by male Marines. This shirt may be worn as a uniform of the day and on leave or liberty, unless otherwise prescribed by the commander. The short sleeve shirt may be worn with the service coat; however, the neck tab must be worn.

c. The blue dress uniform with long-sleeve shirt and black necktab is designated as blue dress "C". The short sleeve shirt without black necktab is worn with the blue dress skirt and cap and is designated as the blue dress "D" uniform. These uniforms will not be worn on leave or liberty. The short sleeve shirt will never be worn with the blue dress coat.

d. The khaki shirts will not be tucked-in, but will be worn outside the skirt at all times, except by those women who are required to wear a duty belt.

e. The green necktabs will be worn in accordance with the following instructions:

(1) The necktab will be worn at all times when the long sleeve shirt is worn, both with and without the service coat.

(2) When the short sleeve shirt is worn with the service coat it will include the wearing of a green neck tab. When the short sleeve shirt is worn as an outer garment it will not include the green neck tab.

(3) When the necktabs are worn, the outer edge of the tabs should be parallel to the outer edge of the collar. Necktabs will vary in width according to the size of the woman Marine and manufacture of necktab; however, an equal amount of collar tab should show on each side of the shirt collar.

g. Grade insignia will be worn on the long sleeve shirt 4 inches down from the shoulder seam and centered on the sleeve.

h. On the short sleeve khaki shirt, grade insignia (green on khaki) will be worn centered on the outer half of each sleeve, midway between the shoulder seam and peak of the cuff.

i. When the khaki shirts are worn as outer garments, the wearing of ribbons and badges shall be the option of the individual unless otherwise prescribed by the commander. When the individual wears ribbons, she has two options:

(1) all authorized ribbons may be worn, or
(2) only personal U.S. decorations along with U.S. unit awards and the Good Conduct Medal may be worn.

If worn, ribbons/badges will be placed on the shirt 1-2 inches above the first visible button and centered so that they are in the same approximate position as ribbons/badges worn on the service coat.

6. MATERNITY UNIFORM FOR WOMEN MARINES. The maternity uniform is currently available for issue and purchase by enlisted women. This uniform is a required uniform for wear by pregnant women Marines who do not elect to be separated when they can no longer wear the service uniform. The wearing of civilian clothes in lieu of the maternity uniform by pregnant women is not authorized. Additional information on requisitioning and wearing the maternity uniform is contained in the **MCBUL 1020 SERIES.**

Fig 6-32. Khaki shirt.

7. GREEN SERVICE SWEATER (fig 6-33).

a. The green sweater may be worn in lieu of the service coat when the service uniform is prescribed, except on leave and liberty. The sweater is NOT authorized for leave or liberty, with the blue uniform. The sweater is NOT authorized for wear with any blue dress uniform.

b. The top button of the shirt will be unbuttoned and the collar will be worn outside the sweater. The sleeves of the sweater may be turned up; however, the sleeves should be of sufficient length to cover the shirt cuff. The waistband of the sweater may be turned up but should be of sufficient length to cover the waistband of the skirt.

c. When the sweater is worn with the camouflage utility uniform, it will be worn underneath the camouflage utility coat.

d. Enlisted women Marines shall wear the metal/plastic grade insignia on the collars of the khaki shirt or white shirt and utility coat in the same manner as currently prescribed for wear on the utility coats.

e. The sweater is authorized for wear with civilian clothing and it may also be worn underneath the overcoat, raincoat, field coat, or all-weather coat.

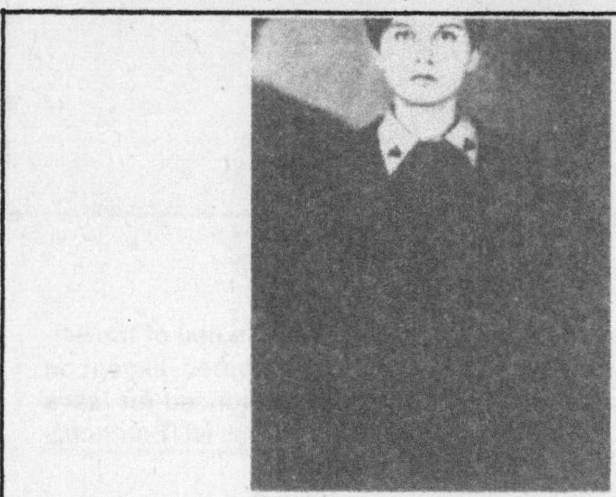

Fig 6-33. Green service sweater.

C. WEARING RIBBONS AND BADGES (figs 6-34 and 6-35)

1. **WEARING RIBBONS.** Ribbons may be worn on a bar or bars, and pinned to the coat or shirt. If ribbons are worn on a bar, no portion of the bar or pin shall be visible.

Ribbon bars are normally worn in rows of three; however, rows of four may be worn when displaying a large number of awards. When more than one row of ribbon bars is worn, all rows except the uppermost will contain the same number of ribbons. When the number of rows is so great as to cause ribbons to be concealed by the service coat lapel (one-third or more of a ribbon concealed), ribbon bars shall be placed in successively decreasing rows; e.g., 4-ribbon rows, 3-ribbon rows, 2-ribbon rows, single ribbon. The left edge of all decreasing rows will be in a line vertically; except that, when the uppermost row presents an unsatisfactory appearance when so alined, it will be placed in the position presenting the neatest appearance (usually centered over the row immediately below it). Women may wear 2-ribbon rows when the coat lapel causes ribbons to be concealed.

All ribbons to which the individual is entitled shall be worn on coats and may be prescribed for wear on shirts by the local commander, except as follows:

Ribbons shall **NOT** be worn on the sweater, overcoat, raincoat, utility coat, or all-weather coat.

When shirts are worn as outer garments, ribbons are not required unless prescribed by the commander. If the individual wears ribbons, he has two options:

(1) all authorized ribbons may be worn, or
(2) only personal U.S. decorations along with U.S. unit awards and the Good Conduct Medal may be worn.

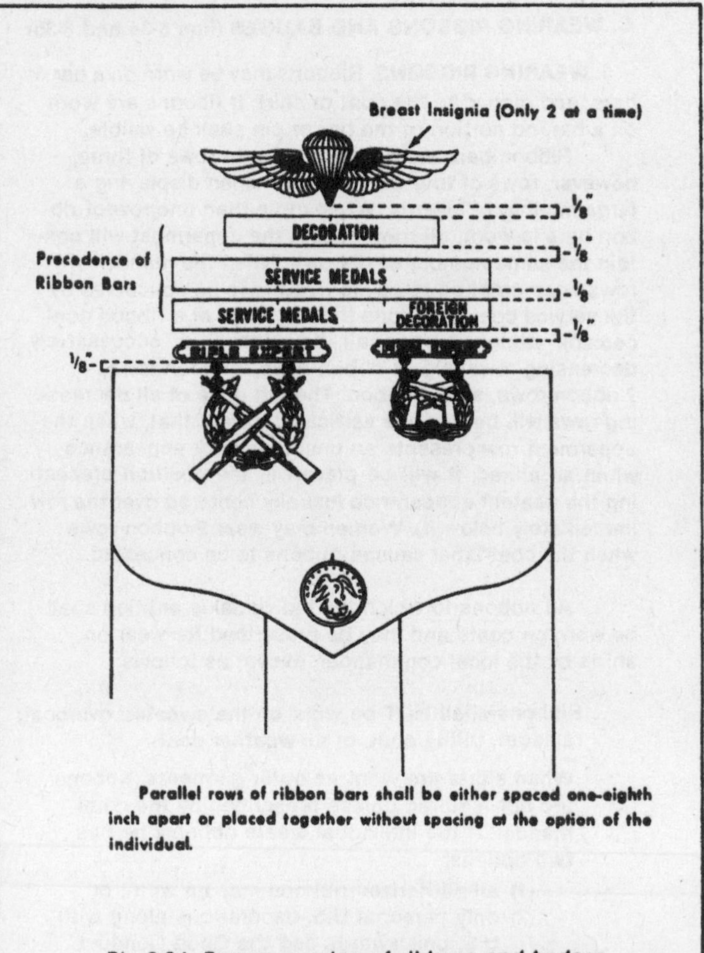

Fig 6-34. Proper wearing of ribbons and badges (male Marines).

Figure 3-34 Legend

1. Bottom edge of rifle bar 1/8 in. above the edge of the pocket.

2. Top of the pistol bar is even with the top of the rifle bar; therefore, the bottom of the pistol bar will be more than 1/8 in. above top edge of the pocket.

3. The first row of ribbons will be 1/8 in. above the top edge of the shooting badges. The second and succeeding row(s) of ribbons will either be worn 1/8 in. apart or flush.

4. Whether or not ribbons are worn, badges will be spaced so that outboard ends would be even with the ends of a ribbon bar, which is 4-1/8 in. long. The center of this ribbon bar (whether real or imaginary) should coincide with the center of the pocket as shown.

5. Ribbons must be worn in proper order of seniority.

6. Stars will be worn with single ray up.

7. Ribbons must be clean, not faded or frayed.

8. When marksmanship badges are worn, ribbon bars will be centered over the pocket with the bottom edge of the ribbon bar 1/8 in. above the widest holding bar of the marksmanship badge(s).

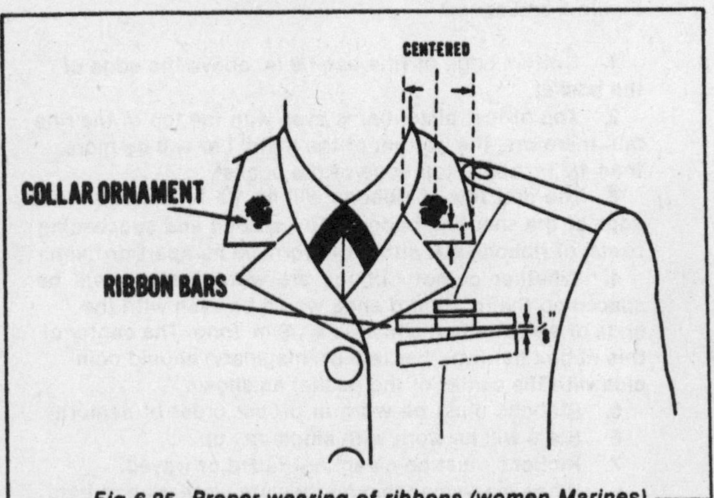

Fig 6-35. *Proper wearing of ribbons (women Marines).*

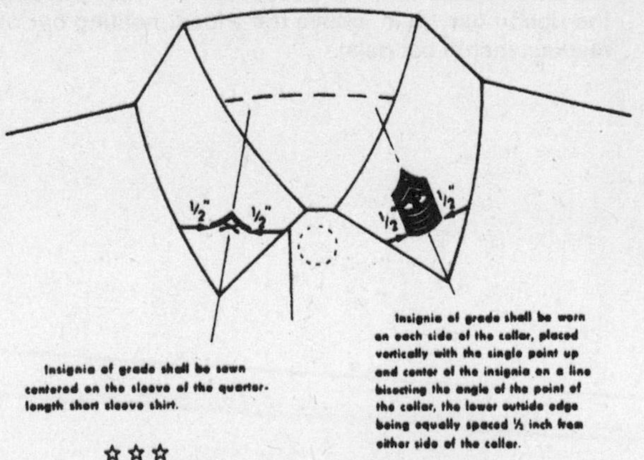

☆☆☆

Fig 6-36. Wearing insignia of grade.

D. WEARING INSIGNIA OF GRADE AND PLACEMENT OF USMC DECAL (figs 6-36 and 6-37)

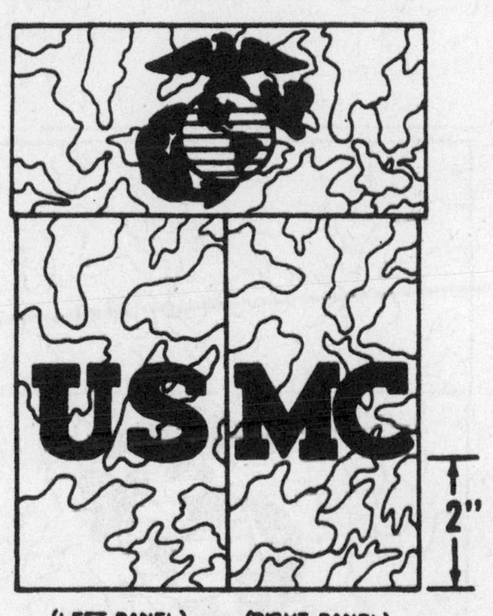

A Marine gets one chance to properly place the iron-on USMC decal on his utility shirt left breast pocket. It must be done right.

The Eagle, Globe, and Anchor is placed on the pocket flap centered right to left, top to bottom.

The "USMC" portion is separated into two parts, "US" and "MC". The "US" is placed on the left panel of the pocket, centered left to right, 2 inches from the bottom edge. The "MC" is placed on the right panel of the pocket, centered left to right, 2 inches from the bottom edge.

Fig 6-36 Contd. Placement of USMC decal (utility shirt, field coat, and raincoat).

On the new poplin camouflage utilities, the pocket is not divided into panels. The Marine Corps emblem and the "USMC" decals are placed as shown in figure 6-37.

Fig 6-37. Placement of USMC decal on poplin utilities.

E. MAINTAINING YOUR UNIFORM

1. GENERAL. After six months in the Marine Corps, you are given a monthly clothing allowance in your pay check. It is to be used to repair or replace unserviceable clothing and alter serviceable clothing for proper fit. Your clothing maintenance allowance is not all that is needed to properly maintain your clothing. Proper care of your uniforms when being worn or stored is important for maximum usage and proper appearance.

When wearing your uniform, avoid carrying long objects (e.g., large key rings or bulky wallets) in your pockets. Wear the appropriate uniform for the job or task that you are to perform.

When not using your uniforms, they should be hung neatly on appropriate hangers to preserve their shapes. Avoid crowding the articles together when hanging the uniforms on hangers. Wooden hangers are ideal for maintaining your uniform. If you store uniforms in a sea bag or trunk, fold them carefully to preserve their shape. Also note item 7 below ("Preventing moth damage") when storing uniforms for a long time.

2. SERVICE UNIFORMS. The service uniform generally shows more wear at creased areas. This may be partially offset by periodically pressing out old creases and reforming them slightly to either side of the previous crease. Sleeve cuffs, trouser hems, and skirt hems should be examined periodically and turned if material permits.

Drycleaning preserves the original appearance and finish of wool and wool-polyester garments and is recommended over hand laundering. However, when drycleaning facilities are not available, and only as a last resort, wool and wool/polyester uniforms may be hand laundered using a neutral soap and fresh lukewarm water, 70° to 80°. Thick suds are necessary for best results. In order to preserve the finish, rubbing should be held to a minimum. Thorough rinsing is necessary to remove all traces of the soap. After washing the garment, squeeze gently to remove water, shape garment by hand, and dry in open air. Colored garments should not be hung in the sun to dry. If this is unavoidable, turn the garments inside out. Never use chlorine bleaches on wool and wool/polyester materials.

3. **BUTTONS AND INSIGNIA.** Gold buttons should be cleaned with a weak solution of household ammonia and water. Do not use abrasives or polishing cloths containing chemicals. Gold-plated buttons that have had the plating removed are likely to turn green due to exposure to moist air. This can be removed by rubbing gently with acetic acid or any substance containing this acid, such as vinegar, followed by a thorough washing in fresh water and drying.

Marine Corps emblems will not be polished. If emblems lose their finish, replace them or refinish them with USMC approved liquid, black protective coating as sold through the Marine Corps Exchange. Do not use paint or other unauthorized coloring agents.

4. **FOOTWEAR.**

a. **LEATHER.** Leather shoes and boots must be properly cared for to ensure optimum wear and to protect the feet. When shoes are not in use, the shape should be maintained by shoe trees. Footpowder should be sprinkled liberally inside shoes to absorb moisture. Shoes should be kept clean of sand, dirt, grit, and other substances that could produce a deteriorating action on shoe threads and shoe leather. Clean shoes periodically with saddle soap.

b. **SYNTHETIC SHOES.** For normal care, just wipe with a damp cloth or sponge. Regular shoe polish may be used to increase the shine. To cover abrasions or scuff marks, use a paste wax shoe polish. Stains should be wiped off as quickly as possible and then the shoes should be cleaned. For stubborn stains, try lighter fluid.

It is recommended that you do not attempt to dye synthetic shoes. Also, do not use acetone, nail polish removers, chlorinated dry cleaning solvent, or alcohol. When in doubt about a cleaner or polish, try a little on the instep near the sole.

5. **LAUNDERING WEB BELTS.** When belts are laundered, shrinkage is normal. To compensate for this, the belts are manufactured 3 inches longer than the waist size. Belts should be washed at least three times before cutting to normal waist size. To prevent excessive shrinkage after laundering, hand stretch the belt while wet.

6. **REPAIRING CUTS IN CLOTH.** A tailor can repair a clean cut in a uniform by weaving the material.

7. **PREVENTING MOTH DAMAGE.** Frequent brushing and exposure to sunshine and fresh air will effectively prevent moths. If uniforms are to be put away for a long time and left undisturbed, they should be thoroughly cleaned and packed in an airtight plastic bag, or protected with camphor balls, cedar wood, or other commercial preparations.

8. REMOVING STAINS, SHINE, AND SINGE MARKS.

a. **BLOOD STAINS.** To remove dried blood, stains should first be brushed with a dry brush to break up and remove as much of the stain as possible. Then soak in cold water for at least an hour followed by regular washing. Should a slight trace of the stain remain, apply a solution of ammonia.

b. **CHOCOLATE STAINS.** To remove chocolate stains, cover the stain with borax and wash with cold water. Then pour boiling water on the stain and rub vigorously between the hands. When dry, sponge with a little naphtha or benzine.

c. **FOOD STAINS.** To remove a food stain, sponge the stain thoroughly with cold water. If a grease stain persists, dry thoroughly and then sponge with a little naphtha or benzine.

d. **IODINE STAINS.** To remove iodine stains, apply a solution of "Hypo" as used in photography or sodium hyposulphite and then thoroughly rinse with water. Sodium hyposulphite should be limited to use on white cotton only. Iodine stains may also be removed by using laundry starch or a solution of ammonia.

e. **KEROSENE STAINS.** To remove kerosene stains, wash in a solution of warm soapy water.

f. **MILDEW STAINS.** To remove recent mildew stains, simply use cold water. Old mildew stains on white cotton can be removed by using bleach.

g. **OIL OR GREASE STAINS.** To remove oil or grease stains, place a clean cloth or other absorbent material under the stain and apply benzine or benzol on the stain and tamp it, driving oil and grease into the absorbent material. If stain is heavy, shift cloth to a clean place and flush again with cleaning solvent. To eliminate the ring, saturate a clean cloth with cleaning solvent and sponge lightly, working from the center of the stained area outward.

h. **PAINT STAINS.** To remove fresh paint stains, follow the method given above for oil or grease stains. Old and hard paint stains are extremely difficult to remove and should be entrusted to a reliable drycleaner. A possible treatment of old paint stains is to soak the stain in turpentine for at least one hour. Then with a teaspoon or other blunt object, break up the stain and flush out as outlined for oil and grease stains. Always use a patting action when spotting fabrics, as brushing or rubbing may destroy the weave, or leave a chaffed area with subsequent damage in color.

i. **PARAFFIN AND WAX STAINS.** To remove paraffin and wax stains, scrape off excess paraffin and wax, place blotting paper over the spot and apply a hot iron to blotting paper. Continue this procedure using clean blotting paper until the spot is removed.

j. **RUST, INK, AND FRUIT STAINS.** To remove rust, ink, and fruit stains from white uniforms, soak the stain in a solution of oxalic acid or moisten the stain and put powdered oxalic acid or sodium or potassium acid oxalate over the stained area. As the stain dissolves, rub gently with a piece of white cotton or linen. Wash with warm water. Do not allow the solution to dry in the fabric. Oxalic acid and its soluble salts are very poisonous and care should be exercised in handling them.

k. **SHINE.** To remove shine from the service or dress uniforms, the spot to be treated should be steamed by laying a wet cloth over it and pressing with a hot iron, and then rubbing it very gently with a piece of "00" sandpaper or emery cloth. This should be done by a tailor. Sponging diluted (1:20) solution of ammonia prior to steaming is also recommended.

l. **SINGE MARK.** To remove a light singe mark, the area should be rubbed vigorously with the flat side of a silver coin. This will make a great improvement in appearance; however, it is not effective in the case of bad singes or scorches. Singe marks may also be removed by sponging with a 3 percent solution of hydrogen peroxide and allowing to dry in direct sunlight; however, hydrogen peroxide is not recommended for woolen or dyed fabrics.

F. MAINTAINING INDIVIDUAL EQUIPMENT

1. **General.** When equipment is entrusted to your custody by your unit, not only are you expected to account for each item, but you are responsible for properly maintaining each item. Proper maintenance of your equipment will prolong its wear and serviceability. The proper care of your equipment not only determines the success of the unit's mission, but also you and your fellow Marine's survival in combat.

2. **CANVAS EQUIPMENT.** The following are representative items of canvas type equipment:

Bag, waterproof clothing.
Cover, canteen.
Cover, helmet.
Pack, ALICE.
Carrier, entrenching tool.
Pouch, ammunition cal. 45, M14, M16.
Case, sleeping bag.
Shelterhalf, tent.
Vest, armor (armor, upper torso).
Carrier, protective mask.

Clean canvas type items by dipping them vigorously in a pail of warm water containing a mild soap or detergent. This prolongs the life of the item and prevents discoloration.

If soiled spots remain after washing, scrub the spots with a white or colorfast cloth, using warm, soapy water or detergent solution. Do not use chlorine bleaches, wet stiff brushes, cleaning fluids, or dyes which will discolor the item. Dry canvas type items in shade or indoors. Do not dry them in the sun because direct sunlight will discolor them.

NOTE: Certain canvas type items, may be provided with fiberboard or plastic stiffeners. If so, clean these cases with a damp, soft brush and cool water only.

3. **WEB EQUIPMENT.** The following are representative items of web equipment:

Belt, cartridge or pistol.
Straps for helmet, helmet liner, pack, lanyards, suspenders, etc.

Clean web equipment the same way you clean canvas equipment. Do not use chlorine, cleaning fluids, or dyes. Rinse all soap carefully from web equipment after washing, and stretch the item back to its original shape while it dries. Dry equipment in shade or indoors. Never use direct sunlight for drying. Do not launder or dry webbing in automatic laundry equipment.

4. **COATED ITEMS.** Items such as the poncho, pneumatic mattress, and protective mask are cleaned as described below.

Wipe soiled, coated items with clean cloth, shampoo by hand with a soft-bristle brush using warm water and mild soap or synthetic detergent, and rinse thoroughly. Air dry the items. Do not machine wash, machine dry, or hot press iron coated items.

5. **PLASTIC CANTEEN AND METAL CUP.** Your plastic (polyethylene) water canteen holds 1 quart. Wash the canteen and cup with warm, soapy water and rinse thoroughly. Keep them drained and dry when not in use.

When required, replace the cap with the M-1 drinking device. This device allows you to drink water from the canteen while you are wearing a protective mask. Do not put the plastic canteen near an open flame or burner plate. The metal canteen cup should be scrubbed as soon as possible after use over an open flame or a hot plate to avoid discoloration of the metal.

6. **STEEL HELMET.** Although the helmet is a sturdy item that can withstand rough treatment, you should not use it as a cooking pan as heat destroys the temper of the metal, weakens the helmet, and reduces the protective qualities. Also, do not use the helmet as a shovel or hammer. Changing the shape of the helmet will also affect the protective quality of the helmet.

7. **SLEEPING BAG.** The sleeping bag requires special attention in cleaning. Do not dry clean the sleeping bag, as the cleaning fluids will cause toxic fumes to linger within the bag. Consult your unit supply department for professional cleaning.

8. **BLANKETS, FIELD JACKET AND LINER, PONCHO LINER.** Wash frequently with lukewarm water and mild soap. Do not use hot or boiling water. **CAUTION:** Drying these items in intense heat will reduce the water repellent quality. Stretch each item back into shape while it is drying.

For additional training in this area, references are provided below:

1. FM 21-15 — Care of Individual Equipment
2. MCO P1020.34 — Marine Corps Uniform Regulations

Chapter 7. Physical Fitness

Objective: Pass the physical fitness test.

A. GENERAL

It is essential to the combat effectiveness of the Marine Corps that every Marine be physically fit. The implementation of the Commandant of the Marine Corps' policies on physical fitness requires that every Marine, regardless of age, grade, or duty assignment, engage in an effective physical conditioning program on a continuing and progressive basis.

The responsibility of maintaining a satisfactory level of physical fitness is shared by each Marine and his commanding officer. The time required for the maintenance of these standards is traditional in the Marine Corps way-of-life and the necessary self-discipline that must be part of the character of all Marines. A program of regular, vigorous and progressive physical fitness training results in an increase in work efficiency, self-confidence, and personal as well as unit pride. A Marine who is not physically fit is a burden to the readiness and combat efficiency of his unit and detracts from the professionalism of the Marine Corps.

B. DEFINITIONS

1. **PHYSICAL FITNESS.** In the Marine Corps, this means a healthy body, the endurance to withstand the stresses of prolonged activity and adverse environment, the capacity to endure the discomforts that accompany fatigue, and the ability to maintain combat effectiveness.

2. **STAMINA.** This is a combination of muscular and cardiovascular endurance. It is the most important aspect of fitness for Marines. Cardiovascular fitness should be the basis for all physical training because of its contribution to the overall health and longer life of the individual. Muscular endurance, which is closely associated with cardiovascular endurance, is the physical characteristic that will allow prolonged activity of a moderate tempo. For Marines, this represents the ability to march long distances with heavy loads or to work long hours and still maintain the reserve to carry on in an emergency.

3. **STRENGTH.** This is the ability to manipulate weight or, for a Marine, his own body weight. A certain amount of body strength is also necessary for appearance, confidence, and load-carrying ability. It is essential that a Marine be able to handle his own body weight; if he cannot, he is either too heavy or too weak.

C. PHYSICAL FITNESS TEST FOR MEN

1. **GENERAL.** The Marine Corps physical fitness test represents acceptable standards of physical fitness for male Marines 45 years of age and under. All eligible Marines must maintain the ability to pass the test at any time. All Marines will be tested at least semiannually. Those who fail the test will be placed on a supervised program until they attain the minimum acceptable level of fitness for their age group.

2. **CONDUCT.** The three events will be conducted in a single session of one morning or afternoon. Movement from one event to another should provide adequate rest before starting the next event. Events may be conducted in any sequence except that the 3-mile run should be last. Marines may wear appropriate gym attire or seasonally

modified utility uniform including gym shoes.

3. EVENTS/STANDARDS. The physical fitness test (PFT) consists of three events: pullups/chinups, bent knee situps, and a 3-mile run. These events are designed to test the strength and stamina of the upper body, the abdomen, and the lower body. To successfully pass the test, a Marine must complete the minimum repetitions or time for each of the three events, plus earn the required additional points listed by age group in figure 7-1. Failure to meet the required minimum in any event constitutes failure of the entire test regardless of total points earned. Minimum acceptable performance standards are listed in figure 7-1. Additional points may be earned in any of the three events. These are listed in the performance chart in figure 7-2.

Required minimum acceptable performance:

Age	Pullups	Situps	3-Mile Run minutes	Subtotal Points	Required Additional Points	Passing Score
17-26	3	40	28	95	40	135
27-39	3	35	29	84	26	110
40-45	3	35	30	78	7	85

Required minimum scores:

Age	Unsatisfactory	3d Class	2d Class	1st Class
17-26	0-134	135	175	225
27-39	0-109	110	150	200
40-45	0- 84	85	125	175

Fig 7-1. Minumum acceptable performance.

Point system. The table below will be used to assign a point value to each of the three events. Maximum attainable score for any one event is 100 points, while 300 points represents a perfect score.

Example:	*6 pullups*	=	*30 points*
	40 situps	=	*40 points*
	23.50 run	=	*65 points*
	Total score		*135 points*

Points	Pullups	Situps	3-mile run	Points	Pullups	Situps	3-mile run	Points	Pullups	Situps	3-mile run	Points	Pullups	Situps	3-mile run
100	20	80	18:00	75	15		22:10	50	10	50	26:20	25	5	25	30:30
99			18:10	74		67	22:20	49		49	26:30	24		24	30:40
98		79	18:20	73			22:30	48		48	26:40	23		23	30:50
97			18:30	72		66	22:40	47		47	26:50	22		22	31:00
96		78	18:40	71			22:50	46		46	27:00	21		21	31:10
95	19		18:50	70	14	65	23:00	45	9	45	27:10	20	4	20	31:20
94		77	19:00	69			23:10	44		44	27:20	19		19	31:30
93			19:10	68		64	23:20	43		43	27:30	18		18	31:40
92		76	19:20	67			23:30	42		42	27:40	17		17	31:50
91			19:30	66		63	23:40	41		41	27:50	16		16	32:00
90	18	75	19:40	65	13		23:50	40	8	40	28:00	15	3	15	32:10
89			19:50	64		62	24:00	39		39	28:10	14		14	32:20
88		74	20:00	63			24:10	38		38	28:20	13		13	32:30
87			20:10	62		61	24:20	37		37	28:30	12		12	32:40
86		73	20:20	61			24:30	36		36	28:40	11		11	32:50
85	17		20:30	60	12	60	24:40	35	7	35	28:50	10	2	10	33:00
84		72	20:40	59		59	24:50	34		34	29:00	9		9	33:10
83			20:50	58		58	25:00	33		33	29:10	8		8	33:20
82		71	21:00	57		57	25:10	32		32	29:20	7		7	33:30
81			21:10	56		56	25:20	31		31	29:30	6		6	33:40
80	16	70	21:20	55	11	55	25:30	30	6	30	29:40	5	1	5	33:50
79			21:30	54		54	25:40	29		29	29:50	4		4	34:00
78		69	21:40	53		53	25:50	28		28	30:00	3		3	34:30
77			21:50	52		52	26:00	27		27	30:10	2		2	35:00
76		68	22:00	51		51	26:10	26		26	30:20	1		1	36:00

Fig 7-2. Performance chart.

4. PERFORMACE OF EVENTS.

a. **PULLUPS** (fig 7-3). The bar is grasped with palms facing either forward or to the rear depending on individual preference, and the body is fully extended to a "dead" hanging position. Feet must be free of the ground. The position of the hands may be changed during the exercise as long as the performer is not assisted, does not dismount from the bar, or does not rest on some support. Pull your body up with arms until chin is over the bar, lower body until elbows are fully extended and the body is again in the "dead" hanging position; this is one repetition. Repeat as many times as possible. Kicking motions such that the feet and/or knees do not rise above waist

Fig 7-3. Pullups.

level are permitted as long as the pullup remains a vertical movement. The body will be kept from swinging by an assistant holding an extended arm in the front of the knees of the Marine on the bar. The movement must be fully completed to count.

b. **BENT-KNEE SITUPS** (fig 7-4). Time limit is 2 minutes. To assume the correct starting position, the Marine lies flat on his back with his knees flexed, both feet on the ground. The correct angle of the thighs to the ground beneath them is 45°. If the heels are too near the buttocks, the individual will not be able to sit up. The legs are spread shoulder-width apart and fingers interlaced behind his head in contact with the ground. The feet are held by another person. From this starting position, bend forward at the waist and raise the upper body until the head is directly over the knees. The heels are not to leave the ground. The upper body is lowered to the starting position until the shoulder blades touch the ground; neither the head nor the hands need to touch the ground. Repeat as many times as possible within the 2-minute time limit. Resting during performance of the exercise is permitted.

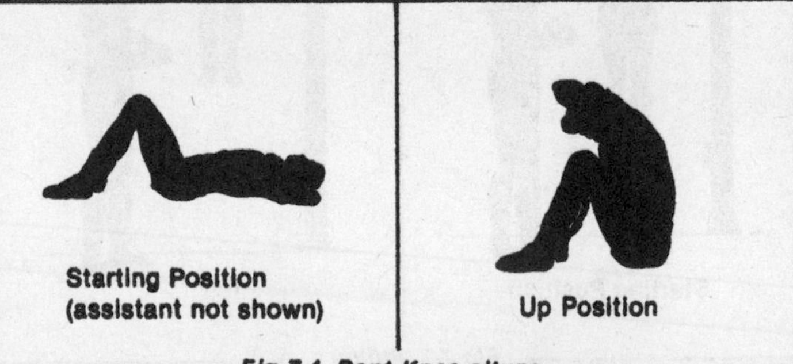

Fig 7-4. Bent-Knee situps.

c. **THREE-MILE RUN.** The object of this event is to complete the 3-mile measured course as rapidly as possible. Walking is allowed.

D. PHYSICAL FITNESS TEST FOR WOMEN

1. **GENERAL.** The Marine Corps physical fitness test represents acceptable standards of physical fitness for women Marines 45 years of age and under. All eligible Marines must maintain the ability to pass the test at any time. All Marines will be tested at least semiannually. Those who fail the test will be placed on a supervised program until they attain the minimum acceptable level of fitness for their age group.

2. **CONDUCT.** The three events will be conducted in a single session of one morning or afternoon. Movement from one event to another should provide adequate rest before starting the next event. Events may be conducted in any sequence except that the 1½ mile run should be last. Marines may wear appropriate gym attire or seasonally modified including gym shoes.

3. **EVENTS/STANDARDS.** The PFT consists of three events; the flexed arm hang, bent-knee situps and a 1½-mile run. These events are designed to test the strength and stamina of the upper body (shoulder girdle), midsection, and lower body. Additionally, the 1½-mile run measures the efficency of the cardiovascular system. To successfully pass the test, personnel must complete the minimum repetitions or time listed for each of the three events (fig 7-5). See figure 7-6 for the point scoring system which is used to determine superior achievement levels. The following figure indicates the minimum acceptable performance for each event, the minimum passing scores for each age group and the total number of points required for the superior achievements levels.

Age	Flexed Arm Hang (seconds)	Situps (repetitions)	1½-Mile Run (minutes)	Total Points
17-26	16	22	15	100
27-39	13	19	16:30	73
40-45	10	18	18	56

Required Minimum scores:

Age	Unsatisfactory	3d Class	2d Class	1st Class
17-26	0-99	100	150	200
27-39	0-72	73	123	173
40-45	0-55	56	106	156

Fig 7-5. Minimum acceptable performance.

a. **FLEXED ARM HANG** (fig 7-7). The individual stands on a support or, if necessary, is assisted by others to reach the starting position. Both palms must face in the same direction. The elbows are flexed so that the chin is over or level with the bar. Once the individual is set in the starting position, the support or assistance is removed and she attempts to maintain elbow flexion for as long as possible. The score is the length of time in seconds that some degree of flexion at the elbow is maintained. The chin may not rest on the bar during the exercise.

Maximum attainable score for any one event is 100 points, while 300 points represents a perfect score.

Example: Flexed Arm Hang	*45 seconds*	=	*50 points*
	30 situps	=	*60 points*
	13:50 run	=	*54 points*
	Total score		*164 points*

Points	Flexed Arm Hang	Situps	1½-Mile Run	Points	Flexed Arm Hang	Situps	1½-Mile Run	Points	Flexed Arm Hang	Situps	1½-Mile Run	Points	Flexed Arm Hang	Situps	1½-Mile Run
100	70	50	10:00	75			12:05	50	45	25	14:10	25	25		16:15
99			:05	74	57	37	:10	49			:15	24	24	12	:20
98	69	49	:10	73			:15	48	44	24	:20	23	23		:25
97			:15	72	56	36	:20	47			:25	22	22	11	.30
96	68	48	:20	71			:25	46	43	23	:30	21	21		:35
95			:25	70	55	35	:30	45			:35	20	20	10	:40
94	67	47	:30	69			:35	44	42	22	:40	19	19		45
93			:35	68	54	34	:40	43			:45	18	18	9	.50
92	66	46	:40	67			:45	42	41	21	:50	17	17		16:55
91			:45	66	53	33	:50	41			14:55	16	16	8	17:00
90	65	45	:50	65			12:55	40	40	20	15.00	15	15		:10
89			10:55	64	52	32	13.00	39	39		:05	14	14	7	20
88	64	44	11.00	63			:05	38	38	19	:10	13	13		30
87			:05	62	51	31	:10	37	37		:15	12	12	6	:40
86	63	43	:10	61			15	36	36	18	:20	11	11		17:50
85			:15	60	50	30	.20	35	35		:25	10	10	5	18:00
84	62	42	:20	59			:25	34	34	17	:30	9	9		.10
83			:25	58	49	29	:30	33	33		:35	8	8	4	.20
82	61	41	:30	57			:35	32	32	16	:40	7	7		:30
81			:35	56	48	28	:40	31	31		45	6	6	3	:40
80	60	40	:40	55			:45	30	30	15	.50	5	5		18.50
79			:45	54	47	27	:50	29	29		15:55	4	4	2	19:00
78	59	39	:50	53			13:55	28	28	14	16:00	3	3	1	:30
77			11:55	52	46	26	14:00	27	27		:05	2	2	1	20.00
76	58	38	12:00	51			:05	26	26	13	:10	1	1		30

Fig 7-6. Point system.

Fig 7-7. Flexed arm hang.

b. **BENT-KNEE SITUPS** (fig 7-8). Time limit is 1 minute. In the correct starting position, the Marine lies on her back (supine position) with knees flexed and both feet flat on the ground. One repetition consists of raising the upper body from the supine position until the head breaks an imaginary plane through the knees and returns to the supine position. Repeat as many times as possible during the time limit. During this movement, the hands must remain behind the head and the feet must remain on the ground. Upon return to the supine position, the shoulder blades must touch the ground to complete the repetion; neither the head nor the hands need touch. As assistant will grasp the participant's feet or her legs below the knee in whatever manner is most comfortable for the participant. Kneeling or sitting on the feet is permitted. Resting during the exercise is permitted in either the up or the down position.

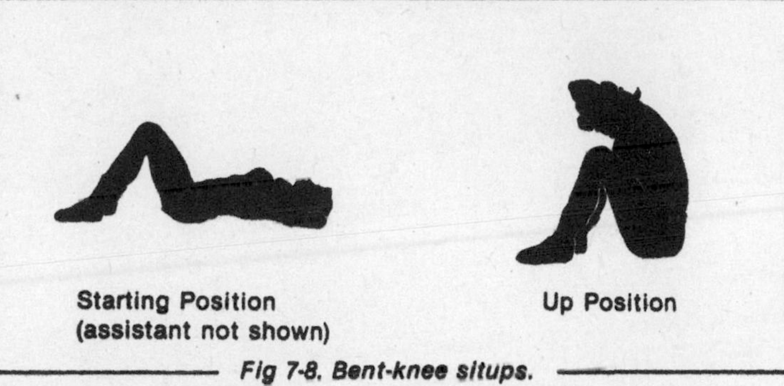

Fig 7-8. Bent-knee situps.

c. **1½-MILE RUN.** The object of this event is to complete the 1½-mile measured course as rapidly as possible. Walking is allowed.

Chapter 8. NBC Defense (Nuclear, Biological, Chemical)

Section I. Chemical and Biological Defense

Objectives:

1. When the alarm is sounded or when faced with the appropriate situation, remove the mask from its carrier and don, seat, clear, and check for proper seal the field protective mask within nine seconds and give the alarm if no one has done so.

2. At the command "SPRAY" or upon being told that an aircraft is spraying a cloud, properly mask, kneel, crouch or sit and cover the body with a poncho within twenty seconds.

3. When directed to move through a contaminated area, don available equipment and properly move through the contaminated area.

4. When provided with filters and a field protective mask, remove and replace the filters in the mask.

5. Explain the symptoms of nerve and blood chemical agent casualties and demonstrate the treatment.

You must be able to protect yourself from the effects of chemical and biological agents in order to perform your mission. The use of correct individual defensive measures can protect you from many of the hazards; therefore, you must learn these measures so that you will not become a casualty and so that you may assist your unit in accomplishing its mission. You must be able to take the correct protective action and correctly use your protective equipment.

A. BIOLOGICAL AND CHEMICAL EFFECTS

Detection of a chemical or biological attack may be difficult. Usually for a chemical attack you will have to rely on your senses to give you indication of the presence of an agent. Biological agents, however, are hard to detect. You will have to watch for certain clues that give indications of their presence. There are some obvious items or events that should make you suspicious of a chemical or biological attack.

1. GENERAL INDICATORS OF BIOLOGICAL OR CHEMICAL ATTACK.

a. Suspicious liquids or solids on the ground or on vegetation

b. Unexplained smoke or mist

c. Dead or sick animals or birds

d. Suspicious odors

2. CHEMICAL AGENT DETECTION. Detection will be primarily by the senses.

a. Irritation of eyes, nose, throat, skin

b. Headache, dizziness, nausea

c. Difficulty with or increased rate of breathing

d. A feeling of choking or tightness in the throat or chest

e. Strange or out-of-the-ordinary odors

f. Strange flavors in food or water

3. BIOLOGICAL AGENT DETECTION. Be aware of clues that may identify the presence of biological agents.

a. Enemy aircraft dropping unidentified material or spraying unidentified substances

b. New and unusual types of shells and bombs,

particularly those which burst with little or no blast

c. Smoke from an unknown source or of an unknown nature

d. An increase in sick or dead animals

e. Unusual or unexplained increase in the number of insects

f. Weapons that do not seem to have an immediate casualty effect

B. ALARM SYSTEMS

Two types of alarm systems may be used to alert you in the event of a chemical or biological attack (fig 8-1). Your unit SOP sets forth how and when local alarms will be given, but they are normally some form of percussion sound. In an emergency, it may be necessary to give visual signals or to sound a vocal alarm. Because of the danger of breathing in the agent if you give a vocal alarm, you should mask first and then shout "GAS" or "SPRAY" giving the visual alarm simultaneously (if you see an aircraft spraying a cloud).

Fig 8-1. Alarm systems for chemical or biological attack.

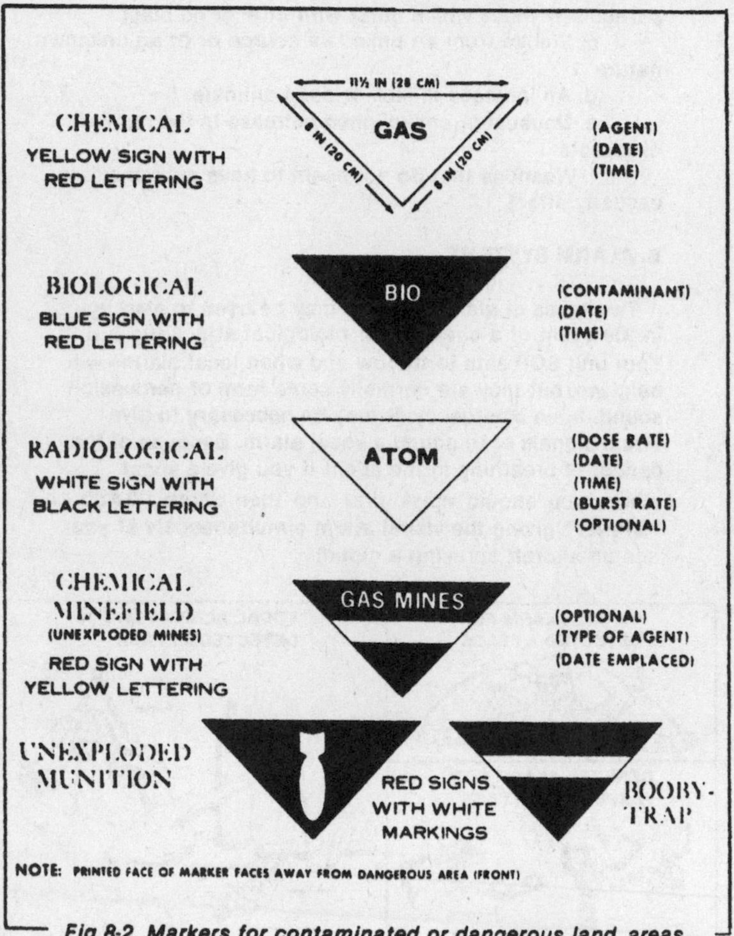

Fig 8-2. Markers for contaminated or dangerous land areas.

C. STANDARD NATO MARKERS

Known or suspected contaminated areas are marked with standard triangular markers. They are color coded and labeled to indicate the contaminating agent. All Marines should be able to recognize the markers shown in figure 8-2.

D. M17 SERIES FIELD PROTECTIVE MASK

1. **GENERAL.** The field protective mask is the most important single item of individual protective equipment in NBC warfare! As such, it must be properly stored and maintained. It is the individual Marine's responsibility to make sure the mask is put together right and that the filters are in good shape! Some tips in maintaining your mask are:

- Check filters. **REMEMBER,** wet filters **DO NOT** work!!
- Check the nosecup to make sure it's in the right position and not loose from the crimping ring (seals the voicemitter and nosecup together).
- Make sure the nosecup and cheek pouches are buttoned.
- Check the rubber faceblank for any dry rot or rips.
- Check the eye lens for scratches that would impair your vision.
- Check your head harness for elasticity.

2. **STORING THE MASK.** Proper storage of the mask with and without the hood is shown in figure 8-3. This must be done properly in order that the mask can be donned quickly and seated properly.

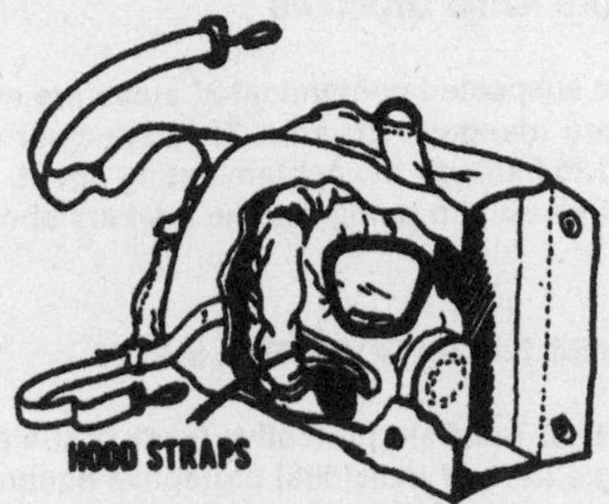

Fig 8-3. Proper storing of mask.

In using the hood with the field protective mask, make sure the mask is stowed properly in the carrier.

The hood will protect the neck and shoulders from being contaminated. The hood will be unzipped and rolled back over the sides and top of the mask with the straps extended out while stored in the carrier.

3. DONNING AND CLEARING THE FIELD PROTECTIVE MASK (fig 8-4). Upon hearing or seeing the alarm for gas:

a. Stop breathing.

b. Remove your headgear with your right hand and open the carrier with your left hand. Place headgear as directed.

c. Hold the carrier open with your left hand; grasp the facepiece just below the eyepieces and remove the mask with your right hand.

Fig 8-4. Donning the mask.

d. Grasp the facepiece with both hands, sliding your thumbs up inside the facepiece under the lower head harness straps. Lift your chin slightly.

e. Seat the chin pocket of the facepiece firmly on the chin. Bring head harness smoothly over head, ensuring that the head harness straps are straight and the head pad is centered.

Fig 8-4. Contd

f. Smooth edges of facepiece on your face with upward and backward motion of hands, pressing out all bulges to secure an airtight seal.

g. Close outlet valve by cupping the heel of your right hand firmly over the opening; blow hard to cleai agent from the facepiece.

Fig 8-4. Contd

h. Block air inlet holes of filter elements, shutting off the air supply. When you inhale, the facepiece should collapse.

j. Resume breathing. (give the alarm).

Fig 8-4. Contd

E. ACTION UPON HEARING OR SEEING THE ALARM "SPRAY"

At the alarm **"SPRAY"** or upon being told that an aircraft is spraying a cloud, mask; sound the alarm; kneel, crouch or sit; and cover your body with a poncho within 20 seconds, as shown in figure 8-5.

Fig 8-5. Action at the command SPRAY.

Open your poncho and cover yourself and your equipment.

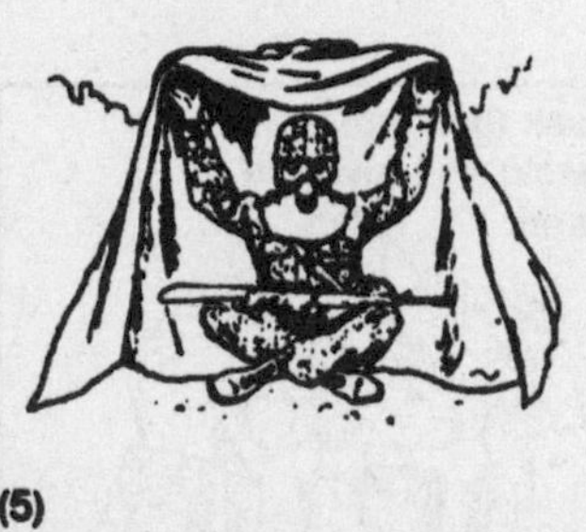

(5)

Check to ensure that the poncho is fully draped around you.

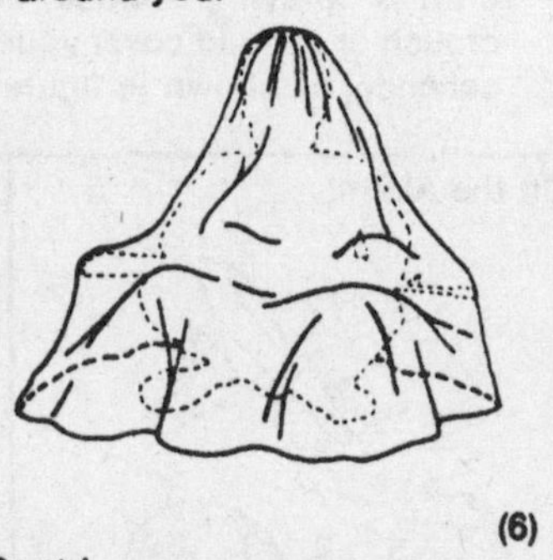

(6)

Fig 8-5. Contd

F. MOVEMENT THROUGH A CONTAMINATED AREA

Avoid contaminated areas or pass through these areas as rapidly as possible, if your mission permits. If you must remain in or pass through contaminated areas, you should:

- Use all the protective equipment you have to prevent chemical agents from entering your body.
- When possible, use vehicles and travel upwind of the contaminated area.
- Select routes or bivouac areas on high ground since chemical agents tend to be heavier than air and settle in low places. Avoid cellars, trenches, gullies, valleys and other low places where agents may collect.

- Avoid unnecessary contact with contaminated surfaces (such as buildings, debris, woods, shrubbery, tall grass, and puddles) which tend to hold the agent.
- Do not stir up dust unnecessarily.

G. FILTER REPLACEMENT PROCEDURE

The M17 series mask has two M13 series filter elements installed in the left and right cheek pouches. These filter elements provide protection to the wearer from all known toxic chemical agents. However, when exposed to agents for long periods of time or if immersed in water or if damaged, the filters break down and must be replaced. In any future conflict, the individual Marine must be able to change the filter elements himself.

1. To remove the filter elements in the M17 series mask, follow the steps outlined in figure 8-6.

1 REMOVE INLET VALVES BY PUSHING UP ON BOTTOM EDGE OF VALVE FLANGE WITH THUMBS.

2 WORK COLLAR FROM UNDER FILTER ELEMENT CONNECTOR FLANGE.

NOTE: TO AVOID RIPS, DON'T STRETCH RUBBER ANY MORE THAN NECESSARY TO REMOVE OR INSTALL MASK COMPONENTS.

Fig 8-6. Removing Filter Elements.

3 REVERSE HEAD HARNESS BY LENGTHENING ALL STRAPS AND LOOPING HARNESS OVER FRONT OF MASK. TO AVOID DISTORTION, DON'T PULL PAD BELOW LENSES.

4 UNBUTTON NOSE CUP FROM FLAP BUTTON.

5 UNBUTTON TOP POUCH FLAP FROM BOTH FLAP BUTTONS. UNBUTTON BOTH SIDES OF MASK BEFORE PROCEEDING.

FLAP BUTTON

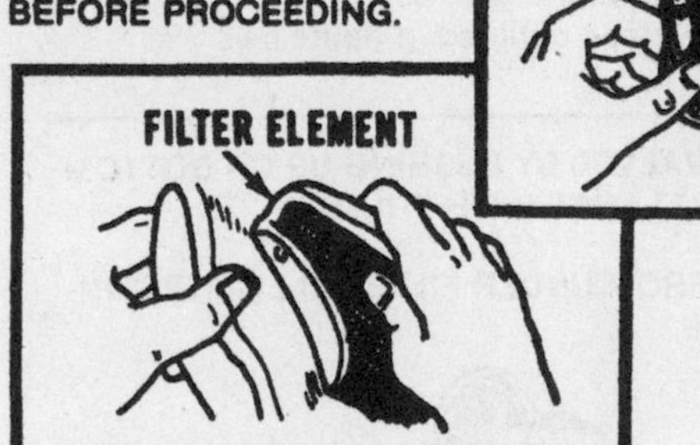

6 GRASP UPPER PART OF ONE FILTER ELEMENT BETWEEN FINGERS AND THUMB. GRASP OUTSIDE OF FACEPIECE BETWEEN VOICEMITTER-OUTLET VALVE ASSEMBLY AND CONNECTOR WITH OTHER HAND. PULL FILTER ELEMENT FROM MASK. REMOVE SECOND FILTER IN SAME MANNER.

Fig. 8-6. Contd

2. To replace the filter elements, follow the steps outined in figure 8-7.

1 FILTER ELEMENTS ARE MARKED EITHER RIGHT OR LEFT. ALINE FILTER ELEMENTS WITH OUTSIDE CONTOURS OF CHEEK POUCHES TO BE SURE YOU'RE INSTALLING THEM CORRECTLY.

2 HOLD FILTER ELEMENT BY SQUARE CORNER WITH YOUR FINGERS ON CONNECTOR SIDE. PULL LOWER POUCH FLAP OUTWARD JUST ENOUGH TO OPEN CHEEK POUCH. INSERT CURVED EDGE OF ELEMENT INTO POUCH WITH A SLIGHT TURNING MOTION. PUSH ELEMENT UP INTO POUCH.

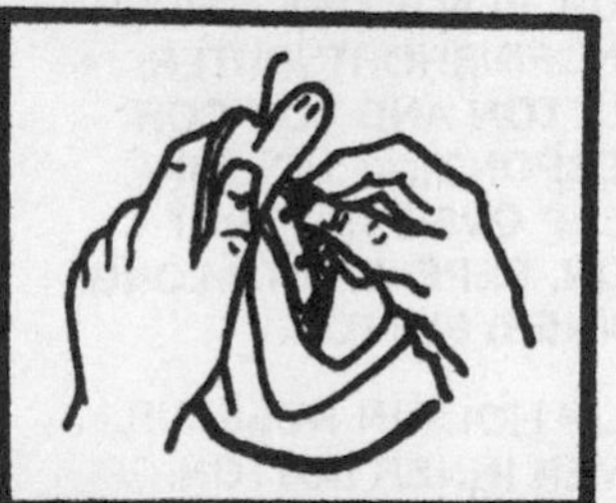

3 GRASP CORNER OF ELEMENT FIRST INSERTED INTO MASK AND WORK ELEMENT INTO PLACE.

Fig 8-7. Installing filter elements.

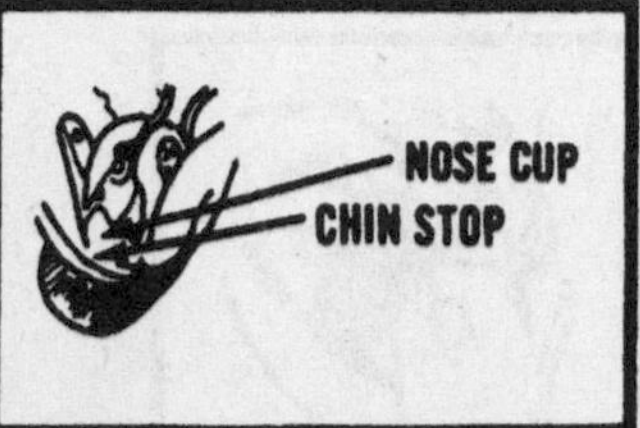

4 ALLOW NOSECUP AND POUCH FLAPS TO FALL INTO NORMAL POSITION. ENSURE THAT BOTTOM OF NOSECUP LIES ON TOP OF CHIN STOP SO MOIST, EXHALED AIR DOESN'T ENTER POUCHES AND DAMAGE FILTER ELEMENTS

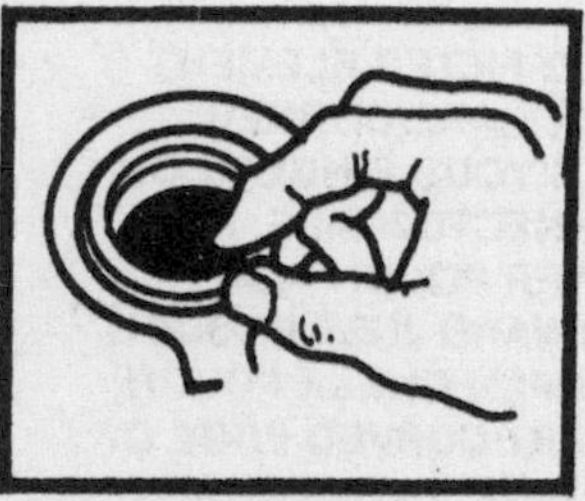

5 WORK COLLAR UNDER CONNECTOR FLANGE AND RECHECK FILTER ELEMENT POSITION. ADJUST IF NECESSARY.

6 AFTER BOTH ELEMENTS ARE INSTALLED, BUTTON POUCH FLAPS AND NOSE-CUP. PLACE ONE FINGER UNDER SHORT (OUTER) BUTTON AND SLIP COR-RESPONDING HOLE IN FLAP OVER THAT BUT-TON. REPEAT WITH LONG (INNER) BUTTON.

7 SLIP HOLE IN NOSECUP OVER INNER BUTTON.

Fig 8-7. Contd

8 BUTTON BOTH SIDES IN LIKE MANNER.

9 RETURN HEAD HARNESS TO NORMAL POSITION AND ADJUST STRAPS AS REQUIRED.

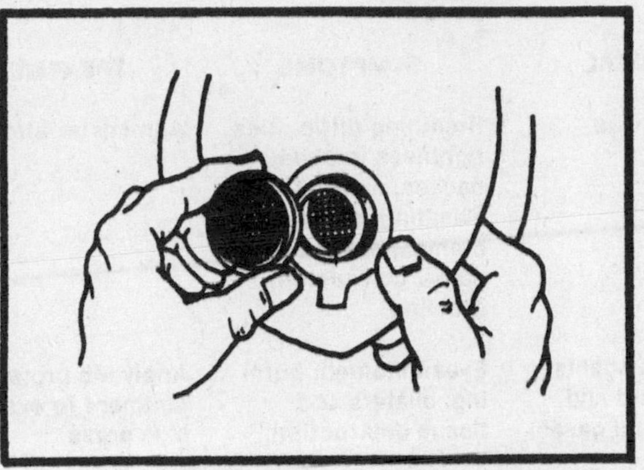

10 INSTALL INLET VALVES.

Fig 8-7. Contd

H. SYMPTOMS AND TREATMENT OF CHEMICAL AGENTS

To master the proper protective measures to protect yourself against a chemical attack, you need to know the effects on your body of those chemical agents that may be used against you, your means of protection against those agents, and their treatment. Your M17 Series Field Protective Mask is the most important single item of protective equipment you have against chemical and biological agents! !

Some of the more common agents which you are likely to encounter and their treatment are contained in table 8-1.

Table 8-1. Chemical Agent Characteristics

CHEMICAL	SYMPTOMS	TREATMENT
Nerve Gas	Breathing difficulties, tightness in chest, nausea, excessive sweating, vomiting, cramps, headache, coma, convulsions, drooling.	Administer atropine.
Blister Agents (Mustard and arsenical gases)	Eyes inflamed, burning; blisters and tissue destruction.	Apply M5 protective ointment to exposed skin areas.
Choking Agents	Difficulty in breathing, tightness of chest.	Loosen clothing, avoid unnecessary exertion, keep warm.
Blood Agents (cyanide, arsine gases)	Breathing difficulties tightness in chest.	Administer Amyl Nitrite and artificial respiration.
Tear Agents	Eyes water, intense eye pain, irritation of upper respiratory tract.	Air skin, flush irritated surfaces with water.
Vomiting Agents (DM, DA, DC)	Sneezing, nausea, salivation, vomiting	Vigorous activity helps reduce nausea and its duration.

Incapacitating Agents	Abnormal behavior, muscle weakness, central nervous systems disorders.	Supportive first aid and physical restraints in some situations.

For additional training in this area, the following references are provided below:

1. FM 21-11	First Aid for Soldiers
2. FM 21-15	Care and Use of Individual Clothing and Equipment
3. FM 21-40	NBC Defense
4. FM 21-41	Individual Defense NBC
5. FM 21-48	NBC Defense Training
6. FMFM 11-1	NBC Defensive Biological Operations in FMF
7. FMFM 11-3	Employment of Chemical Agents
8. FMFM 11-4B	Staff Officers Field Manual Nuclear Weapons Employment Effects Data
9. FMFM 11-5	Operational Aspects of Radiological Defense
10. FMFM 11-6	Armed Forces Doctrine for Chemical Warfare and Biological Defense

11. TM 3-4240-279-10	OM Chem-Bio Field NBC Mask M17/M17A1
12. TM 3-4240-279-20&P	Maint Manual for Mask NBC M17/M17A1
13. TM 8-285	Treatment of Chemical Agent Casualties and Conventional Military Chemical Injuries
14. TM 10-277	Chemical Toxological and Missile Fuel Handlers Protective Clothing
15. MCI Course 57.6	Chemical Warfare Defense

Section II. Nuclear Defense

Objectives:

1. When in an open area, without warning, demonstrate the measures used to protect against nuclear explosion.

2. When given a two minute warning and near a sheltered area, demonstrate the measures used to protect against a nuclear explosion.

A. REACTION TO NUCLEAR EXPLOSION WITHOUT WARNING

Drop flat on your stomach with your feet toward the explosion, close your eyes, place your hands under your body, and put your head down (fig 8-8).

Fig 8-8. No-warning reaction position.

NOTE: Remain in position for 90 seconds from the time of the blast.

B. REACTION TO NUCLEAR EXPLOSION WITH WARNING

While in defensive positions, you are notified that there will be a nuclear explosion in two minutes. You actions should be those as illustrated in figure 8-9. However, if time does not permit, take the best shelter available.

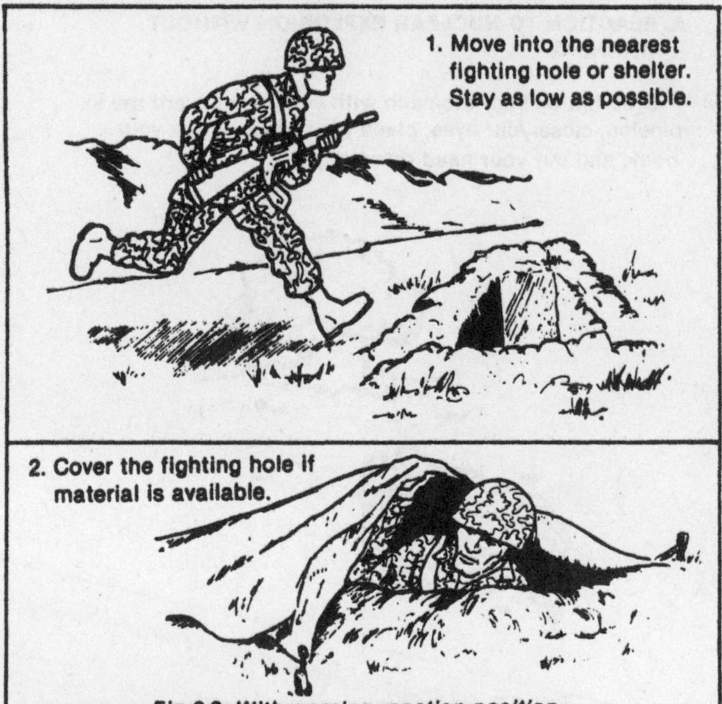

Fig 8-9. With-warning reaction position.

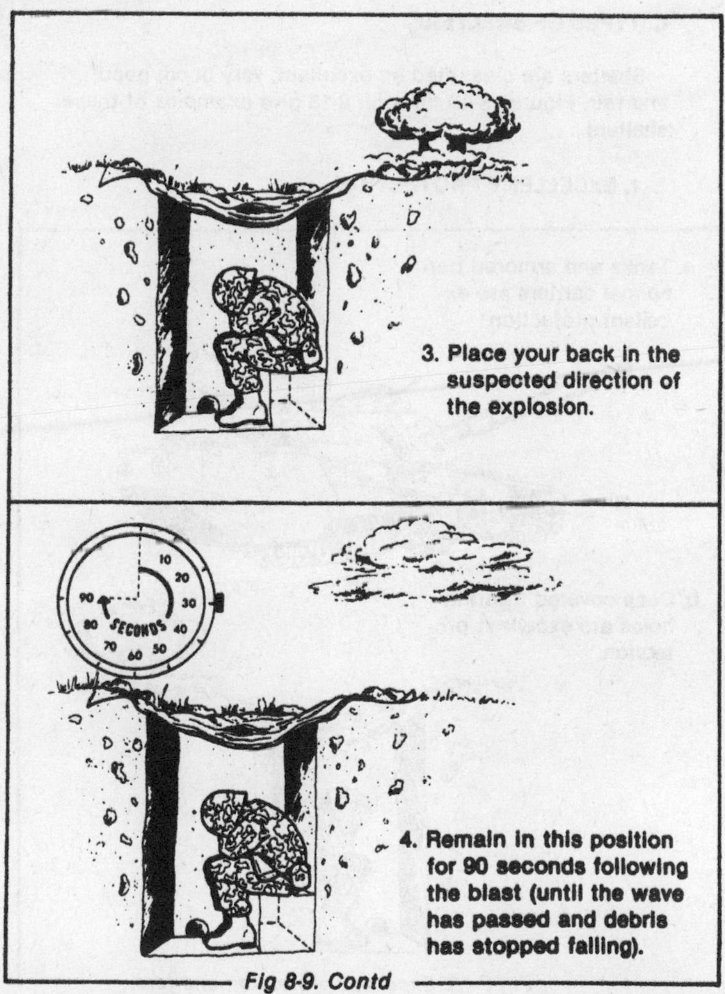
3. Place your back in the suspected direction of the explosion.
10
20
30
40
50
60
70
80
90
SECONDS
4. Remain in this position for 90 seconds following the blast (until the wave has passed and debris has stopped falling).

Fig 8-9. Contd

C. TYPES OF SHELTERS

Shelters are classified as excellent, very good, good, and fair. Figures 8-10 through 8-13 give examples of these shelters.

1. EXCELLENT PROTECTION.

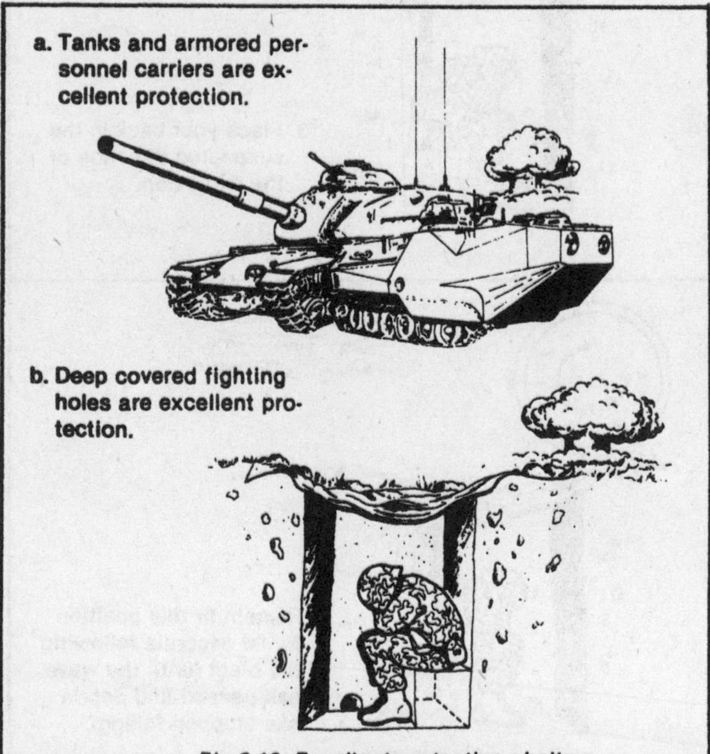

Fig 8-10. Excellent protection shelters.

Fig 8-10. Contd

2. VERY GOOD PROTECTION.

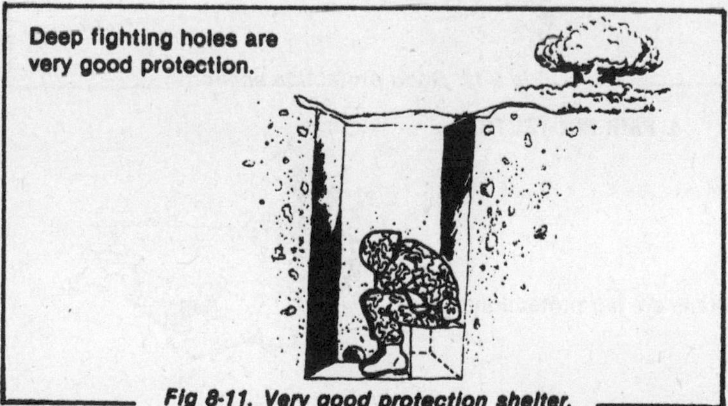

Fig 8-11. Very good protection shelter.

3. GOOD PROTECTION.

a. Ditches are good protection.

b. Hills are good protection.

Fig 8-12. Good protection shelter.

4. FAIR PROTECTION.

Walls are fair protection.

Fig 8-13. Fair protection shelter.

For additional training in this area, references are provided below:

1. FM 21-11	First Aid for Soldiers
2. FM 21-15	Care and Use of Individual Clothing and Equipment
3. FM 21-40	NBC Defense
4. FM 21-41	Individual Defense NBC
5. FM 21-48	NBC Defense Training
6. FMFM 11-4B	Staff Officers Field Manual Nuclear Weapons Employment Effects Data
7. FMFM 11-5	Operational Aspects of Radiological Defense
8. MCI Course 57.7	Nuclear Warfare Defense

Chapter 9. Service Rifle and Marksmanship

Section I. The Service Rifle

Objectives:

1. Explain the meaning of the term sustained rate of fire and state the sustained rate of fire for the appropriate service rifle.

2. Explain the meaning of the term maximum effective range and state the maximum effective range of the appropriate service rifle.

A. DESCRIPTION

The M-16A1 rifle is a 5.56mm, magazine-fed, gas-operated, air-cooled, shoulder weapon. See table 9-1 for general data.

Table 9-1. General Data

1. Gas operated.

2. Air cooled.

3. Magazine-fed (20 or 30-round box type).

4. In-line stock.

5. Semiautomatic and automatic capability.

   a. Cyclic rate of fire: 700-800 rounds per minute.

b. Maximum effective rate of fire (semi): 45-65 rounds per minute.

c. Maximum effective rate of fire (auto): 150-200 rounds per minute.

d. Sustained rate of fire: 12-15 rounds per minute.

6. Maximum effective range: 460 meters.

7. Maximum range: 2,653 meters.

8. Muzzle velocity: 3,250 feet per second (approximate).

9. Muzzle energy (at the muzzle): 1,200 foot pounds (approximate).

10. Mechanical features:

a. Rifling: six grooves, one turn in 12 inches.

b. Sight radius: 19.75 inches.

c. Trigger pull: 8.5 pounds maximum; 5.0 pounds minimum.

d. Sights: rear, flip type, adjustable for windage; front, click type, adjustable for elevation.

e. Sight adjustment: each click in elevation or windage moves the strike of the bullet 2.8 centimeters (or 1.1 inches) per 100 yards.

B. THE SUSTAINED RATE OF FIRE

The rate of fire which a weapon can maintain for an indefinite length of time is its sustained rate of fire.

C. MAXIMUM EFFECTIVE RANGE

The maximum effective range of a weapon is the distance to which a weapon may be expected to fire accurately to inflict casualties or damage. The maximum effective range is 460 meters for both the M-16 and the M-14 rifle.

For additional training in this area, the following references are provided below:

1. FM 23-8	M14 & M14A1 Rifle and Rifle Marksmanship
2. FM 23-9	M16A1 Rifle and Rifle Marksmanship
3. FMFM 1-3	Basic Marksmanship

Section II. Field Stripping the M16A1 Rifle

Objective: When provided with a cartridge or other pointed object, disassemble (field strip) and assemble the service rifle.

A. DISASSEMBLY

1. The first step in disassembly is to render the rifle safe by clearing it.

2. Ensure the selector is on safe and allow the bolt to go forward.

3. Remove the sling.

4. Remove the handguards (fig 9-1). To remove the handguards, place the butt of the assembled weapon firmly on the ground or on a table.

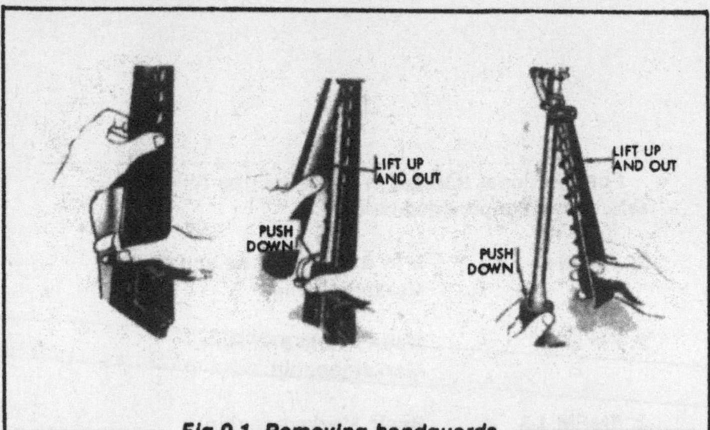

Fig 9-1. Removing handguards.

5. The next step in field stripping the M16A1 rifle is to separate it into its two main groups, the upper and lower receiver groups (fig 9-2). Use the nose of a cartridge or other pointed object to press the takedown pin toward the right side of the receiver (fig 9-2a) until the upper receiver swings free of the lower receiver (fig 9-2b). The takedown pin does **NOT** come out of the receiver. Use the cartridge to press the receiver pivot pin to the right (fig 9-2c), then separate the lower receiver group from the upper receiver group (fig 9-3).

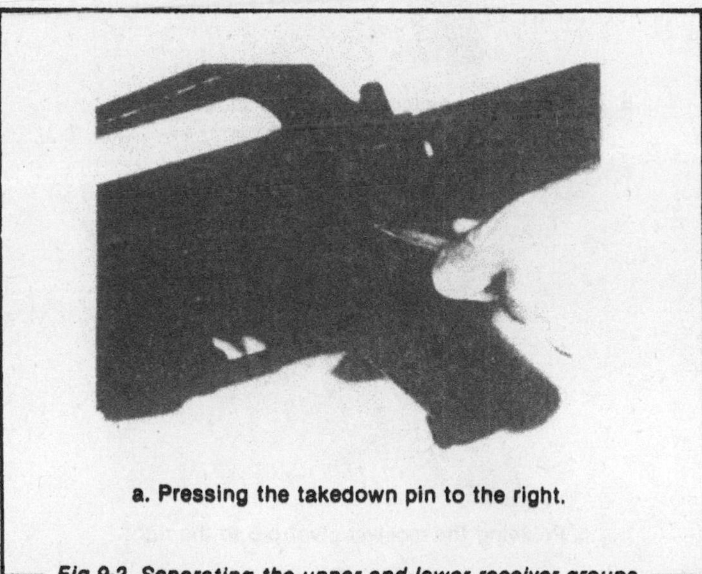

a. Pressing the takedown pin to the right.

Fig 9-2. Separating the upper and lower receiver groups.

b. Upper receiver swings free of the lower receiver.

c. Pressing the receiver pivot pin to the right.

Fig 9-2. Contd

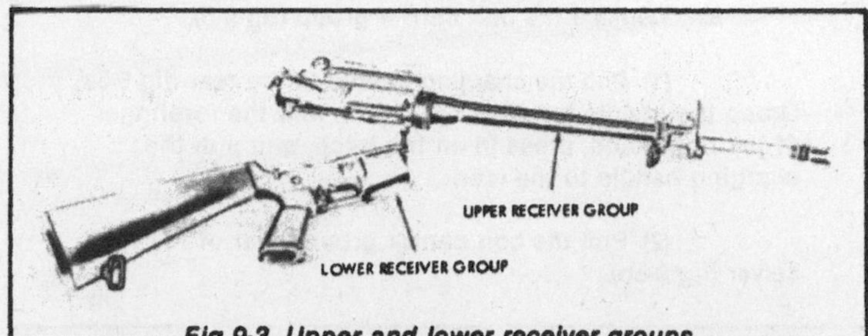

Fig 9-3. Upper and lower receiver groups.

6. Disassembly of the upper receiver group. Breaking the rifle into the main groups and disassembly of the upper and lower receiver groups constitute field stripping of the M16A1 rifle (fig 9-4).

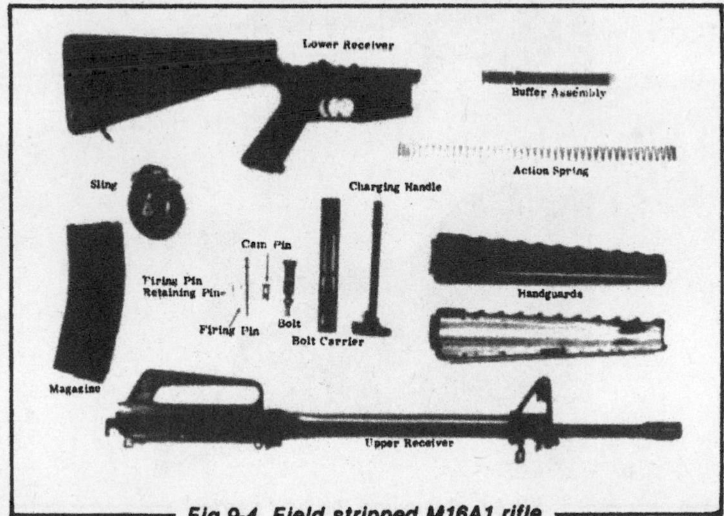

Fig 9-4. Field stripped M16A1 rifle.

a. Remove the bolt carrier group (fig 9-5).

(1) Pull the charging handle to the rear (fig 9-5a). Grasp the handle between the thumb and the forefinger of the right hand, press in on the latch, and pull the charging handle to the rear.

(2) Pull the bolt carrier group clear of the receiver (fig 9-5b).

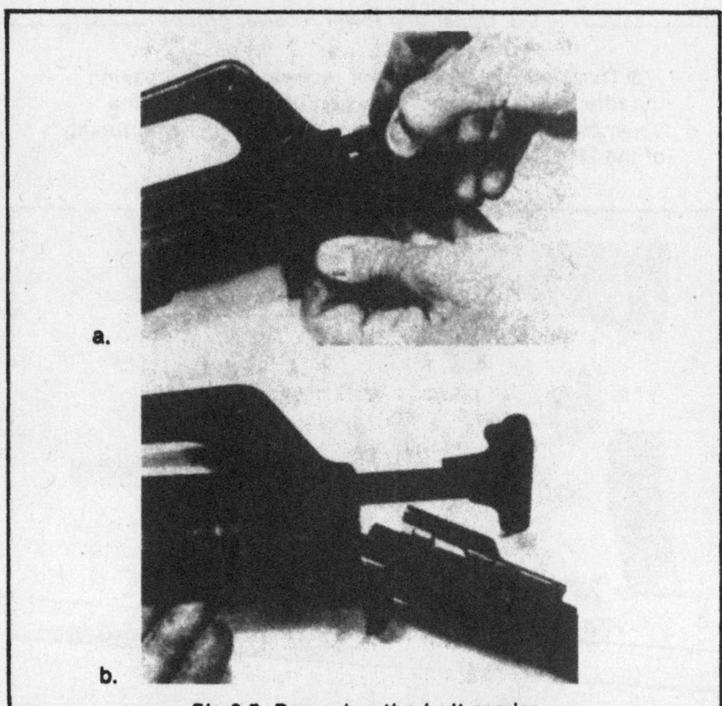

Fig 9-5. Removing the bolt carrier.

b. Remove the charging handle (fig 9-6). Pull until it falls from the receiver group.

Fig 9-6. Removing the charging handle.

c. Disassemble the bolt carrier group (fig 9-7).

a.

Fig 9-7. Disassembly of bolt carrier group.

(1) Use the point of a cartridge or other pointed object to press out the firing pin retaining pin (fig 9-7a).

(2) Raise the front end of the carrier and allow the firing pin to drop from its well in the bolt (fig 9-7b).

(3) Rotate the bolt until the cam pin is clear of the bolt carrier key. Remove the cam pin by rotating it one-quarter turn and lifting it out of the well in the bolt and bolt carrier (fig 9-7c).

(4) Slide the bolt out of the recess in the bolt carrier (fig 9-7d).

NOTE: No part of the bolt should be disassembled.

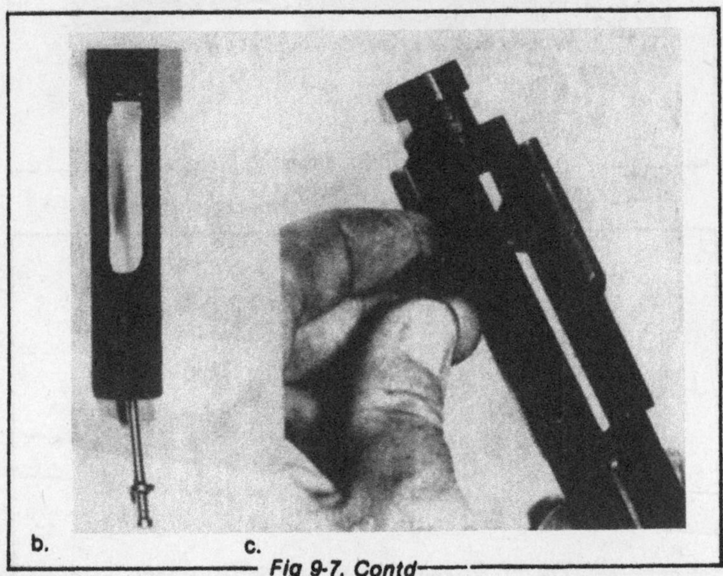

b. c.

Fig 9-7. Contd

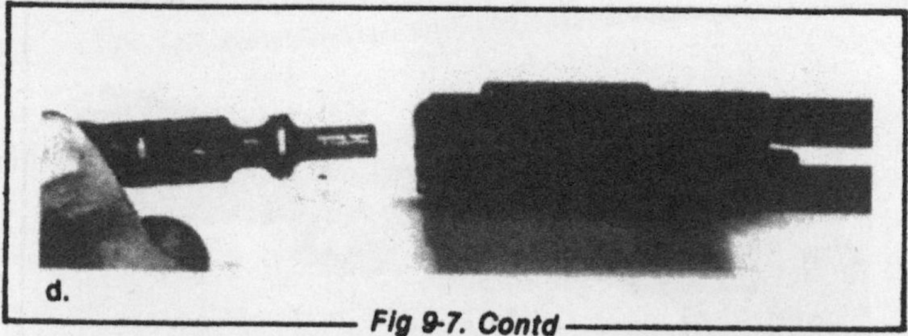

Fig 9-7. Contd

7. Disassembly of the lower receiver group. Make sure the hammer is cocked. Remove the buffer assembly and spring by depressing the buffer retainer and allowing the buffer assembly to be forced out of the lower receiver extension by the action spring (fig 9-8). Remove the action spring from the receiver extension and separate the buffer assembly from the spring (fig 9-9).

Fig 9-8. Remove the buffer assembly.

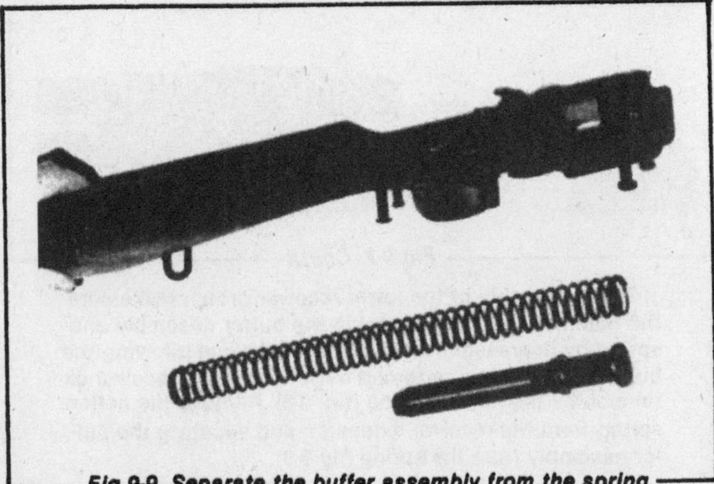

Fig 9-9. Separate the buffer assembly from the spring.

B. REASSEMBLY

Reassembly of the M16A1 is accomplished by reversing the procedures described above.

For additional training in this area, references are provided below:

1. FM 23-9	M16A1 Rifle and Rifle Marksmanship
2. FMFM 1-3	Basic Marksmanship
3. TEC Lsn 939-071-0010-F	Disassembling and Assembling the M16A1 Rifle

Section III. Cleaning and Lubricating the M16A1 Service Rifle

Objective: When provided with the appropriate materials, properly clean and lubricate the service rifle.

A. GENERAL

The rifle should be inspected daily, when in use, for evidence of rust and for overall serviceability. A clean, properly lubricated, well-maintained rifle will fire when needed. Under adverse conditions, key parts of the rifle may need special care and cleaning several times a day. See that dirt, rust, gummed oil, ice, snow, and mud are removed as they will cause rapid deterioration of the inner mechanism and outer surfaces. Keep all surfaces clean and properly lubricated. Use only approved cleaners, lubricants, and tools (fig 9-10) to take care of your rifle. Do not clean outer surfaces with a treated cloth or other commercial compounds.

B. M16A1 RIFLE

1. CLEANING AND LUBRICATION BEFORE FIRING. The bore and chamber should be cleaned and dried. Clean by pushing patches through the bore until they protrude through the flash suppressor.

NOTE: When cleaning the M16A1, run patches or a brush through the bore from chamber to muzzle.

The bolt carrier group may be removed and dirt and oil cleaned off the firing pin, outer and inner sur-

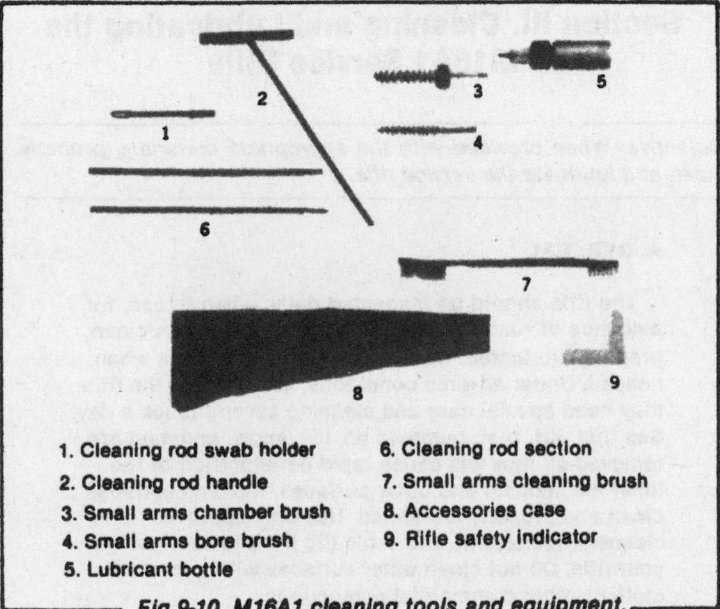

Fig 9-10. M16A1 cleaning tools and equipment.

faces of the bolt, and bolt (piston) rings. Make certain rings are well lubricated and staggered. Apply a coat of lubricating oil to the inner surfaces of the bolt carrier. Give special attention to the slide and cam pin area.

2. **CLEANING.** Clean the rifle daily.

a. **MAGAZINES.** Disassemble and wipe dirt from the magazine tube, spring, and follower. Apply a light coat of lubricant to the magazine spring.

b. **BOLT CARRIER GROUP.** Disassemble the bolt carrier group and wash all components and outer surfaces with patches saturated with bore cleaner. Clean the bolt carrier key with a WORN bore brush dipped in bore cleaner. Dry the bolt carrier key with pipe cleaners.

Using a small brush dipped in bore cleaner, scrub carbon deposits and dirt from the locking lugs of the bolt.

CAUTION: Brush the outer surface of the bolt paying particular attention to the area behind the bolt rings and under lip of the extractor. Do not attempt to remove discoloration caused by heat.

When dry and before assembly, apply a generous coat of lubricant to the outside bolt body and rings. Put a drop of lubricant in the bolt carrier key.

CAUTION: The firing pin and firing pin recess in the bolt should have a light coat of lubricant.

c. **UPPER RECEIVER.** Clean with rifle bore cleaner.

CAUTION: Do not use WIRE brush on any external surfaces.

Clean the outside surface of the protruding gas tube in the receiver with a worn brush attached to a section of the cleaning rod. Clean the top of the gas tube by inserting the rod and brush through the back of the receiver. After cleaning, coat the inner surface of the upper receiver with lubricant and apply a light coat to the outer surfaces.

CAUTION: Do not use abrasive material to clean the gas tube.

d. **BARREL.** Attach the bore brush to the rod, dip it in bore cleaner, and brush through the bore until it extends beyond the muzzle. Do not reverse direction of the brush while in the bore.

Clean the chamber with the chamber brush soaked in bore cleaner. Dry the bore and chamber with rifle patches until they come out clean. Lightly lubricate the bore, and chamber, and the lugs in the barrel extension.

Lightly lubricate all outer surfaces of the barrel and sight including surfaces under the handguard.

Generously lubricate the front sight post screw, detent, and spring.

e. **LOWER RECEIVER GROUP.** Wipe dirt from the trigger mechanism with a clean patch or brush or pipe cleaner.

CAUTION: Do not use wire brush on aluminum surface.

Remove carbon build up with bore cleaner and soft bristle brush and wipe dry.

Clean drain holes in bolt cap screw with a pipe cleaner.

Apply a light coat of oil to the buffer, action spring, and inner surface of lower receiver extensions. Apply a generous coat of oil inside the lower receiver and all components including the takedown and pivot pins.

For additional training in this area, references are provided below:

1. FM 28-9	M16A1 Rifle and Rifle Marksmanship
2. FMFM 1-3	Basic Marksmanship
3. TEC Lsn 939-071-0011-F	Maintaining the M16A1 Rifle

Section IV. Stoppages and Immediate Action

Objectives:

1. When a service rifle has a stoppage, apply immediate action to reduce the stoppage.

2. When a service rifle has a malfunction, identify, locate, and correct the malfunction.

A. GENERAL

A stoppage is an unintentional interruption in the cycle of operation. Common causes are faulty ammunition or a faulty magazine. A stoppage may result from malfunctioning of one of the operating parts.

Proper care of the rifle will prevent most stoppages. When one does occur, the Marine rifleman promptly reduces it and continues his fire mission. The first step in reducing a stoppage is to apply IMMEDIATE ACTION.

B. IMMEDIATE ACTION FOR THE M16A1

1. Tap up on the bottom of magazine to fully seat it.
2. Pull charging handle to rear.
3. Look for ejection of casing or cartridge.
4. Release charging handle.
5. Strike forward assist assembly to seat bolt.

6. Aim and attempt to fire. Should the weapon fail to fire, investigate the cause and take corrective action.

7. **REMEMBER:** TAP, PULL, LOOK, RELEASE, STRIKE, AIM, FIRE.

C. REDUCING MALFUNCTIONS OF THE M16A1 RIFLE

There are six major categories of malfunctions due to stoppages caused by mechanical failure of the weapon, magazine, or ammunition. The malfunctions, their usual causes, and corrective actions are shown in table 9-2.

Table 9-2. Malfunctions, Causes, and Corrective Actions

CATEGORY	DESCRIPTION	PROBABLE CAUSE	CORRECTIVE ACTION
Failure to feed and chamber a cartridge and to lock a chambered cartridge.	It occurs during the initial loading of the rifle and occasionally during the rifle's cycle of operation. When the rifle is initially loaded, the forward movement of the bolt carrier group may lack the sufficient force required to feed, chamber, and lock the first cartridge from the magazine.	1. Excess accumulation of dirt, or powder fouling in or around the bolt carrier. 2. Defective magazine. 3. Magazine improperly loaded. 4. Magazine improperly inserted in the rifle. 5. Damaged or dirty ammunition. 6. Damaged or broken action spring. 7. Excess accumulation of dirt in lower receiver extension. 8. Damaged or fouled gas tube resulting in short recoil.	1. Apply immediate action and ensure the upper receiver is free of loose cartridges. 2. Apply remedial action for any reoccurrences by field stripping, inspecting, and lubricating the rifle at the earliest opportunity. 3. Have rifle inspected by qualified ordnance personnel if remedial action does not correct the malfunction.

(continues)

Table 9-2. Malfunctions, Causes, and Corrective Actions

CATEGORY	DESCRIPTION	PROBABLE CAUSE	CORRECTIVE ACTION
Failure of a cartridge to fire despite the fact that it is chambered and locked and trigger or automatic sear has released the hammer	It occurs when the firing pin fails to strike the primer or strikes the primer with insufficient force. Note: With the bolt carrier forward, a quick visual inspection will not reveal this malfunction.	1. Powder fouling or dirt accumulation on the firing pin. 2. A defective or broken firing pin. 3. Failure of the bolt carrier to fully close on the bolt. Note: This will not be apparent upon inspection due to the hammer striking the bolt carrier, causing it to move forward.	1. Apply immediate action. 2. Apply remedial action for any reoccurrences by inspecting, cleaning, and lubricating the firing pin, bolt, bolt carrier, and locking recesses. 3. Inspect ammunition for firing pin indent on the cartridge primer when remedial action does not correct malfunction. If primer is indented, notify qualified ammunition personnel. 4. Have rifle inspected by qualified ordnance personnel if remedial action does not correct the malfunction and the cartridge primer does not reveal an indent.

(continues)

CATEGORY	DESCRIPTION	PROBABLE CAUSE	CORRECTIVE ACTION
Failure of a cartridge to be completely ejected from the rifle.	It occurs when the cartridge is not ejected through the ejection port or becomes jammed in the upper receiver as the bolt closes during the cycle of operation. On some occasions the cartridge, while initially clearing the rifle, may strike an outside surface and bounce back into the path of the bolt.	1. Weak or damaged extractor spring. 2. Accumulation of powder fouling or dirt around the ejector spring. 3. Weak or damaged ejector spring. 4. Short recoil due to an accumulation of powder fouling in the gas mechanism. 4. Resistance caused by an extremely carboned or corroded chamber impeding the extraction and subsequently the cartridge ejection.	1. Apply immediate action, but release the charging handle only after the receiver is clear of all obstructions which could cause the rifle to malfunction again. 2. Apply remedial action for any reoccurrences by cleaning, inspecting and lubricating the extractor, extractor spring, ejector spring, and chamber. Replace the extractor and extractor spring if damaged * 3. Have rifle inspected by qualified ordnance personnel if remedial action does not correct the malfunction.
Failure of a cartridge to be successfully extracted from the chamber.	It occurs when the cartridge remains in the chamber while the bolt and bolt carrier move a short distance rearward or recoils fully. This malfunction is considered to be the most difficult to correct.	1. Short recoil due to an accumulation of powder fouling in the gas mechanism. 2. Dirty or corroded chamber. 3. A damaged, weak, or broken extractor or extractor spring.	1. Remove magazine, and lock the bolt to the rear. Insert the assembled cleaning rod into the muzzle and force the cartridge from the chamber by tapping the rod against the inside base of the expended cartridge.

Table 9-2. Malfunctions, Causes, and Corrective Actions (Continued)

CATEGORY	DESCRIPTION	PROBABLE CAUSE	CORRECTIVE ACTION
			2. Replace extractor and extractor spring if inspection does not reveal defects in the chamber or on the bolt.*
Failure of the bolt to remain in a rearward position, engaged by the bolt catch, after the last round has been fired from the magazine.	The rifle will appear normal as there are no immediate visual checks which will determine if the cycle of operation is interrupted or the last round has been fired.	1. Short recoil which does not allow the bolt catch to hold the bolt rearward. 2. Excess fouling or dirt which restricts the movement of the bolt catch. 3. Dented or dirty magazine which restricts the movement of the magazine follower. 4. Weak or broken magazine spring which restricts movement of the magazine follower. 5. Defective action spring, caused by stretching, which creates a faster cycle of operation than normal and insufficient time is allowed for the bolt catch to lock the bolt to the rear.	1. Apply immediate action to determine if rounds are still remaining in magazine. A magazine with rounds remaining indicates some other category of malfunction. 2. Clean, inspect, lubricate, and replace as necessary if the magazine is empty upon inspection. 3. Replace defective action spring.*

CATEGORY	DESCRIPTION	PROBABLE CAUSE	CORRECTIVE ACTION
Any malfunction which cannot be defined under the previous categories.	1. Firing of two rounds on single pull of the trigger in the semiautomatic mode. 2. Bolt catch engages bolt during firing when rounds still remain in the magazine. 3. Failure of the trigger to return to a forward position after release. 4. Failure of the magazine to lock in the rifle. 5. Damaged or broken parts. 6. Incorrectly assembled or loose parts. 7. Short recoil.	1. Trigger pin loosens or backs out of its seat in the receiver due to a broken or incorrectly assembled hammer spring. 2. Firing rifle from a rigid mount or defective bolt catch and spring. 3. Accumulation of dirt or fouling in the mechanism and/or the lack of lubrication. 4. Accumulation of dirt around magazine catch, defective magazine, or improperly adjusted magazine catch. 5. N/A 6. N/A 7. Fouled or damaged gas tube.	1. Field strip rifle and manipulate the trigger pin back in place. Inspect and have the hammer spring replaced or correctly assembled. 2. Replace bolt catch and spring if malfunction occurs frequently.* 3. Immediate corrective action is to manually reposition trigger. Permanent corrective action requires disassembling, cleaning and lubricating.* Sometimes the hammer and disconnector may require replacement due to improper engagement surfaces.* 4. Clean and lubricate magazine catch area, replace defective magazine, and readjust magazine catch. 5. Replace damaged and broken parts.* 6. Reassemble and tighten parts correctly.* 7. Replace gas tube.*

*Must be done by ordnance personnel.

For additional training in this area, references are provided below:

1. FM 23-9 — M16A1 Rifle and Marksmanship
2. TEC Lsn 939-071-0012-F — M16A1 Rifle, Preventing and Correcting Common Malfunctions

Section V. Safety Procedures for the Service Rifle

Objective: When handling or employing the service rifle, explain and demonstrate the safety measures used.

A. GENERAL RULES

1. Consider every weapon to be loaded until you examine it and find it to be unloaded. Never trust your memory in this respect. There is an old saying among hunters that, "the empty gun shoots the loudest."

2. Never point a weapon at anyone you do not intend to shoot, or in a direction where an accidental discharge may do harm.

3. Never fire a weapon until it has been inspected to see that nothing is in the bore or chamber. Firing a weapon with any obstruction in the bore may burst the barrel, resulting in serious injury to you or your fellow Marines.

4. Never grease or oil your ammunition. Some foreign weapons are designed to use greased or oiled ammunition, but the use of such ammunition in your weapon will result in dangerously high pressure in the chamber and barrel.

5. Never place a cartridge in a hot chamber unless you intend to fire it immediately. Excessive heat may cause the cartridge to cook off.

6. Do not allow your ammunition to be exposed

to the direct rays of the sun for any length of time. The powder will deteriorate from the heat.

B. RIFLE RANGE SAFETY

1. When dry firing, each dummy round will be checked to ensure that no live ammunition is present.

2. Each rifle will be inspected by an officer, NCO, or coach to ensure no obstruction is in the bore. Upon completion of firing, each rifle will be inspected to ensure that all live ammunition has been removed from the weapon.

3. Except while being used to conduct live or dry fire exercises, all rifles will have magazines removed, bolts opened and locked to the rear, and safeties on.

4. When carrying a rifle on the range, the muzzle will be pointed upward and downrange.

5. Ammunition will be issued only on command from the control tower.

6. Rifles will be loaded only on command from the control tower.

7. When not in use rifles will be elevated (muzzle up).

8. Dry firing will not be conducted to the rear of the firing line.

For additional training in this area, references are provided below:

1. FM 23-9	M16A1 Rifle and Rifle Marksmanship
2. FMFM 1-3	Basic Marksmanship

Section VI. Rifle Qualification

Objectives:

1. Qualify with the service rifle.

2. While wearing a field protective mask and provided with ten rounds of ammunition, engage a stationary target with the service rifle.

3. Explain the meaning of the term battlesight zero.

A. SIGHT SETTING

M16A1 rifle (fig 9-11). Windage adjustments are made on the rear sight, and elevation adjustments on the front sight. The rear sight consists of two flip-type apertures and a windage drum with a spring-loaded detent. The aperture marked (L) is used for ranges of 300 meters or greater and the unmarked aperture for ranges from 0-300 meters. The front sight consists of a rotating sight post with a spring-loaded detent. Adjustments for either windage or elevation are made by pressing in on the spring-loaded detent with a sharp instrument, or the tip of a cartridge, and rotating the windage drum or the front sight post in the desired direction of change. To indicate direction for movement of the sights, the rear sight is stamped with an arrow and R. The front sight is stamped UP. One click of either elevation or windage will move the point of impact on the target approximately 2.8 centimeters for each 100 meters (or 1.1 inch for 100 yards) of range.

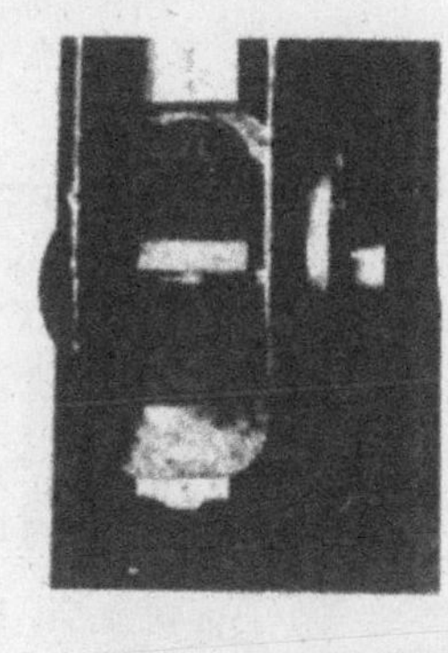

a. Top-rear

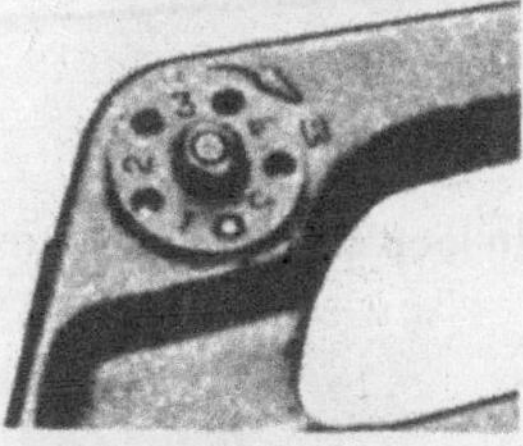

b. Side-rear

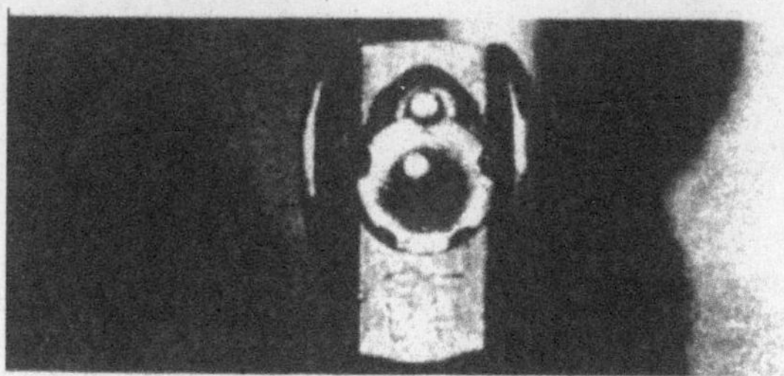

c. Top-front

Fig 9-11. M16A1 standard rifle sight.

B. FIRING POSITIONS (M16A1 RIFLE)

1. PRONE (fig 9-12).

a. Stand at the ready...

b. with loop sling high on arm.

c. Drop to knees holding rifle securely.

d. Place butt of rifle on ground under center of body. Pivot down to left side.

Fig 9-12. Steps in assuming a prone position.

e. Place left elbow right and forward so that it will be directly under the piece.

f. Force butt of rifle into right shoulder.

g. Relax into the sling and obtain your stock weld.

Fig 9-12. Contd

h. Feet apart. Shoulders level with ground.

i. Reloading-Press magazine release button.

j. Place magazine in magazine well and push up.

k. Press bolt catch allowing bolt carrier to go forward.

Fig 9-12 Contd

2. **SITTING** (fig 9-13).

a. Stand at the ready. Loop sling high on arm.

b. Drop to the ground, breaking fall with right hand.

c. Place upper left arm inside left knee.

Fig 9-13. Steps in assuming a sitting position.

d. Force the butt of the rifle into the right shoulder.

e. Lower right arm until it rests inside the right knee. Relax forward into the sling and obtain stock weld. Crossed ankle shown.

f. Crossed leg position.

g. Open leg. Left upper arm is placed down along the left shinbone.

Fig 9-13. Contd

h. Reloading-Press magazine release button.

i. Place magazine into feedway and push up.

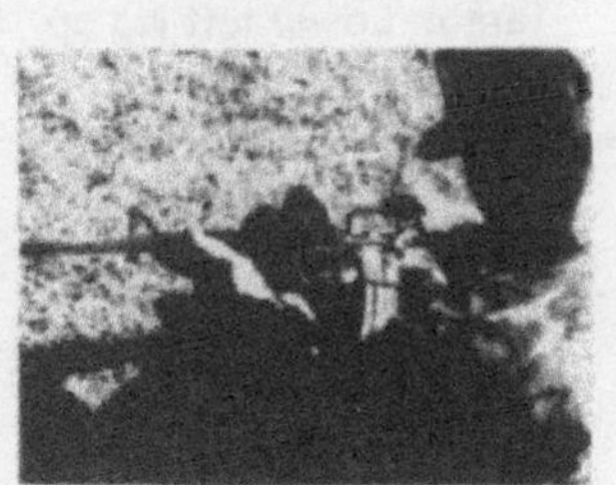

j. Press bolt catch allowing the bolt carrier to go forward.

Fig 9-13. Contd

3. **KNEELING** (fig 9-14).

a. Drop to right knee. Right leg is parallel to target. Left foot toward target. Lower left leg approximately vertical.

b. Lower right buttock to right foot. Place flat surface of left upper arm on the flat surface of left knee.

c. Force butt of rifle into right shoulder.

d. Relax forward into sling and obtain stock weld. High kneeling position shown.

Fig 9-14. Steps in assuming a kneeling position.

e. Low kneeling position

f. Medium kneeling position

g. High kneeling position

Fig 9-14. Contd

4. **STANDING** (fig 9-15).

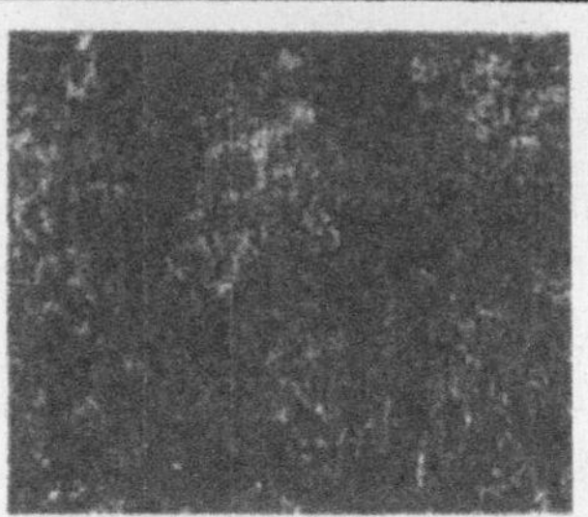

a. Spread feet a comfortable distance.

Fig 9-15. Steps in assuming a standing position.

b. Using a modified parade sling (sling cannot be used for support), place the left hand in a place to best support the rifle.

c. Grasp the pistol grip and place the rifle into right shoulder. Obtain stock weld.

d. Hold right elbow high to form pocket for rifle butt.

e. Standing position.

Fig 9-15. Contd

C. FIRING WITH THE FIELD PROTECTIVE MASK

MCO 1510.2J states that: While wearing the field protective mask, fire 10 rounds from the service rifle (with battle sights zeroed) to effectively engage stationary multiple targets at ranges up to 457 meters, (firing from a distance of 457 meters, the individual is capable of sustaining 60 percent first-round hits.) Normally when you fire with the field protective mask on, you will find it difficult to aline the sights of your weapon. This may be accomplished by placing the butt of the stock slightly down and outward in your shoulder. This enables you to effectively accomplish your mission.

D. BATTLESIGHT ZERO

Current doctrine of the United States Marine Corps prescribes a battlesight zero for 274 meters (300 yards). That is, the sight of the rifle should be so adjusted that the trajectory of the bullet and the line of aim intersect at a range of 274 meters (300 yards). Battlesight zero is a predetermined sight adjustment that, set on the weapon, will enable the shooter to engage targets effectively at battle ranges when conditions do not permit exact sight settings. When engaging targets up to 274 meters (300 yards), use the short range sight. Flip the "L" or long range sight up to engage targets beyond 274 meters (300 yards).

For additional training in this area, references are provided below:

1. FM 23-9	M16A1 Rifle and Rifle Marksmanship
2. FMFM 1-3	Basic Marksmanship
3. MCO 3574.2F	Marksmanship and Familiarization Firing

Chapter 10. Individual Tactical Measures

Section I. Squad in the Defense

***Objectives:** Upon completion of this section, you should, as a member of a unit conducting a defense and having been assigned a primary position, supplementary position, and sector of fire, be able to:*

1. Construct a fighting hole.

2. Clear fields of fire and mark right and left lateral limits of fire.

3. Demonstrate the correct application of camouflage to a fighting position.

4. Demonstrate the correct application of camouflage to the individual Marine and his equipment.

5. Properly defend a fighting position against infantry and/or armor mechanized attack by notifying the unit leader of any enemy activity observed, commencing fire on command, and defending the position by fire and close combat as required.

A. PLANNING THE DEFENSE

The defensive mission of the Marine rifle squad is to repel the enemy's assault by fire and close combat. This requires that the squad be assigned a definite position and sector of fire so as to take advantage of the expected attack. Certain tasks must be accomplished to prepare the assigned position for the actual conduct of the defense. The tasks are carried out concurrently, if possible, but the situation may require that priorities be established.

1. **ESTABLISH SECURITY.** Ensure enough squad members are kept alert to maintain an effective warning system.

a. During daylight with the enemy not close, a minimum of one sentinel is posted in each squad area.

b. When contact with the enemy is probable or during periods of limited visibility, additional security will be necessary. If one-man fighting holes are employed, alternate men will be posted; if two-man fighting holes, one man per hole will be posted.

c. Depending on the situation, members of the squad may be required to patrol areas outside the squad's position.

d. The frequency of relief for sentinels and listening posts is affected by considerations such as the physical condition of the men, effects of weather, morale, and unit strength. As a guide, relief occurs whenever the commander orders it.

2. **ASSIGN POSITIONS.** The squad leader positions his fire teams to cover the front and flanks of the squad area by overlapping sectors of fire and observation.

a. The squad leader, in conjunction with the fire team leaders, selects firing positions for each rifleman and assigns sectors of fire.

b. The squad leader selects firing positions and sectors of fire for the squad automatic weapons which includes assignment of a principal direction of fire (PDF) covering a likely avenue of approach or deadspace in machinegun final protective lines (FPL). The PDF is within the sector of fire or on one edge of the sector. Each member of the unit will mark the left and right limits of his sector of fire. The method used should be an aid to delivering pre-planned fires during periods of reduced visibility. Figure 10-1 illustrates two expedient methods for marking limits.

c. If not previously selected by the platoon commander, the firing positions and sectors of fire for the grenadiers will be assigned by the squad leader.

3. **ORGANIZE THE GROUND.** This begins immediately after positions have been assigned. The tasks involved are: clearing fields of fire, digging fighting holes, and camouflaging.

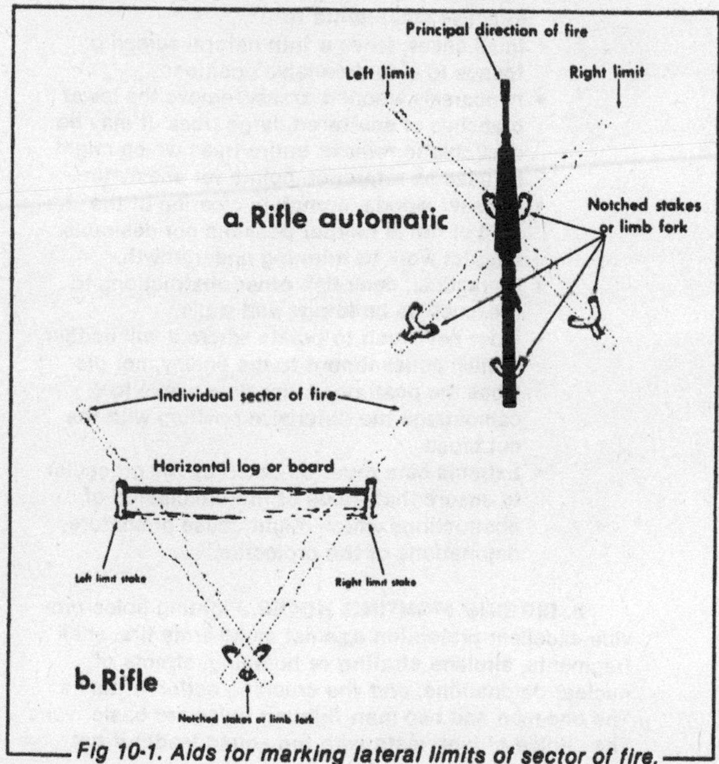

Fig 10-1. Aids for marking lateral limits of sector of fire.

a. CLEARING FIELDS OF FIRE. In clearing fields of fire forward of each fighting-hole, the following principles are observed:

- Do not disclose the squad's position by excessive or careless clearing.
- Start clearing near the forward edge of the fighting hole and work forward to the limits of effective small arms fire.
- In all cases, leave a thin natural screen of foliage to hide defensive positions.
- In sparsely wooded areas, remove the lower branches of scattered, large trees. It may be desirable to remove entire trees which might be used as reference points for enemy fire.
- In heavy woods, complete clearing of the field of fire is neither possible nor desirable. Restrict work to thinning undergrowth.
- If practical, demolish other obstructions to fire, such as buildings and walls.
- Move cut brush to points where it will neither furnish concealment to the enemy, nor disclose the position. A possible use is to camouflage the defensive position with the cut brush.
- Extreme care must be taken by the grenadier to ensure that fields of fire are cleared of obstructions which might cause premature detonations of the projectile.

b. DIGGING FIGHTING HOLES. Fighting holes provide excellent protection against small-arms fire, shell fragments, airplane strafing or bombing, effects of nuclear detonations, and the crushing action of tanks. The one-man and two-man fighting holes are basic types The choice of type rests with the squad leader if not prescribed by higher authority. The type of fighting hole used is based on squad strength, fields of fire, and size of the squad sector.

(1) Construction of two-man fighting hole (figs 10-2 & 10-3). In most types of soil, the fighting hole gives protection against the crushing action of tanks provided the occupants crouch at least two feet below the ground surface. In sandy or soft soils, it may be necessary to revet the sides with sandbags to prevent caving in. The soil is piled around the hole as a parapet, approximately three feet thick and six inches high, leaving a shelf wide enough to be used as an elbow rest by a Marine firing his weapon.

Fig 10-2. Two-man fighting hole (side-view).

(2) Advantages and disadvantages of two-man fighting hole. Since it is longer than the one-man type, it offers somewhat less protection against tanks crossing the long axis, as well as protection against strafing, bombing, and shell fragments. Some advantages of the two-man fighting hole are continuous observation (one man rests while the other man maintains security), assistance and reassurance for each other, and redistribution of ammunition between the two Marines.

c. Camouflage and concealment. Camouflage is protection from energy observation. Concealment is protection from enemy fire. Camouflage measures are strictly carried out from the moment the position is occupied.

(1) **POSITION.**

(a) Do not disclose the position by excessive clearing of fields of fire.

(b) Use the same turf or topsoil that has been removed from the area of the fighting hole to camouflage the parapet.

(c) Dispose of all soil from the fighting hole not used on the parapet. Carry the soil away in sandbags or shelter halves. Dispose of it under low bushes, on dirt roads or paths, in streams or ponds, or camouflage it.

(d) Avoid digging in next to an isolated bush, tree, or clump of vegetation.

(e) Conceal the fighting hole from observation, both from overhead and from ground level, by the use of a camouflaged cover. Construct the cover from natural materials.

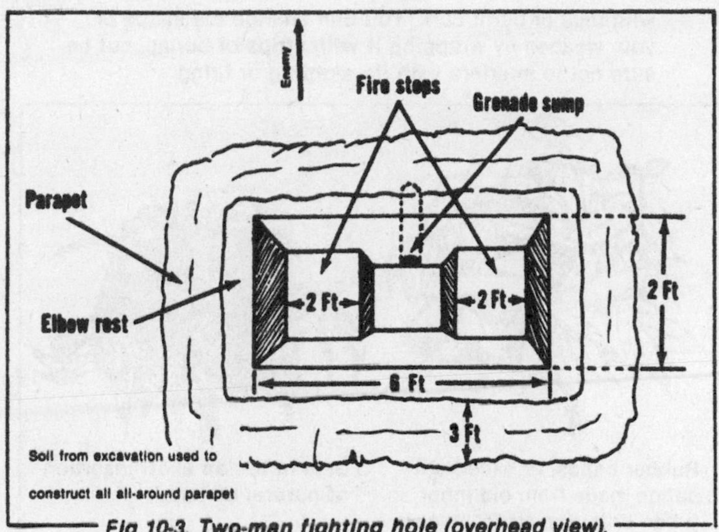

Fig 10-3. Two-man fighting hole (overhead view).

(f) Replace natural material used in camouflage before it wilts or changes color.

(g) Avoid creating fresh paths near the position. Use old paths or vary the route followed to and from the position.

(h) Avoid littering the area near the position with paper, tin cans, and other debris.

(2) **EQUIPMENT.** The outline of the helmet is one of the striking characteristics of a Marine's equipment. Take steps to change the form of the helmet (fig 10-4). If your pack or other 782 gear has faded, darken it

with mud or burnt cork. You can change the shape of your weapon by wrapping it with strips of burlap, but be sure not to interfere with its sighting or firing.

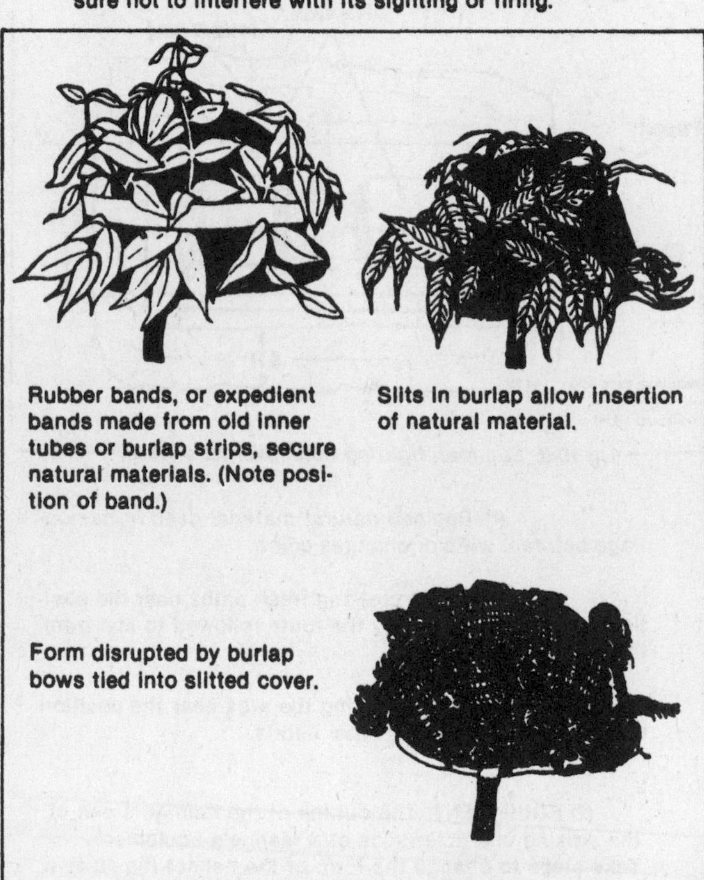

Fig 10-4. Techniques of camouflaging the helmet.

Be especially careful with shiny objects such as belt buckles, mess gear, goggles, binoculars, and personal items such as rings and watches.

(3) **BODY AND CLOTHING.** Your face, neck and hands should be toned down by painting them with a disrupted pattern. Pay particular attention to areas that will reflect light, such as nose, cheekbones, chin, and eye sockets. Use camouflage paint or burnt cork, (fig 10-5).

Fig 10-5. Camouflaging the face.

(4) **SELECT AND PREPARE SUPPLEMENTARY POSITIONS.** These positions are organized the same as the primary positions. They are used by the squad to fire on targets that cannot be engaged from the primary position. For example, firing on enemy troops attacking the

flanks or rear of the platoon defense area. This constitutes a mission other than the primary mission. These should not be confused with alternate positions which are additional positions from which the primary mission may be accomplished.

B. CONDUCTING THE DEFENSE

1. INFANTRY ATTACK.

a. **ENEMY PREPARATORY BOMBARDMENT.** The enemy will normally precede his attack with fire from any or all of the following weapons: artillery, naval gunfire, mortars, machineguns, tanks, and aircraft. During this attack, the squad will take cover in its prepared position, maintaining surveillance of the squad's sector to determine if the enemy is advancing closely behind their supporting fires. Any member of the squad who observes enemy activity will report it immediately to his unit leader. Local security will be withdrawn to the friendly lines when ordered, under the cover of the other members in the squad position.

b. **OPENING FIRE AND FIRE CONTROL.** Fire is withheld on approaching enemy troops until they come within effective small arms range of the squad's position. Squad members open fire upon the approaching enemy on command of the squad leader, or when the enemy reaches a predetermined line. Once fire is opened, direct control passes to the fire team leaders. The fire team leaders, in accordance with the squad leader's previous plan, designate new targets, change rates of fire when necessary, and give the order to cease fire.

c. **FINAL PROTECTIVE FIRES.** If the enemy's attack is not broken and he begins his assualt, final protective fires are called for by the company commander. These are fires delivered immediately in front of the defensive lines. When final protective fires are called for, all squad members fire in their individual sectors at a maximum effective rate until told to stop.

d. **ENEMY REACHES THE SQUAD POSITION.** Enemy infantry reaching the squad position are driven out by fire, grenades, and the bayonet (close combat). The success of the defense depends upon each rifle squad defending in place. A stubborn defense by frontline squads breaks up enemy attack formations and makes him vulnerable to counterattack by reserve units. The squad does not withdraw except when specifically directed by higher authority.

2. **INFANTRY/MECHANIZED ATTACK.** When tanks or other armored vehicles support an enemy infantry attack, the primary target of the squad is the hostile infantry. When hostile infantry does not afford a target, the squad directs its small-arms fire against the aiming devices and vision slits of enemy armor. Under no circumstances will the squad be diverted from its basic mission of engaging and destroying the hostile infantry. Antitank weapons are used against armor. Every effort is made to separate the tanks from dismounted enemy infantry.

For additional training in this area, references are provided below:

1. FM 5-15	Field Fortifications
2. FM 5-20	Camouflage
3. FM 5-34	Engineer Field Data
4. TEC Lsn 937-061-0130-F	Camouflage, Cover and Concealment Part I
5. TEC Lsn 937-061-0131-F	Camouflage, Cover and Concealment Part II
6. TEC Lsn 937-061-0132-F	Camouflage, Cover and Concealment Part III
7. TEC Lsn 010-071-1044-F	Hasty Fighting Positions
8. TEC Lsn 010-071-1072-F	Supervise the Preparation of a Squad Defensive Position
9. MCI Course 03.7	Tactics of the Marine Rifle Squad
10. MCI Course 03.15	Individual Protective Measures
11. MCI Course 03.34	The Marine Infantry Small Unit in Defensive Operations
12. MCI Course 03.61	Marine Rifleman

Section II. Hand Grenades

Objectives: When provided with grenades, you will be able to:

1. Identify the shape and designation and explain the purpose of the standard fragmentation hand grenade and illumination hand grenade.

2. Properly employ hand grenades against targets at ranges to twenty-five meters.

A. PURPOSE

Hand grenades are designed for projection to a target by means of throwing. They assist the individual Marine in the accomplishment of the following missions:

- Producing casualties
- Signaling
- Screening
- Illuminating
- Producing incendiary effects
- Riot control (gas only)

B. IDENTIFICATION

You should be able to identify, by sight and touch (for night employment), the fragmentation hand grenade M67 (fig 10-6a) and the illuminating hand grenade MK1 (fig 10-6b). The fragmentation hand grenade is baseball-shaped with a smooth body while the illuminating hand grenade is elliptical with a flat bottom and a flange running around the center.

a. Fragmentation

b. Illumination

Fig 10-6. Hand grenades.

C. THROWING

1. **REMOVAL OF THE SAFETY CLIP** (fig 10-7). The safety clip must be removed before you attempt to throw the M67 fragmentation grenade.

a. Snap safety clip handle around fuze safety lever.

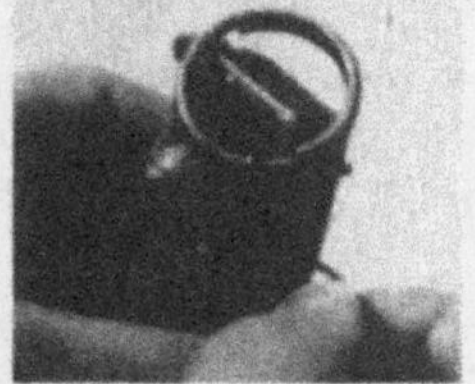

b. Remove small loop of safety clip from slot on fuze body.

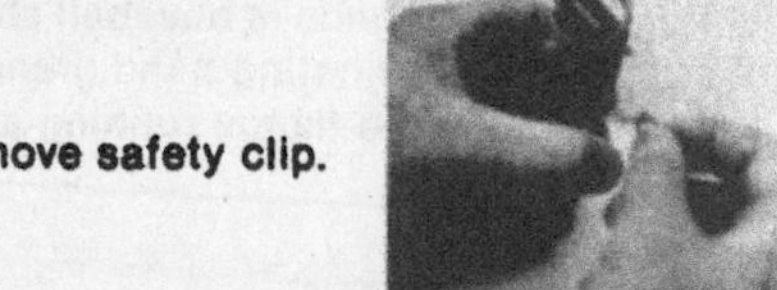

c. Remove safety clip.

Fig 10-7. Removal of safety clip.

2. **HOLDING THE GRENADE** (fig 10-8). Safety is the primary factor to be considered when determining the proper method of holding the grenade.

a. Right-handed thrower.

b. Left-handed thrower.

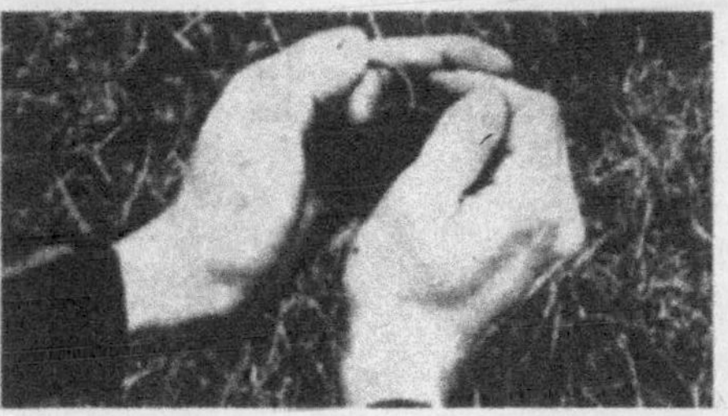

c. Holding the riot control grenade.

Fig 10-8. Holding the grenade.

3. **TECHNIQUE.**

a. Observe the target to fix the throwing distance in your mind.

b. Hold the grenade at shoulder level and grasp the safety ring or clip with the index finger of your opposite hand. Pull the pin with a twisting motion.

c. Look back at the target.

d. Throw the grenade with an overhand motion that is most natural to you and that will allow the grenade to spin in flight.

e. Follow through as you release the grenade.

4. **POSITIONS.** The positions illustrated are used primarily for training purposes to ensure uniformity and control. In combat, your position will be dictated by the amount of cover and distance to the target.

a. **STANDING** (fig 10-9).

(a) Balance your weight. Grenade shoulder high. Pull pin with twisting motion.

(b) Look at the target.

(c) Throw with natural motion. Follow through.

(d) Take cover. If none available, drop to prone position with helmet facing the target.

Fig 10-9. Standing position.

b. **KNEELING** (fig 10-10).

(a) Kneel comfortably.

(b) Look at the target.

(c) Throw naturally. Push off with foot.

(d) Take cover.

Fig 10-10. Kneeling position.

c. **PRONE TO KNEELING** (fig 10-11).

(a) Hold grenade forward so that you can see the safety pin.

(b) Assume kneeling position. Throw and take cover as above.

Fig 10-11. Prone to kneeling.

d. **ALTERNATE PRONE** (fig 10-12).

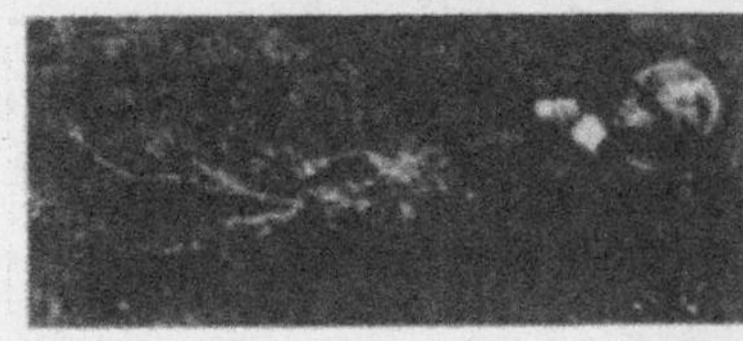

(a) Body perpendicular to intended flight.

(b) Brace right foot firmly on ground. Pull pin and hold grenade away from your body, arm cocked for throwing.

Fig 10-12. Alternate prone.

(c) Throw grenade by pushing off with foot and pulling downward with outstretched left arm.

(d) Follow through. Take cover.

Fig 10-12. Contd

For additional training in this area, references are provided below:

1. FM 23-30 — Grenades and Pyrotechnic Signals
2. TEC Lsn 645-093-7315-F — Identification of Hand Grenade and Grenade Ammunition
3. MCI Course 03.15 — Individual Protective Measures

Section III: Mines and Boobytraps

Objectives: When operating in an environment where the enemy is known or suspected to be employing mines and boobytraps, you will be able to:

1. Employ physical protective, detection, and avoidance countermeasures.

2. Upon tripping a mine or boobytrap, apply immediate action.

A. PHYSICAL PROTECTIVE COUNTERMEASURES

1. Wear body armor and helmet.

2. Sandbag vehicle flooring.

3. Keep arms and legs inside vehicle.

4. Maintain an appropriate distance from other personnel.

5. Don't travel alone.

6. Don't pick up souvenirs.

B. DETECTION COUNTERMEASURES

The three detection countermeasures can be categorized as visual inspection, probing, and mine detection.

1. **VISUAL INSPECTION.** Be alert and observant for:

- Mud smear, mudballs, dung, or boards on a road.
- Apparent road repair.

- Wire leading away from the side of a road.
- Tripwires across trails.
- Unusual terrain features.
- Suspicious items in trees or bushes.
- Enemy markings (the enemy will mark most boobytrap locations in some way).

2. **PROBING** (fig 10-13). Suspicious spots must be probed with a pointed stick. All metal should be removed from an individual who is probing an area to ensure metal sensitive mines are not accidentally activitated.

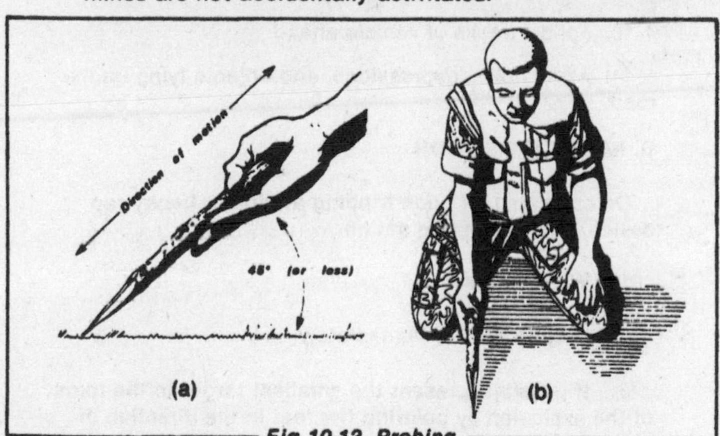

Fig 10-13. Probing.

C. AVOIDANCE COUNTERMEASURES

1. Stay off trails, footpaths, etc., as much as possible.

2. Move where local inhabitants move.

3. Avoid patterns.

4. Maintain appropriate intervals.

5. Move slowly if possible.

6. Be alert when pursuing the enemy.

7. Use artillery and mortar fire to help neutralize boobytraps.

8. Mark detected mines and boobytraps.

9. If on roads, stay in well-used portions.

10. Follow tracks of vehicle ahead.

11. Avoid holes, depressions, and objects lying on the road.

D. IMMEDIATE ACTION

On command, or upon tripping a mine or boobytrap device, take immediate action.

1. Warn others.

2. Drop to ground immediately.

3. If possible, present the smallest target to the force of the explosion by pointing the feet in the direction of the charge.

For additional training in this area, references are provided below:

1.	FM 20-32	Mine/Counter Mine Operations at Company Level
2.	MCI Course 03.4	Landmine Warfare Demolitions

Chapter 11. Security of Military Information

Section I. Security Classification, Classified Information, and Access to Classified Documents

---

Objectives:

1. Name and define three levels of security classification.

2. Define classified information and explain how it must be protected, stored, and destroyed.

3. State who should have access to classified documents.

Security is a protective condition that prevents unauthorized persons from obtaining information of military value. Such information is afforded a greater degree of protection than other material, and is given a special designation or classification.

A. SECURITY CLASSIFICATION

Classified matter which requires protection in the interest of national defense shall be limited to three categories of classification and will carry one of the following designations: TOP SECRET, SECRET, CONFIDENTIAL.

1. TOP SECRET—a "Top Secret" classification is limited to information or material which requires the highest degree of protection of the three categories. The defense of this material is vital and unauthorized disclosure could result in exceptionally grave damage to the nation. Examples of "exceptionally grave damage" in-

clude war against the United States or its allies, the breaking down of foreign relations vitally affecting the national security, the compromise of vital national defense plans or complex cryptologic and communications intelligence systems, the revealing of sensitive intelligence operations, and the disclosure of scientific or technological developments vital to national security.

2. **SECRET**—The "Secret" classification is limited to information or material the unauthorized disclosure of which could result in serious damage to the nation. Examples of "serious damage" include the breaking down of foreign relations significantly affecting national security.

3. **CONFIDENTIAL**—The "Confidential" classification is limited to information or material the unauthorized disclosure of which could cause "identifiable damage" to the nation, including the compromise of information which indicates the strength of ground, air, and naval forces in the United States and overseas areas; the disclosure of technical information used for training, maintenance, and inspection of classified munitions of war; the revealing of performance characteristics, test data, design, and production data on munitions of war.

B. CLASSIFIED INFORMATION

Classified information is any official information which has been determined to require, in the interest of national security, protection against unauthorized disclosure and which has been so designated.

1. **PROTECTING CLASSIFIED INFORMATION.** Custodians of classified material shall be responsible for safeguarding classified material at all times and particularly for locking classified material in appropriate security containers.

whenever it is not in use or under direct supervision of authorized persons. During working hours when classified information is removed from storage for use by authorized persons in officially designated offices or working areas, the material shall be kept under constant surveillance and face down when not in use. Classified information or material shall not be removed from officially designated office or working areas for the purpose of working on such material during off duty hours unless specifically approved by the commanding officer or his representative who must be designated in writing. At the end of the working day, commanding officers will require a security check of all work spaces to ensure that all classified material is properly secured.

a. Each individual is responsible for assuring that classified information which they prepare, receive, or handles is properly accounted for and made available only to those who have the appropriate clearance and the need to know. The individual having knowledge and/or custody of classified matter is responsible for any failure, on his part, which may contribute to its loss, compromise, or unauthorized disclosure.

b. Effective physical security is attained only when all the established methods and procedures are carefully carried out. These include: the proper storage of material when not in use; the proper handling when in use, to include constant surveillance and accountability; and by ensuring that classified information is not discussed over the telephone or in an area where unauthorized persons may overhear the discussion.

2. **STORAGE, DISPOSAL AND DESTRUCTION OF CLASSIFIED INFORMATION.** Whenever classified information is not under the personal control and observation of an authorized person, it will be protected or stored in

a locked security container. Those Marines who serve in billets in which classified information is used received detailed instruction on their responsibilities regarding the storage, disposal, and destruction of that information. Most Marines, however, rarely come in contact with classified information, but should know that all classified information, regardless of its classification, should be safeguarded, properly stored, and disposed of or destroyed in accordance with OPNAVINST 5510 Series. All Marines should be aware that it is their responsibility to report any apparent violation of the safeguarding of military information.

3. **ACCESS TO CLASSIFIED DOCUMENTS.** Access is the ability and opportunity to obtain knowledge or possession of classified information.

a. The Department of Defense employs a security system based on the simple principle of circulation control; i.e., control of access to classified information. Knowledge or possession of classified information shall be permitted only to individuals whose official duties require access in the interest of promoting national security and only if they have been determined to be trustworthy.

b. To have access to classified information, one must have a "need to know" in addition to possessing the proper level of clearance.

c. These principles are equally applicable if the prospective recipient is an organizational unit, including commands, other Federal agencies, defense contractors, foreign governments, and others.

4. Commanding officers should ensure that personnel under their jurisdiction are briefed in accordance with chapter 3, OPNAVINST 5510 Series before granting access to classified information.

For additional training in this area, references are provided below:

1. DOD 5200.1-R	Information Security Program Regulations Dec. 78
2. OPNAVINST 5510 Series	Department of the Navy Information Security Program Regulations Sep. 78
3.	Security Manager's Handbook

Section II. Collection and Use of Military Information

Objectives:

1. Identify the various types of unclassified and classified information of value to foreign nations.

2. Name six methods by which foreign nations collect information on U.S. Forces.

3. Explain how foreign nations make use of seemingly insignificant military facts.

Intelligence collection activities are directed toward obtaining detailed knowledge concerning our forces. Spies or intelligence officers, as they are officially known, and their agents are at this moment gathering information within the United States. A nation such as the United States can be weakened by the theft of its vital information, and its enemies can be strengthened by the acquisition of that information, whether it be classified or unclassified. It is the responsibility of each individual who has been entrusted with sensitive information to protect America's military information.

A. TYPES OF UNCLASSIFIED AND CLASSIFIED INFORMATION OF VALUE

1. Valuable unclassified information. Unclassified information most likely sought by intelligence officers or agents is:

- Names, duties, personal data, and characteristics of military personnel.
- Technical orders, manuals, or regulations.

- Base directives.
- Personnel rosters.
- Unit manning tables.
- Information about the designation, strength, mission, or combat posture of a unit.
- Development of ships, aircraft, and weapons systems.

2. Classified Information. Classified information most likely to be sought by intelligence officers or agents includes:

- Military plans, weapons, or operations
- Foreign government information.
- Intelligence activities, sources, or methods.
- Foreign relations or foreign activities of the United States.
- Scientific, technological, or economic matters relating to national security.
- United States Government programs for safeguarding nuclear materials or facilities.
- Communications security material to include: cryptographic systems, their codes, cipher devices, and machines.

B. METHODS BY WHICH FOREIGN NATIONS COLLECT INFORMATION

1. Methods by which foreign nations obtain information are as follows:

- Air, sea, and ground reconnaissance and surveillance.
- Communications intelligence through intercepting unsecure telephone, radio, and microwave telecommunications.
- Electronic surveillance using devices which monitor conversations.
- Eavesdropping or wiretapping.
- Prisoners of war and refugees.
- Documents, newspapers, and magazines.
- Press and radio/television releases, photographs and editorials.
- Careless talk.

2. Agents, both male and female, will use several of the above sources to obtain intelligence and will resort to other subversive actions such as:

- Cultivating friendships with U.S. citizens to the extent of placing personnel under obligation which may prove embarrassing or by offering money to obtain information.
- Coercion of personnel by blackmail, threats, or promises of harm to relatives living in foreign countries.
- Exploitation of personnel who may be dissatisfied or in personal difficulties.
- Intimidation, harassment, entrapment, discrediting, searching, spying on, or recruiting personnel traveling in unfriendly countries.

- Persuading personnel to defect.
- Obtaining information from personnel by correspondence (including "pen pals"), questionnaires, amateur radio activities, and other forms of communications.

C. USE OF SEEMINGLY INSIGNIFICANT MILITARY FACTS

Foreign agents use many single, seemingly insignificant facts to piece together a total picture of an operation or plan. As the illustrations below show, each single fact, by itself, means little, but once put together these seemingly insignificant facts could prove to be very damaging.

Bill's unit is leaving for Norway for a five week operation

Well,....business should be slow for you all next week with 2/6 leaving Monday

KGB INTELLIGENCE REPORT:

UNIT	2d Bn 6th Marines
STRENGTH	900
DESTINATION	Norway
DATE OF DEPARTURE	Monday 17 Jan 1983
LENGTH OF OPERATION	5 Weeks

The agent of a foreign intelligence service need not be a foreigner. The individual you meet at a disco could be a foreign diplomat or a fellow American who has been recruited as an agent. Do not expect the agent to expose his role. Usually there is a long period of cultivation during which your conversations could be completely normal. However, at any time someone may begin to inquire into activities which are classified. Then you should stop to consider whether the inquiry is innocent curiosity or the beginning of an attempt to secure intelligence information.

You should report the circumstances to a responsible official, e.g., your OIC, security manager, or commanding officer.

For additional training in this area, references are provided below:

1.	FM 30-17	Counterintelligence Operations
2.	FMFM 2-4	Counterintelligence
3.	OPNAVINST 5510.1	Department of the Navy Information Security Program Regulations Sep. 78

Section III. Information Used to Gain Tactical Advantage in Combat and How It Is Collected During Peace and War

Objective: Name three types of information, concerning U.S. Forces. that the enemy can use to gain tactical advantage in combat and state how such information is collected in peace and war.

Combat intelligence is derived from the evaluation of information on the enemy (both his capabilities and his weaknesses), the weather, and the terrain. The objective of combat intelligence is to minimize uncertainty concerning the effects of these factors on the accomplishment of the mission.

A. INFORMATION CONCERNING U.S. FORCES THAT WILL GIVE AN ENEMY TACTICAL ADVANTAGE IN COMBAT

The following are four examples of information that would give an enemy tactical advantage over U.S. Forces.

1. **COMPOSITION** (the identification and organization of a unit). This type of information identifies the unit's size and type.

a. In combat, this information can be collected from captured U.S. military personnel, by intercepting and analyzing radio messages from U.S. Forces, or by ground or air reconnaissance.

b. In peacetime, this type of information can be collected by intercepting unsecure telephone, radio, or microwave communications; from careless talk by members of a unit or the news media; or by air reconnaissance.

2. **TACTICS** (the manner in which U.S. Forces conduct an operation).

a. During combat, this information can be collected through prisoners of war or by studying the tactics used by a U.S. Force during a previous encounter.

b. During peacetime, this information can be collected by observing U.S. Forces during training operations or by obtaining copies of unit SOP's and Training Manuals (TM's) or Field Manuals (FM's) or Fleet Marine Force Manuals (FMFM's).

3. **STRENGTH** (in terms of men, weapons and equipment).

a. During war, this information may be collected from prisoners, air and ground reconnaissance, and by intercepting foreign radio communications.

b. During peacetime, this information can be collected by observing U.S. Forces during training operations, by obtaining copies of unit tables of organization (T/O's) and tables of equipment (T/E's), or by gaining information from unit members (loose talk).

4. **LOGISTICS** (the ability to support combat operations).

a. During war, this information can be collected by air and ground reconnaissance, from U.S. prisoners or civilians who have been within U.S. controlled areas, from captured U.S. documents, or by intercepting unsecure radio communications.

b. During peacetime, this information can be collected by observing U.S. Forces during training operations; from loose talk by unit personnel; or from intercepting unsecure radio, telephone, or microwave communications.

There are other types of information which would give the enemy tactical advantages over U.S. Forces such as disposition or location of U.S. Forces, training status and combat effectiveness. This information can be collected by enemy forces in the same way as in items 1-4 above.

For additional training in this area, a reference is provided below:

1. FM 30-5 Combat Intelligence

Section IV. Hypothetical Situations and Your Responsibility as a Marine to Safeguard Military Information

Objective: When given hypothetical situations, recognize and explain the responsibilities of a Marine to safeguard military information.

A. SITUATION 1

While attending a party with several of your friends (both civilian and military), you overhear a member of your unit discussing classified information with a group of people.

YOUR RESPONSIBILITY:

- Attempt to protect the classified information from further compromise or risk of compromise.
- Report the circumstances to a responsible official, e.g., your section head, OIC, security manager, or commanding officer.

B. SITUATION 2

You have been assigned duty at the battalion/squadron headquarters. At 1930 all offices are empty and you have started your security check. While checking the S-3 office, you find a Secret document which has been left out on the top of a desk.

YOUR RESPONSIBILITY:

- Safeguard the document.
- Call the OOD, security manager/unit S&C files NCO, or commanding officer and report

the finding of an unsecured classified document.

C. SITUATION 3

While waiting to use the public phone located in your barracks, you overhear the person using the phone discussing your unit's pending deployment.

YOUR RESPONSIBILITY:

- You stop the person from making any other comments, and advise him that such information is not to be discussed over a telephone.
- Report the unauthorized disclosure to your unit's security manager, your OIC, or commanding officer.

D. SITUATION 4

You are a stereo hobbyist and you frequently do business at the stereo store just outside the main gate. The storekeeper is a likeable person and enjoys chatting with Marines about their work. On your next visit he strikes up a conversation about military electronics and asks if he could borrow one or two military electronic technical manuals.

YOUR RESPONSIBILITY:

- You are not a counterintelligence agent. Your first responsibility is to simply tell the store owner that it will not be possible for you to obtain the technical manuals.

- Your second responsibility is to immediately report to your OIC that you have been asked to supply military information.

Chapter 12. Substance Abuse

Section I. Illegal Drug Use

Objectives:

1. State the Marine Corps policy on illegal drug use.

2. State at least three effects of illegal drug use for each of the following: stimulants, depressants, narcotics, hallucinogens, cannabis, and inhalents.

3. State the Marine's responsibility to himself and to his fellow Marines concerning illegal drug use.

4. State the purpose of the Marine Corps Voluntary Drug Disclosure Program.

5. State the eligibility criteria for a Marine to receive assistance under the Voluntary Drug Disclosure Program.

6. State the benefits of participating in constructive off-duty activities.

7. State the legal consequences of use, possession, or distribution of illegal drugs.

8. State the purpose of the Marine Corps Urinalysis Testing Program.

9. State the administrative actions that can result from use, possession, or distribution of illegal drugs.

A. MARINE CORPS POLICY ON ILLEGAL DRUG USE

The distribution, possession, or use of illegal drugs is not tolerated in the United States Marine Corps. Distribution means selling or giving drugs to another person in any given quantity. It is also illegal to own roach clips, coke spoons, syringes, wrapping papers, and any other items intended to illegally use drugs.

B. DEFINITION OF ILLEGAL DRUG USE

A drug is a substance that changes the functions of the body or mind when taken. Many drugs are legal and can be bought "off-the-shelf." Others are controlled by law. Of these controlled substances, some have no known medical use and are illegal. Examples of these are heroin, LSD, and hashish. Other controlled substances are available with a doctor's prescription. Using prescription drugs when you have no prescription, or taking more than the prescribed amount is also illegal.

C. DRUGS AND THE INDIVIDUAL

1. Most drugs that are used illegally affect the body's central nervous system. The central nervous system controls our senses of sight, hearing, taste, smell, and touch; our movements and thoughts; and our hearts and lungs. The effects of drugs depend on the type of drug and the amount taken, and can range from mild changes in sensation or mood to death.

2. The human body has the capacity to develop a tolerance to many drugs. When this happens, larger and larger doses of drugs are required to achieve the same effect. This results in physical dependence. The body requires the drug in order to function normally. If the drug is not taken, withdrawal symptoms (which can be very dangerous) occur. After withdrawal, the body returns to normal if no damage has been done.

3. Another kind of dependence is psychological. The mind needs the drug. This is caused by the desire to repeat the artificial sensations of illegal drug use, and results in more and more frequent use. Nearly all illegal drug use can result in psychological dependence.

4. The chart (Table 12-1) on the following pages gives the effects of each general class of drug on the body. Notice that some legal drugs (caffeine, nicotine, and alcohol) are included as a reference. The effects listed are for use of a single drug. When different drugs are taken at the same time, they can often multiply each other's effects. This is called the synergistic effect, and is extremely dangerous. It makes drug overdose easy, and makes treatment by medical personnel more difficult.

STIMULANTS	
Common Names	amphetamines, speed, cocaine, snow, caffeine, nicotine, uppers, meth, bennies, dexies, co-pilots, footballs
Immediate Effects	increased heart rate and blood pressure, wakefulness, loss of appetite, feeling of alertness and well being, dilated pupils, dry mouth, sweating, restlessness, rapid talking, shallow breathing, delirium, panic, aggression, hallucinations, bizarre and violent behavior.
After Effects	exhaustion, hunger, depression, apathy, sore muscles and joints, headache, dehydration, irritability, long periods of sleep

Table 12-1. Drug Classes and Effects

Long Term Effects	weight loss, nervousness, heart or circulatory complications severe headaches, mental illness, tolerance development
Danger of Dependency	physical: possible, psychological: high probability
DEPRESSANTS	
Common Names	barbituates, downers, methaqualone, quaalude, chloral hydrate, alcohol, tranquilizers, valium, librium, goofballs, reds, yellow jackets
Immediate Effects	decreased heart rate and blood pressure, drowsiness, loss of coordination, slurred speech, mood changes, confusion, nausea, difficulty in breathing, unconsciousness, loss of memory
Note: These effects are severely magnified when different depressants are used together.	
After Effects	depression, nausea, headache, anxiety, insomnia
Long Term Effects	tolerance, addiction
Danger of Dependency	physical: high probability, psychological: high probability, withdrawal very dangerous

Table 12-1. Contd

NARCOTICS	
Common Names	heroin, morphine, codeine, methadone, H, junk, smack, snow, horse, loads
Immediate Effects	insensitivity to pain, euphoria, sedation, initially acts as a stimulant and then as a depressant
After Effects	depression, itching, nervousness, sweating, hunger, watery eyes, runny nose, constipation
Long Term Effects	tolerance, addiction
Danger of Dependency	physical: high probability psychological: high probability, withdrawal dangerous

CANNABIS	
Common Names	marijuana, hashish, THC, pot, grass, weed
Immediate Effects	mild intoxication, mild euphoria, sense of well being, relaxation, impaired memory, altered depth and time perception, occasional nausea and lack of coordination, red eyes, increased heart rate, hunger, sweating

Table 12-1. Contd

After Effects	possible drowsiness, withdrawn behavior, mild withdrawal symptoms
Long Term Effects	increased tolerance, impaired lung function, respiratory illness, hormone imbalance, loss of sex drive in males, loss of motivation, brain damage
Danger of Dependency	physical: possible psychological: moderate probability
HALLUCINOGENS	
Common Names	LSD, PCP, peyote, mescaline, STP, DMT, morning glory seeds, mushrooms
Immediate Effects	mood and perception altered, hallucination, possible paranoia, experience varies from one time to another
After Effects	confusion, weakness, possible nausea
Long Term Effects	varies widely depending on drug used; flashbacks, genetic defects, brain damage, mental illness, increased tolerance
Danger of Dependency	physical: none known, psychological: moderate probability

Table 12-1 Contd

INHALENTS	
Common Names	Nitrous Oxide, Butyl Nitrite, Amyl Nitrite, Chlorohydrocarbons, Hydrocarbons, poppers, aerosol, cleaning fluid, propellents, glue, paint thinner, whippets
Immediate Effects	excitement, euphoria, giddiness, loss of inhibitions, aggressiveness, delusions, depression, drowsiness, headache, nausea, watery eyes, runny nose, loss of coordination, slurred speech, bad breath
After Effects	insomnia, loss of appetite, depression, irritability, headache
Long Term Effects	possible tolerance; damage to liver, kidneys, blood, bone marrow, and brain; heart failure
Danger of Dependency	physical: possible psychological: moderate probability

Table 12-1. Contd

D. DRUGS AND THE UNIT

1. A Marine under the influence of drugs cannot do his job effectively. Other Marines will have to carry the

weight of the illegal drug user, thus impairing unit efficiency. In combat, one Marine illegally using drugs endangers the survival of the entire unit.

2. Illegal drug use itself is a breach of unit discipline. Since drugs are fairly expensive, their use often leads to theft and other offenses in order to raise the money needed to buy drugs. The result is a breakdown in discipline and morale that can leave a unit ineffective.

3. Trafficking means distributing, either selling or giving drugs to someone else. By providing the drugs that are used illegally, the trafficker contributes to problems of the illegal drug user and the unit. The trafficker wants to increase his business and profits. He takes advantage of the weaknesses of individuals and causes the problem of illegal drug use to grow.

E. YOUR RESPONSIBILITY AS A MARINE

Most people who are well informed about the effects of drugs rarely abuse them. You owe it to yourself to learn what the effects of drugs really are and to avoid them. Do not be satisfied, though, with avoiding drugs yourself. Marines take care of their own. If you cannot convince your fellow Marines that they should not use drugs, report them. Do not let friendship or negative peer pressure stop you from doing what you know is right. In the long run, it is best for all concerned.

F. VOLUNTARY DRUG DISCLOSURE PROGRAM

The Marine Corps has a program that permits Marines who have used illegal drugs, and who sincerely intend to discontinue that use, to obtain assistance. The purpose of the Marine Corps Voluntary Drug Disclosure Program is to provide a method through which Marines can stop using illegal drugs. Any Marine with a drug use problem may obtain treatment or rehabilitation by means of voluntary disclosure. A Marine can obtain assistance under this program only once during his career.

Marines who seek assistance for drug use may initiate the evaluation and treatment process by voluntarily disclosing the nature and extent of their personal drug use to the unit Substance Abuse Control Office (SACO). Voluntary disclosure made to the SACO relating to the Marine's past or present drug use is a privileged communication and may not be used in any disciplinary action under the Uniform Code of Military Justice. Information disclosed to persons other than drug screening, counseling, treatment, or rehabilitation personnel is not privileged.

For a Marine to receive assistance under this program, specific eligibility criteria must be met:

1. The Marine must clearly demonstrate a sincere desire to seek help to eliminate personal drug use.
2. Traffickers in illegal drugs are not eligible.
3. The Marine must not have previously been identified as a drug user, regardless of the means of identification, including pre-service illegal drug use waiver.
4. A Marine identified as a drug user during the disclosure process of another Marine is not eligible.

G. ALTERNATIVE AND PUNISHMENT OF ILLEGAL DRUG USE

1. Off-duty activities such as sports, education, music, hobbies, and volunteer work provide a creative outlet for relief of stress and boredom, and thus are a positive alternative to illegal drug use. Not only do they help you as an individual, but they also build fellowship and camaraderie, strengthen the unit, and help others.

2. Since illegal drug use is illegal, it may result in non-judicial punishment or a court martial under the Uniform Code of Military Justice (UCMJ). The results can be restriction, loss of rank or pay, confinement at hard labor, and even a bad conduct discharge. More importantly, as a Marine, you are responsible for your actions whether you use drugs or not. Even if you are not charged with illegal drug use, your actions while under the drug's influence may cause you to find yourself charged with assault, destruction of government property, or any other misconduct that occurred while you were "high."

H. ADMINISTRATIVE ACTIONS

1. Commanding officers have been instructed by the Commandant of the Marine Corps to use every lawful means at their disposal to identify those who illegally use drugs. One way that commanders do this is by conducting urinalysis tests on a regular basis. Others include random vehicle searches, health and welfare inspections, marijuana dogs, undercover agents, and review of logbook entries and incident reports.

2. Commanding officers have a wide variety of administrative actions available to discourage illegal drug use and to prevent illegal drug use from harming others. Some of these are:

- Unmarried Marines may be denied the privilege of living off base.
- Married Marines may be evicted from government quarters.
- On base driving privileges may be revoked.
- Confirmed incidents of illegal drug use may be recorded in the Service Record Book (or be reported on a Special Fitness Report for Sergeants and above).
- Any Marine trafficking in illegal drugs will be discharged.
- A Marine found illegally using drugs is not eligible for promotion for a period of six months.
- A Marine who illegally uses drugs the first time may be discharged if the commander decides that a pattern of misconduct has been established.
- Marines who illegally use drugs a second time will usually be discharged.
- Any Marine who illegally uses drugs a third time will be discharged.

THE COMMANDANT OF THE MARINE CORPS HAS SAID, "THERE SHOULD BE NO QUESTION IN ANYONE'S MIND THAT THOSE WHO DO NOT MEET THESE STANDARDS WILL BE SEPARATED FROM THE MARINE CORPS. I EXPECT THE FULL SUPPORT OF EVERY MARINE IN COMBATING THE ILLEGAL USE OF DRUGS."

For additional training in this area consult the unit Substance Abuse Control Officer (SACO) or see the references provided below:

1. MCO 5255.1	Marine Corps Drug Abuse Administration and Management Program
2. MCO 5355.2	Marine Corps Urinalysis Testing Program
3. MCO P5300.	Marine Corps Substance Abuse Program
4. SECNAVINST 5300.28	Alcohol and Drug Abuse Control
5. ALMAR 246/81	Marine Corps Policy Concerning Illegal Drugs
6. NAVMC 2750	Marine's War on Drugs

Section II. Alcohol Abuse

Objectives:

1. State the Marine Corps policy on alcohol abuse.

2. Define alcohol abuse.

3. State at least five symptoms of alcohol abuse.

4. State the Marine's responsibility to himself and fellow Marines concerning alcohol abuse.

5. State the administrative actions that can result from alcohol abuse.

6. State how a Marine may obtain assistance for himself and/or his dependents in controlling alcohol abuse.

7. Name the Unit Substance Abuse Control Officer.

A. MARINE CORPS POLICY ON ALCOHOL ABUSE

Alcohol abuse is not tolerated in the United States Marine Corps.

B. DEFINITION OF ALCOHOL ABUSE

Alcohol abuse, as defined in MCO 5370.6A, is any irresponsible use of alcohol which leads to misconduct, unacceptable social behavior, or impairment of an individual's performance of duty, physical or mental health, financial responsibility, or personal relationships.

C. ALCOHOL AND ITS SYMPTOMS

1. Alcohol is the most frequently abused drug in our society. It is listed in table 12-1 as a depressant. Like other depressants, alcohol abuse dangerously affects one's reasoning ability, coordination, social behavior, and performance. It is dangerously addictive both physically

and mentally. Over a period of time, alcohol abuse usually leads to serious illness involving the heart, liver, and other organs. Alcohol abuse can lead to alcoholism, which is a progressive, treatable disease, however, if left untreated, it will result in death or permanent brain damage.

2. Alcohol is legal, but all too often, resulting actions while intoxicated are not. This is the other side of the effects of alcohol. Misconduct, accidental injuries, motor vehicle accidents, and arrest are some of the results of alcohol abuse.

D. SIGNS OF ALCOHOL ABUSE

A few of the many recognizable signs of alcohol abuse are:

1. **HANGOVER.** The nausea, headache, and drymouth following heavy drinking are signs of the irritation of the body that alcohol abuse has caused. A Marine in this condition does not perform well on the job.

2. **BLACKOUT.** Blackout is a loss of memory while drinking. If a Marine cannot remember how he arrived home after a drinking session, then that Marine has had a blackout.

3. **FATIGUE.** The depressant effect of alcohol plus the late night on the town can leave a Marine tired. This might cause the Marine to be late for work or to be absent entirely, jeopardizing the Marine's effectiveness and reliability.

4. **FREQUENT SICK CALLS.** The frequent alcohol abuser may be severely "hungover" and require medical

assistance. Additionally, that trip to sick bay might be used to cover-up a problem with being constantly late for work.

5. **SOCIAL PROBLEMS.** Sometimes the alcohol abuser is the "life of the party," but the frequent abuser becomes embarrassing to himself and to others. Ultimately, this can lead to the loss of family and friends.

E. ALCOHOL AND THE UNIT

A Marine under the influence of alcohol is just as dangerous to the unit as a Marine under the influence of any other drug. Incidents of violent crime, motor vehicle accidents, spouse and child abuse are frequently alcohol related. Drunk drivers are an especially dangerous menace who take the lives of many innocent victims each year. Substandard performance, financial irresponsibility and unacceptable behavior all adversely impact organizational efficiency.

F. YOUR RESPONSIBILITY AS A MARINE

1. Alcohol is legal. However, misconduct as a result of alcohol abuse is illegal. Every Marine is responsible for his or her own actions whether under the influence of alcohol or not and will be held strictly accountable for those actions under the Uniform Code of Military Justice. If you don't drink, don't start. If you do drink, learn not to drink too much. If you think that you need to prove something to your friends, prove that you are responsible for taking care of yourself and avoiding the problems of alcohol abuse.

2. Marines take care of their own. Alcohol abuse by any Marine, on liberty or in garrison, is the responsibility of every other Marine. Alcohol abuse must be avoided or

corrected. Stopping alcohol abuse by Marines is a responsibility of all Marines.

G. ADMINISTRATIVE ACTIONS

In order to protect Marines from the effects of alcohol abuse, the commanding officer may take several administrative actions. Some of these are:

- If a Marine is an alcohol abuser, it is quite possible this abuse will have a negative effect on his proficiency and conduct marks. This can delay promotions.
- Authorization to operate a government vehicle can be denied.
- Base driving privileges for private vehicles will be suspended for one year for any Marine convicted of driving under the influence of alcohol on or off base.
- Unmarried Marines may be denied the privilege of living off base.
- Married Marines may be evicted from government quarters if that Marine's alcohol abuse affects quarters residents.
- Confirmed incidents of alcohol abuse will be entered in the service record book. The Marine involved will be formally counseled by the Commanding Officer.
- Continued alcohol abuse will result in separation from the Marine Corps for reasons of unsuitability.

THE COMMANDANT OF THE MARINE CORPS HAS SAID, " THOSE WHO DO NOT MEET THESE STANDARDS WILL BE SEPARATED FROM THE MARINE CORPS. THE PRIVILEGE OF BEING A MARINE IN-

CLUDES THE RESPONSIBILITY FOR MAINTAINING THE HIGHEST STANDARDS OF DISCIPLINE, CONDUCT, AND PERFORMANCE. ALCOHOL ABUSE IS A FORM OF INDISCIPLINE THAT CAN SERIOUSLY REDUCE THE OVERALL VALUE AND EFFECTIVENESS OF THE INDIVIDUAL MARINE AND DEGRADE THE OPERATIONAL EFFECTIVENESS OF THE MARINE'S ORGANIZATION. THOSE WHO CHOOSE TO ABUSE ALCOHOL WILL BE IDENTIFIED AND ASSISTED TO THE DEGREE POSSIBLE, BUT IN ALL CASES, HELD ACCOUNTABLE FOR THEIR ACTIONS."

H. ASSISTANCE

A Marine may obtain help for himself, his family, or another Marine by contacting the unit Substance Abuse Control Officer, medical personnel, or the Chaplain. These persons have access to a large number of agencies and publications designed to assist those who abuse alcohol.

For additional training in this area, consult the unit Substance Abuse Control Officer, (SACO) or see references provided below:

1. SECNAVINST 5300.28	Alcohol and Drug Abuse Control
2. MCO 5370.6A	Marine Corps Alcohol Abuse Administrative and Management Program
3. NAVMC 2662A	Marine Corps Policy on Alcohol Abuse
4. ALMAR 125/82	A Seminar on Alcohol and Alcoholism

Chapter 13. Land Navigation

Section I. Terrain Features, Colors, and Use of Grid System

Objective: Given a standard military map (scale 1:50,000) identify and record the location, using six-digit coordinates, of a hill, saddle, steep slope, gradual slope, dirt road, junction of two roads, and three manmade objects.

A. TERRAIN AND VEGETATION FEATURES

1. HILL. A hill is shown on the standard military map by a number of closed contour *lines*. Figure 13-1a shows the hills as they would appear when looking at them at ground level. Figure 13-1b shows them as they would appear on the map. Contour lines are *BROWN*.

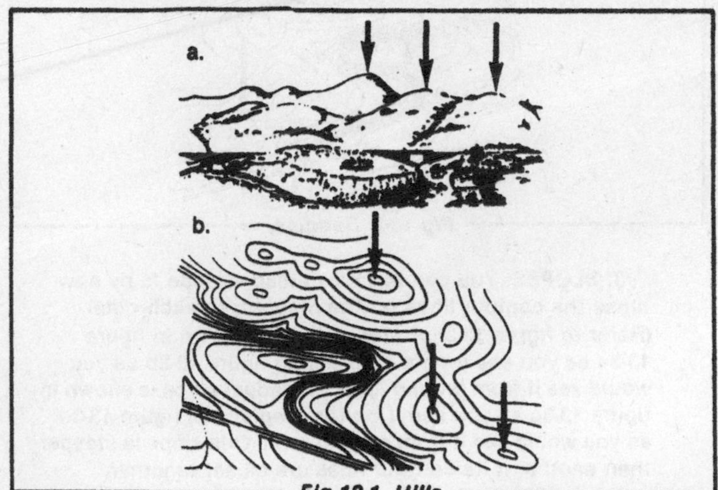

Fig 13-1. Hills.

2. **SADDLE.** A saddle is formed when two hills are close together and the area between the hills is lower than the hill tops but not as low as the surrounding area. Figure 13-2a shows saddles as they would appear from ground level and figure 13-2b shows them as they would appear on the map.

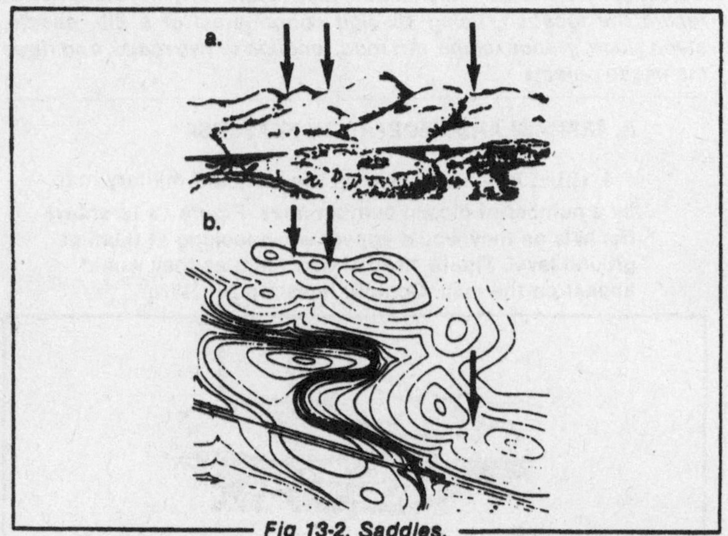

Fig 13-2. Saddles.

3. **SLOPES.** You can tell how steep a slope is by how close the contour lines on the map are to each other (Refer to figure 13-3).A steep slope is shown in figure 13-3a as you see it on a map and in figure 13-3b as you would see it from ground level. A gradual slope is shown in figure 13-3c as you see it on the map and in figure 13-3d as you would see it from ground level. One slope is steeper than another if its contour lines are closer together.

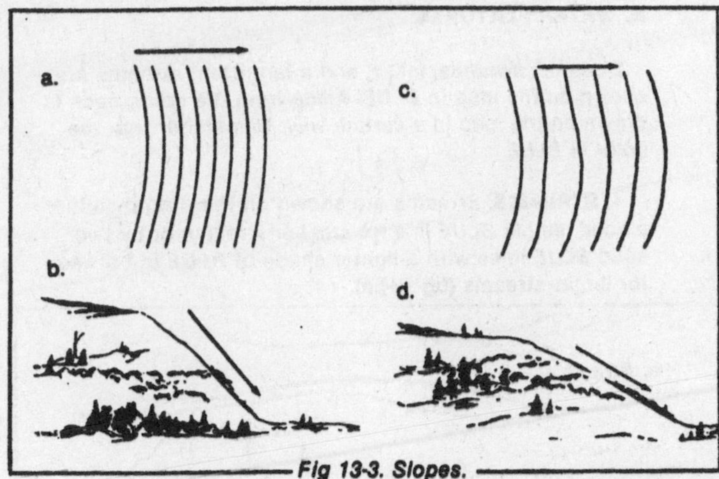

Fig 13-3. Slopes.

4. TREES AND OTHER VEGETATION. Trees and other types of vegetation are shown on the map in GREEN. In most cases when the countryside is shown with its normal covering of vegetation, it is colored an overall light green. At times when orchards, heavy forest or grasslands are shown, they will be shown as illustrated in figure 13-4. Remember that they are GREEN.

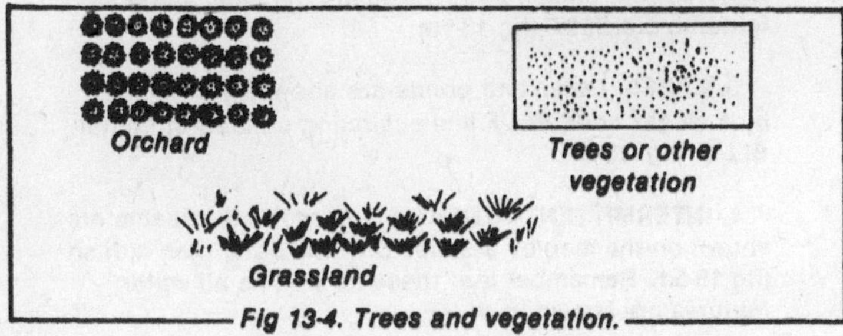

Fig 13-4. Trees and vegetation.

B. WATER FEATURES

Streams, swamps, lakes, and intermittent streams are shown on the map in *BLUE*. Aside from the color, each is drawn on the map in a certain way. Remember that the color is *BLUE*.

1. **STREAMS.** Streams are shown on the map by either a solid, single *BLUE* line for smaller streams or by two solid *BLUE* lines with a lighter shade of *BLUE* in between for larger streams (fig 13-5a).

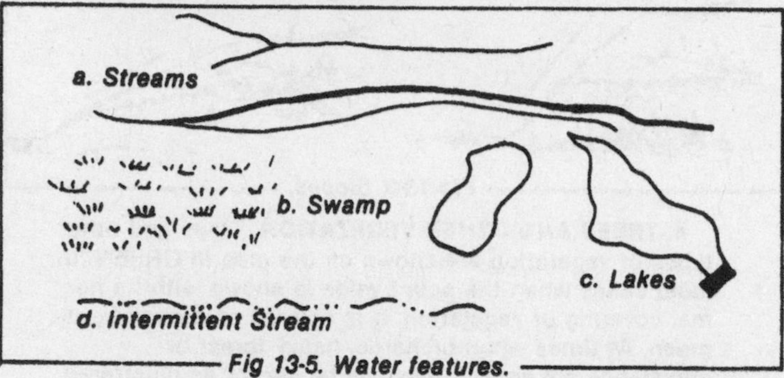

Fig 13-5. Water features.

2. **SWAMPS.** Swamps are shown on a map by grass features with broken lines mixed in. The lines and grass features are *BLUE* (fig 13-5b).

3. **LAKES.** Lakes and ponds are shown on the map by a single, solid *BLUE* line encircling an area of lighter *BLUE* (fig 13-5c).

4. **INTERMITTENT STREAMS.** Intermittent streams are shown on the map by a series of three dots, then a dash (fig 13-5d). Remember that these as well as all water features are shown in *BLUE*.

C. ROADS AND ROAD JUNCTIONS

Normally, major highways and main thoroughfares are shown on the military map in solid *RED* lines (fig 13-6a). Secondary roads are shown by two parallel *BLACK* lines (fig 13-6b), and dirt or gravel roads are shown by two parallel broken *BLACK* lines (fig 13-6c). Road junctions are formed where roads meet.

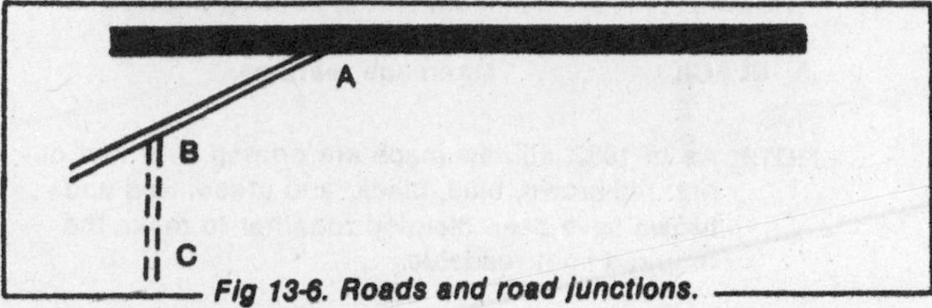

Fig 13-6. Roads and road junctions.

D. MANMADE FEATURES

Manmade features are shown on the military map in *BLACK*. Since it would be difficult for each building in a city to be shown on the map, normally larger towns or cities will be shaded in *RED* with only the prominent or main buildings shown such as schools, hospitals, churches, etc. Figure 13-7 shows some common manmade features which might be found on the military map.

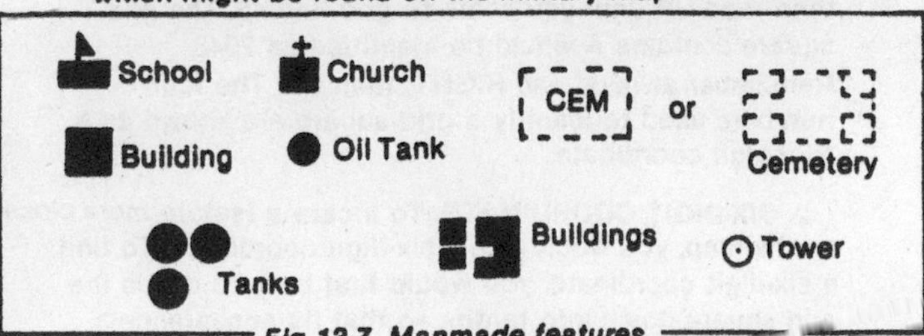

Fig 13-7. Manmade features.

E. SUMMARY OF MAP COLORS

1. **BROWN** .... Contour lines, plowed fields, cuts,
2. **GREEN** .... Trees, orchards, grasslands, and
3. **BLUE** .... Streams, swamps, lakes, and
4. **RED** .... Main roads, built-up areas, and
5. **BLACK** .... Manmade features.

NOTE: As of 1982, all new maps are printed with four colors: red-brown, blue, black, and green. Red and brown have been blended together to make the map red light readable.

1. **GRID SQUARE.** Grid lines are superimposed on the military map. Each line, both horizontal and vertical, is numbered. To find the location of a certain grid square, combine the numbers of the grid lines that form the lower left corner of that square, first the vertical, then the horizontal. If you wanted to find the correct designation of the grid square that contains the A in figure 13-8, FIRST read RIGHT until you come to vertical grid line 29, then read UP until you come to grid line 48. The grid square contains A would be identified as 2948. Remember always read RIGHT, then UP. The four numbers used to identify a grid square are known as a four-digit coordinate.

2. **SIX-DIGIT COORDINATE.** To locate a feature more closely on the map, you would use a six-digit coordinate. To find a six-digit coordinate, you would first have to divide the grid square down into tenths so that its appearance

would be as pictured in figure 13-9. Again, you read all the way RIGHT FIRST so that the first three numbers of the coordinate for points B would be 309; then read all the way UP so that the second three numbers would be 503 or a six-digit coordinate of 309503. It is not recommended that you actually draw the lines within grid square 3050 since such lines obstruct other map information. Use the map scale located on the protractor as shown in figure 13-10. You can make your own scale on a paper corner. With practice you can learn to estimate the tenths in a grid square with fair accuracy.

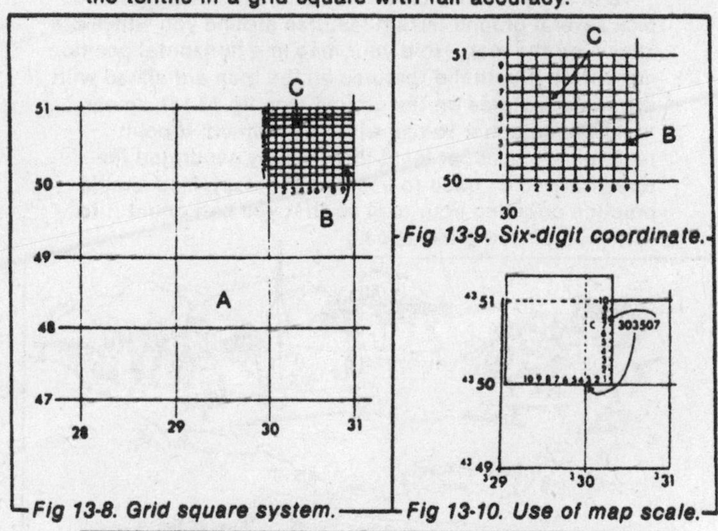

Fig 13-8. Grid square system.

Fig 13-9. Six-digit coordinate.

Fig 13-10. Use of map scale.

For additional training in this area, references are provided below:

1. FM 21-26 — Map Reading
2. TEC Lsn 930-071-0016-F — Terrain Features

Section II. Terrain Association

***Objective:** Given a standard military map (scale 1:50,000), and shown present location, orient the map to surrounding terrain; identify the four primary directions, compute the distance to a designated point at least 6000 meters distant, and use the map to navigate to that point.*

A. MAP ORIENTATION

To orient your map by the terrain association method, pick several ground terrain features around you which are shown on the map. Hold your map in a horizontal position and rotate it until the features on the map are alined with the same features on the ground (see fig 13-11). Linear features are better to use with this method. If point features are used, at least three widely separated features have to be used to improve accuracy. You should practice orienting your map so that you can orient it to within 5° of true orientation.

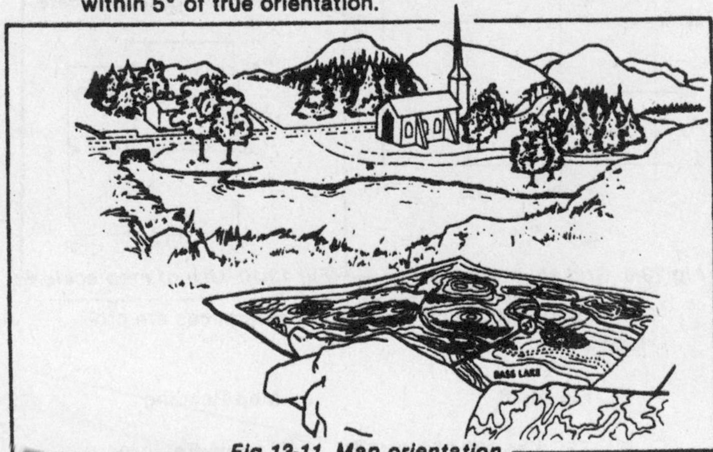

Fig 13-11. Map orientation.

B. PRIMARY DIRECTIONS

Once the map is oriented correctly, the four primary directions can be identified and pointed out very easily. Once the map is oriented, the top of the map will be alined in a northerly direction. If you were standing at the bottom of the map and facing toward the top, as it lies on the ground, north would be to your front, east to your right, west to your left, and south directly to your rear (see fig 13-12).

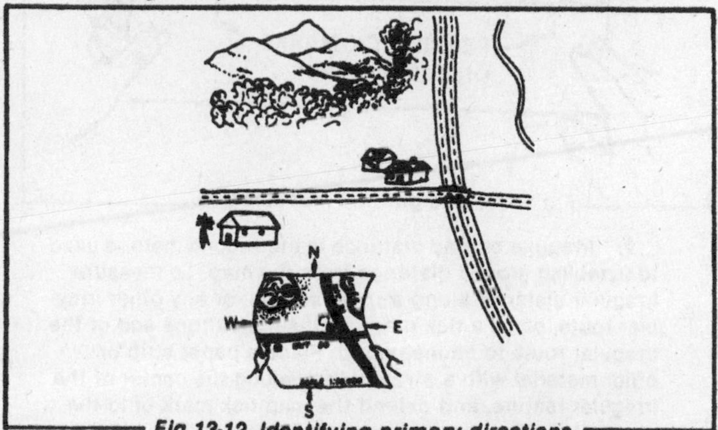

Fig 13-12. Identifying primary directions.

C. DISTANCE COMPUTATION

1. Straight-line measurement is the first method used to establish a ground distance from the map. Once two points have been identified on the map sheet, it is a simple matter to use a straightedge of paper to tick off the distance between the two points. When making map measurements, it is important that all measurements be made from the center of the topographic symbol concerned

as that point most accurately designates the true location of that feature on the ground (see fig 13-13).

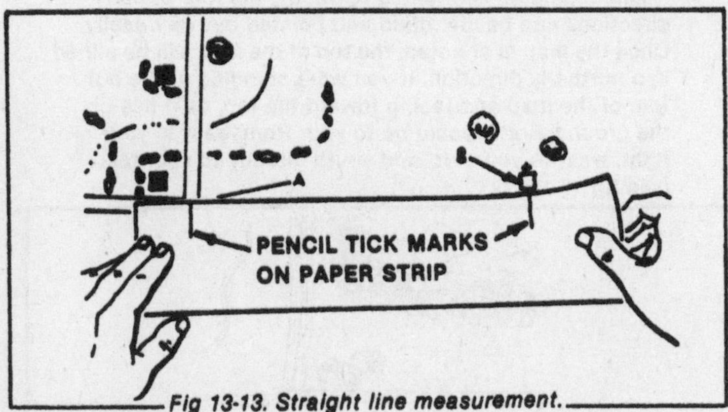

Fig 13-13. Straight line measurement.

2. Irregular or road distance is the second method used to establish ground distance from the map. To measure irregular distance along a road, stream, or any other irregular route, place a tick mark on the map at one end of the irregular route to be measured. Place a paper strip or other material with a straightedge along the center of the irregular feature, and extend the map tick mark onto the paper strip. The straightedge will eventually leave the center of the irregular feature. At the exact point where this occurs, place a tick mark on the map and extend it onto the paper. Rotate the paper strip until its straightedge once again is running along the center of the linear feature. Be sure to aline the last tick mark on your straightedge with the last tick mark on the irregular feature again. Place a tick mark where the straightedge leaves the center of the irregular feature. Repeat this procedure until you have ticked off the desired distance (see fig 13-14).

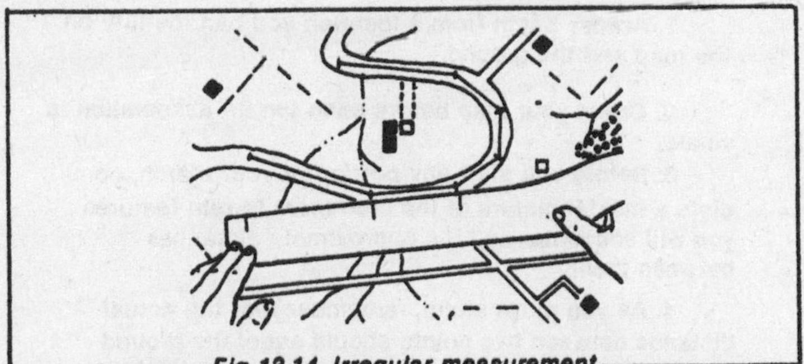

Fig 13-14. Irregular measurement.

3. To convert the map distance to ground distance, place the paper strip with the tick marks along the appropriate graphic scale at the bottom of the map sheet and determine the ground distance (see fig 13-15).

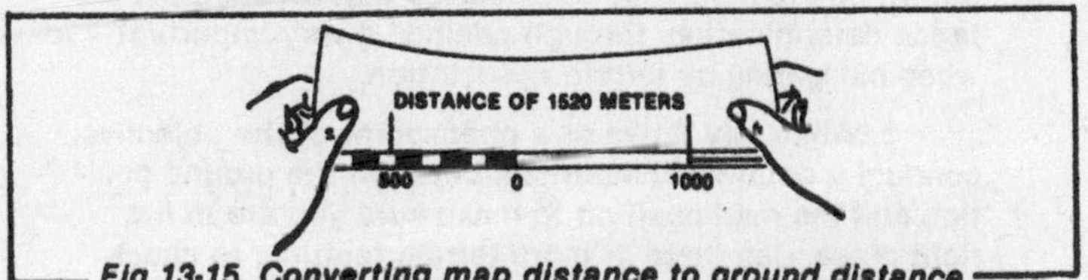

Fig 13-15. Converting map distance to ground distance.

4. The average pace count of a Marine is 120 paces to each 100 meters. The average rate of march for the individual Marine is 4 kilometers per hour. These averages will vary to some degree according to the individual and terrain, but may be used as a guide until each Marine has established an individual pace count and rate of march.

D. LAND NAVIGATION BY TERRAIN ASSOCIATION

1. In employing terrain association, the following points should be remembered:

1. Always begin from a location you can identify on the map and the ground.

2. Orient your map before each terrain association is made.

3. Before you start any portion of your march, complete a mental picture of the prominent terrain features you will encounter and the approximate distances between them.

4. As you move along, remember that the actual distance between two points should equal the ground distance determined from the map. For example, if the map indicates you should cross a stream 200 meters after passing a hill, you should in fact cross a stream at that distance. If you go only 100 meters and come to a stream, you know that it is not the right one and is not shown on the map. This emphasizes that an accurate distance determination, through pacing, is very important when navigating by terrain association.

5. When you arrive at a checkpoint of the objective, conduct a detailed comparison between the ground position and the map position to make sure you are in the right place. Use three or more terrain features to check your position.

6. Navigation by terrain association depends on your ability to visualize what a terrain feature on the ground looks like from its representation on the map.

For additional training in this area, references are provided below:

1.	FM 21-26	Map Reading
2.	TEC Lsn 930-071-0164-F	Determine Distance While Moving

Section III. Land Navigation by Dead-Reckoning

Objective: Given a lensatic compass, a protractor, and a map of the local area, follow a given azimuth for 1,500 meters on the ground to an area of approximately 20 meters in diameter. Both the starting point and the objective must be identifiable on the map.

A. MAP ORIENTATION

Orient your map using the procedure described in section II of this chapter.

B. ROUTE SELECTION

1. Your first step in selecting your route is to locate and plot the starting point (SP) and objective (OBJ) on your map; then draw a straight line between the two points (see fig 13-16).

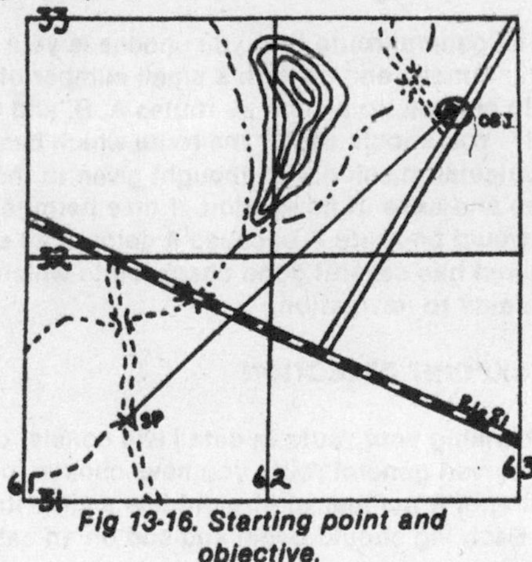

Fig 13-16. Starting point and objective.

2. Next you should plot all areas which you wish to avoid on the map; then draw the general routes which may be used (lines A, B, and C on fig 13-17).

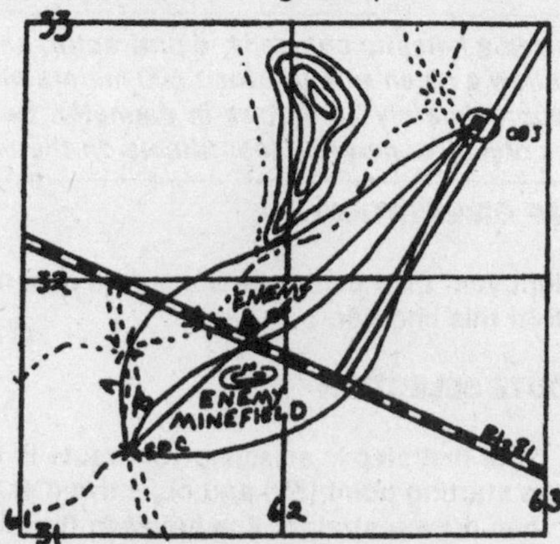

Fig 13-17. General routes.

3. The general route that you choose is your decision. You will normally end up with a small number of possible routes to choose from such as routes A, B, and C in figure 13-17. You should select the route which best suits your particular mission with thought given to the tactical situation and ease of navigation. If time permits, a logical choice would be route A because it detours all enemy activity and has several good checkpoints which may be used as aids to navigation.

C. CHECKPOINT SELECTION

1. Planning your route in detail will consist of converting the curved general route you have chosen into a route consisting of a number of straight line segments called "legs." Each leg should begin and end on an easily iden-

tifiable terrain feature, if possible. These terrain features are called checkpoints (CP) because they will enable you to check your navigation and location periodically during your movement (fig 13-18). Using route A, the first leg could be from the starting point (SP) to the bridge on the dirt road north of the starting point. The second leg could be from the bridge, which is checkpoint one, to the junction of the stream just south of the hill along grid line 62. This will be checkpoint two. The third leg could go from checkpoint two to the objective. In all instances when legs of a route are drawn, they should be drawn or extended long enough so that you can measure a grid azimuth for them.

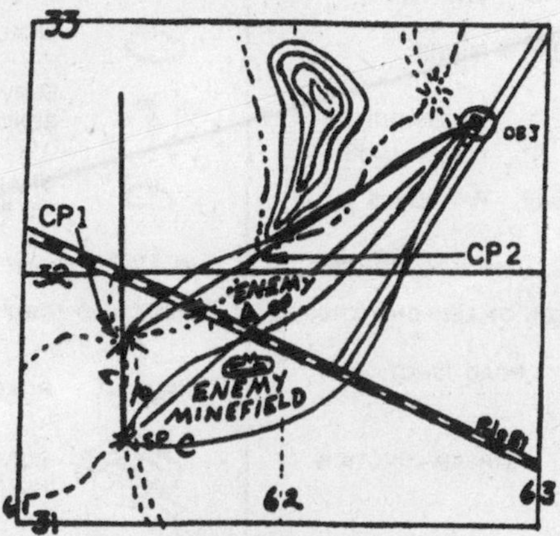

Fig 13-18. Locating checkpoints.

2. There are two basic types of checkpoints: line checkpoints and point checkpoints. A line checkpoint is a natural or manmade linear feature which crosses your line of march (fig 13-19). Point checkpoints are specific

objects or terrain features which, if located and properly identified, help to positively indicate your exact location (fig 13-20). The primary advantage of a point checkpoint over a linear checkpoint is that once you have located a line checkpoint, you still must figure out your exact location along that feature. The ideal checkpoint is one that is a combination of either two line checkpoints (fig 13-21), or a point checkpoint located along a line checkpoint (fig 13-22).

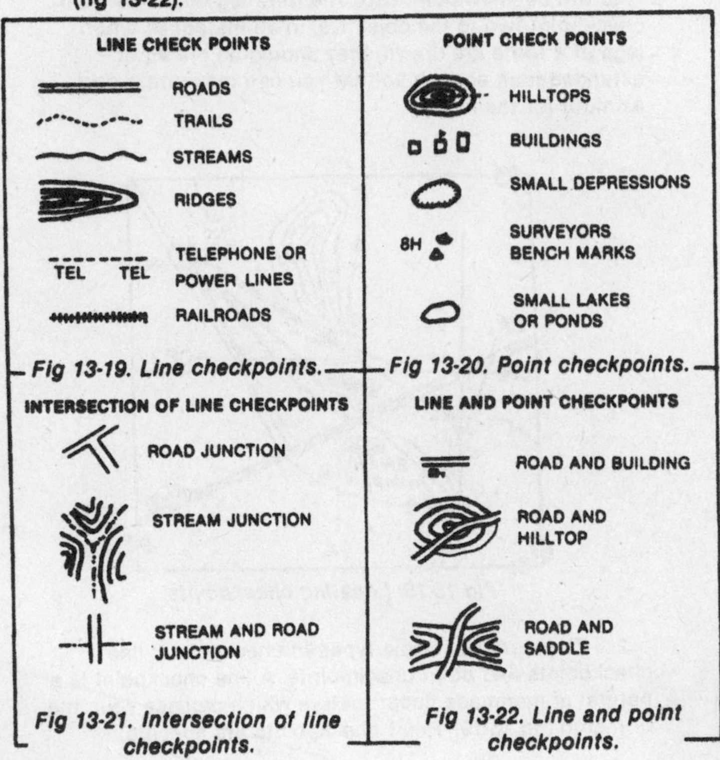

Fig 13-19. Line checkpoints.

Fig 13-20. Point checkpoints.

Fig 13-21. Intersection of line checkpoints.

Fig 13-22. Line and point checkpoints.

D. AZIMUTHS

1. **AZIMUTH DEFINITION.** An azimuth is an "angle" measure within a circle clockwise from the base direction, north. When used with land navigation, the directional circle is broken up into 360 possible azimuths or degrees (fig 13-23).

2. **AZIMUTHS AND LAND NAVIGATION.** When we speak of following an azimuth in land navigation, think of yourself in the center of a circle at the start or origin. A line drawn from you to the objective would be on a certain angle or azimuth, in this case 60 degrees, when measured within a circle from a base direction, north. This system of finding and following an azimuth to an objective is universal within the U.S. military and assures that the objective is found with accuracy each time (fig 13-24).

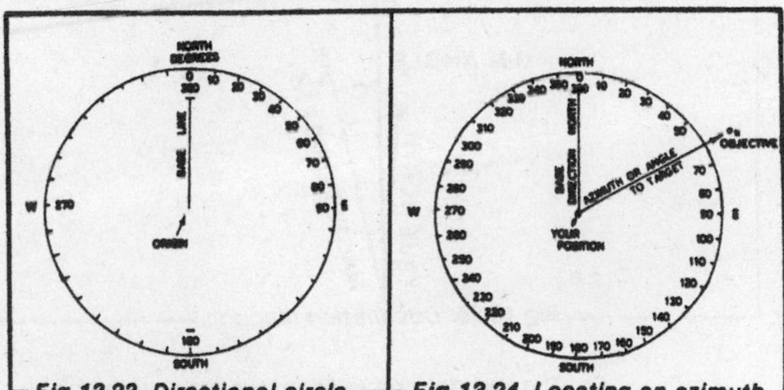

Fig 13-23. Directional circle. *Fig 13-24. Locating an azimuth.*

3. **BASE DIRECTION** (North).

a. There are two base directions or norths used when navigating over land with the aid of the map and compass. These base directions are known as GRID and

MAGNETIC NORTH. The difference between these two points is known as the Grid-Magnetic or G-M angle and is shown on all military maps by what is called a declination diagram (fig 13-25). When navigating over land with the aid of the map and compass, TRUE NORTH, the actual direction of the North Pole, is seldom used so it will not be discussed.

b. **MAGNETIC NORTH** is measured with a lensatic compass. The north-seeking arrow on the compass points to an area in the Hudson Bay region of Canada where the magnetic attractions from the earth's core are the strongest in the northern hemisphere. This is known as magnetic north and is shown by a half arrow on the declination diagram (fig 13-25). Whenever you use an azimuth from a compass to plan or follow a route in the field, keep in mind that it is a magnetic azimuth.

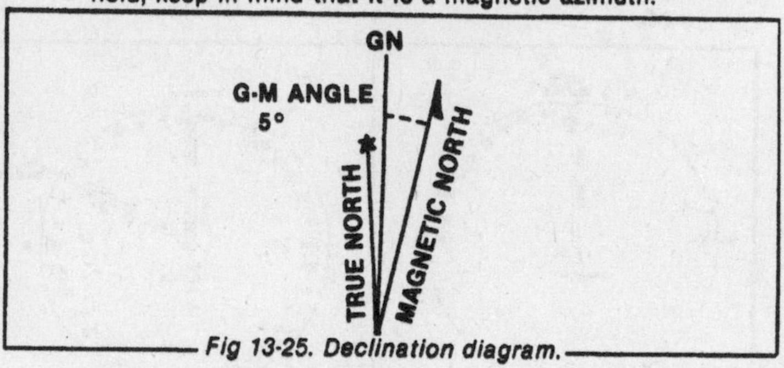

Fig 13-25. Declination diagram.

c. The vertical grid lines on the map run from south at the bottom of the map to north (called GRID NORTH) at the top of the map (fig 13-26). Because the grid lines are placed on each map sheet in the same way, very seldom will the base directions, grid and magnetic north, be on the same angle. The grid north angle is shown in the declination diagram as GN (fig 13-26). Whenever you plot an azimuth with a protractor on a map, keep in mind that it is a grid azimuth (fig 13-27).

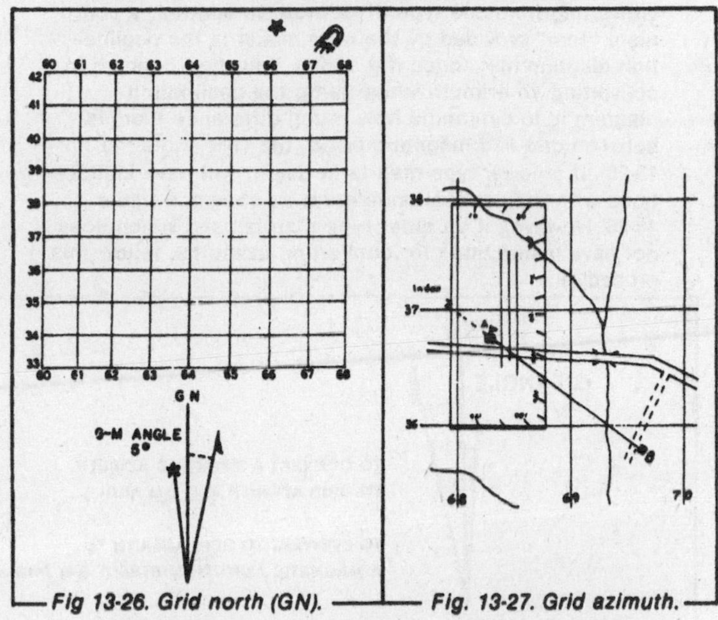

Fig 13-26. Grid north (GN).

Fig. 13-27. Grid azimuth.

4. G-M ANGLE CONVERSION. Before you begin to navigate, it is very important that you determine whether the initial direction you are given to follow is expressed as a magnetic azimuth or a grid azimuth. The angle between the two may vary as much as 20° in some parts of the United States. If an azimuth is determined with the map and protractor, it is called a grid azimuth and cannot be followed on the ground with a compass until it is converted to a magnetic azimuth. By the same token, an azimuth determined with the lensatic compass is a magnetic azimuth and cannot be correctly plotted on the map until it has been converted to a grid azimuth. When converting from one type of azimuth to another, a convenient "tool" provided by the map maker is the declination diagram mentioned (fig 13-28). Your first concern in converting an azimuth when using the declination diagram is to determine how much difference there is between grid and magnetic north, the G-M angle (fig 13-28). If a newer type map is in use, it will have instructions with the declinationdiagram as shown in figure 13-28. However, if an older type map is used which does not have instructions for converting azimuths, follow this procedure:

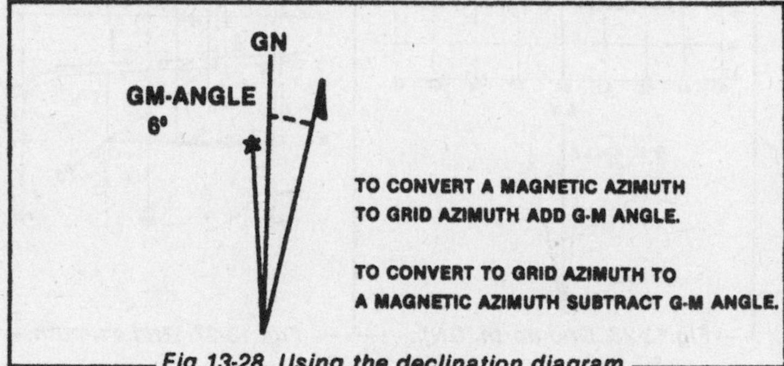

Fig 13-28. Using the declination diagram.

a. Determine the amount of the G-M angle for your map which would be the number of degrees difference between grid and magnetic north.

b. Place your finger on the symbol for the base direction you are converting from (grid north or magnetic north).

c. Move your finger to the symbol for the base direction to which you wish to convert.

d. Apply the **LEFT ADD, RIGHT SUBTRACT (LARS)** rule. This means that if your finger moves to the Left, Add the amount of the G-M angle to the given azimuth. If it moves to the Right, Subtract the amount of the G-M angle from the given azimuth.

e. Using the declination diagram (fig 13-28), a grid azimuth of 36° when converted to a magnetic azimuth would be 30° (RIGHT SUBTRACT, 6° from 36° = 30°). Convert a magnetic azimuth of 16° to a grid azimuth (answer: 16° + 6° = 22°).

5. THE PROTRACTOR.

a. **DESCRIPTION.** A protractor is basically a ruler for measuring angles. It may be circular, semicircular, square, or rectangular. Regardless of its shape, the protractor will consist of an index point, a base line, and a scaled outer edge (fig 13-29). The scaled edge has two sets of numbers: 0 to 180, representing the right side of a circle, and 180 to 360 representing the left side of a circle. As a result, by rotating a semicircular or rectangular protractor it can be made to represent a complete circle. It is important to remember that if the outer edge of such a protractor is to the right, the azimuth is read or plotted using readings between 0° to 180°. If the outer edge is to the left, the values of the readings will be between 180° to 360°.

b. **MEASURING A GRID AZIMUTH** (map direction). To determine the direction from one point to another on the map, you first draw a straight line through the two points, making sure that the line is long enough (3 to 4 inches) to extend beyond the outer edge of the protractor. Then you position your protractor on the map so that the index point is on the starting point and the protractor baseline (0° line) is exactly parallel to the nearest vertical grid line on the map. Then you read the grid azimuth at the point where the line you drew between the two points crosses the protractor scale. For example, in figure 13-29 the line between the points A and B crosses the protractor scale at 40° mark; therefore, the grid azimuth from point A to point B is 40°.

NOTE: it is essential that the protractor straightedge be exactly parallel to a vertical grid line. Even a slight variation from parallel will result in a measurement error of several degrees. It is often difficult to achieve this parallel alinement by visual inspection. Therefore, the following expedient method is suggested for greater accuracy; extend the line between the two points (such as C and D in figure 13-30), until it intersects the nearest vertical grid line. Then place the index arrow exactly at the point of intersection and aline the protractor straightedge exactly on the grid line.

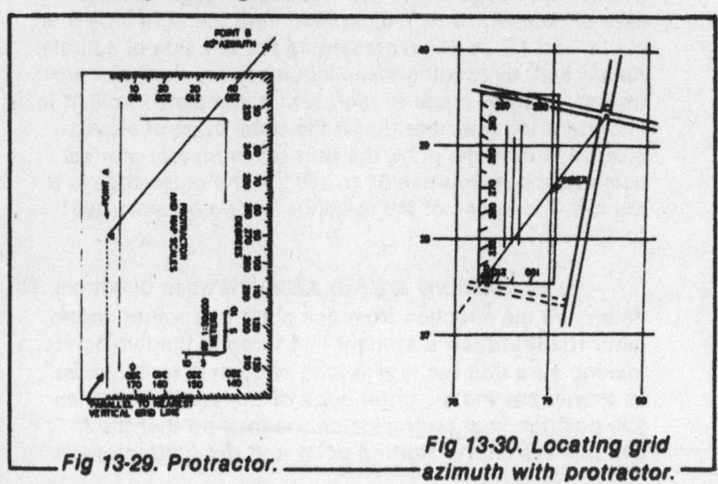

Fig 13-29. Protractor.

Fig 13-30. Locating grid azimuth with protractor.

c. **PLOTTING AN AZIMUTH WITH THE PROTRACTOR.** To plot a grid azimuth from a certain point on a map, place the protractor index at the point and rotate the protractor until the base line exactly parallels the nearest north-south grid line. Make a tick mark on the map at the point indicated by the desired azimuth on the protractor. Remove the protractor and use some form of straightedge to draw a line from the starting point to the tick mark. Figure 13-30 shows a grid azimuth of 215° plotted from point C to point D.

6. SETTING MAGNETIC AZIMUTHS.

a. Setting magnetic azimuths onto the lensatic compass can be accomplished by two methods. The first method is commonly referred to as the "day" method but can be accomplished any time as long as there is sufficient light. With the day method, first rotate the compass until the desired azimuth is under the black index line; then turn the bezel ring until the luminous line is directly over the north arrow. Once this is done, follow a line formed by the black index line and the sighting wire in the compass cover, ensuring that the luminous line remains directly over the north arrow (Use figure 13-31 to clarify the names of the compass components).

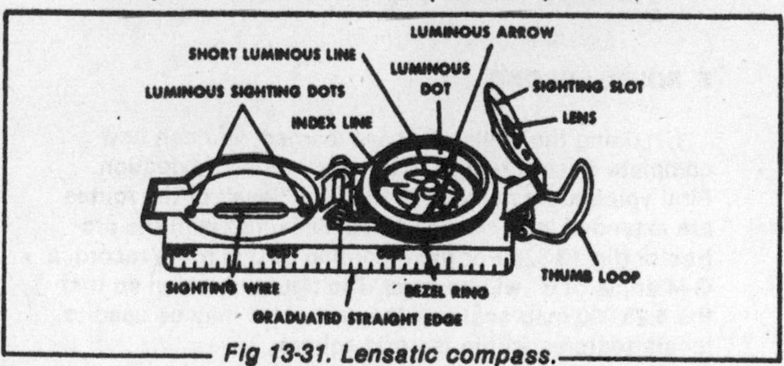

Fig 13-31. Lensatic compass.

b. The second method of setting a magnetic azimuth on the lensatic compass is commonly referred to as the "night" method, as no light is required. Around the base of the bezel ring is a series of 120 notches. On the forward edge of the body of the compass is a bezel detent spring with its tip seated in one of the notches (fig 13-31). As the bezel ring is turned, the spring moves notch to notch producing a click. Each click of the bezel ring is equal to 3° of change in direction. To set an azimuth of 51° onto the lensatic compass at night:

(1) Rotate the bezel ring until the luminous line is over the black index line.

(2) Rotate the bezel ring counterclockwise 17 clicks (51 ÷ 3 = 17, remember each click equals 3°).

(3) Turn the compass until the north arrow is directly under the luminous line. The azimuth is now set; that is, the 51° azimuth is directly under the black index line, and you would go in the direction indicated by a line formed on the two luminous dots in the compass cover.

E. ROUTE RECORD

1. Using the skills you have learned, you can now complete a route record to be used during navigation. First you should make sure that the "legs" of the routes are extended long enough to be measured with the protractor (fig 13-32). For the recording of this route record, a G-M angle of 6° will be used. The figure is drawn so that the 1:25,000 map scale on the protractor may be used to locate features within the grid square.

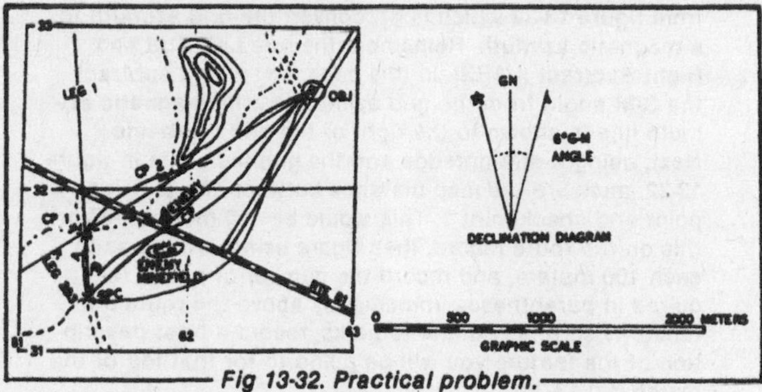

Fig 13-32. Practical problem.

2. Now that the starting point, checkpoints, objective, and legs of your route have been established on the map, it is a simple matter to use the skills that you have already learned to get the information needed for a route record (fig 13-33).

FROM	TO	MAGNETIC AZIMUTH	DISTANCE	REMARKS
SP (614313)	CP (614318)	353°	(480) 400M	BRIDGE

Fig 13-33. Route record format.

a. For each leg of the route to be navigated, you should record the location of the point you are starting from and the location of the point to which you will be proceeding, in this case, from the starting point (grid coordinates 614313), to checkpoint 1 (grid coordinates 614318). Next you will need to find the magnetic azimuth of the leg, in this case 353°. This magnetic azimuth is arrived at by first determining the grid azimuth, in this case 359°, then using the G-M angle of the declination diagram from figure 13-32 which is 6°, convert the grid azimuth to a magnetic azimuth. Remember the rule Left Add and Right Subtract (LARS). In this case, you would subtract the G-M angle from the grid azimuth as the magnetic azimuth line is shown to the right of the grid north-line. Next, using a straightedge and the graphic scale in figure 13-32, measure the map distance between the starting point and checkpoint 1. This would be 400 meters. Record this on the route record, then figure using 120 paces to each 100 meters, and record the number of paces required in parentheses immediately above the route distance. Then finally under remarks, record a brief description of the feature you will be going to for that leg of the march (fig 13-34).

b. Now that you have been given a description of how to record a route record, use the protractor and figure 13-32 to complete a route record. It should match the route record shown in figure 13-34 when completed.

FROM	TO	MAGNETIC AZIMUTH	DISTANCE	REMARKS
SP (614313)	CP_1 (614318)	353°	(480) 400M	BRIDGE
CP1 (614318)	CP_2 (619321)	58°	(720) 600M	STREAM JUNCTION
CP2 (619321)	OBJ (627326)	51°	(190) 950M	CROSS STREAM AFTER 425M

TOTAL 1950 METERS · 2390 PACES

Fig 13-34. Completed route record.

G. LENSATIC COMPASS

1. Success or failure of land navigation by map and compass will depend largely on your ability to determine

from your map the best routes to follow, to plot these routes, and, during actual movement, to follow your desired azimuth with the aid of the lensatic compass.

2. The center hold technique of using the lensatic compass should be used while navigating (fig 13-35). It is easier to use during navigation and more accurate than the compass to eye method. The center hold method can also be used during the day and at night. The center hold method is applied in the following manner:

Fig 13-35. Center hold technique.

a. You need not remove your helmet. If armed with a rifle, it should be slung well back on your shoulder.

All metal objects such as grenades, magazines, etc. should be removed from the front of your body.

b. Open the compass completely. The cover and eyepiece should be completely raised so that it will not obstruct your view of the dial and so that the dial can rotate freely.

c. Hold the compass level in both hands at a point midway between your chin and your belt; then lock your elbows in place so that if a turn must be made, your entire body turns—not just your arms.

d. Holding the compass in this manner, set your compass using the "day" or "night" method as appropriate. If you have correctly set your compass, the desired azimuth will be under the black index line when you have turned the compass so that the north arrow is under the long luminous line.

e. The luminous sighting dots and sighting wire on the compass cover now form a line that points in the direction you want to move. Your body should also be facing in the same direction.

3. When following azimuths during land navigation, steering marks should be used to help stay on course. As you begin your march, sight along the direction you will be going for points that stand out (fig 13-36). A steering mark may be any well defined object in your line of march such as a big tree, big rock, or even another Marine. Steering marks should be selected as the navigation progresses so that you may select the best mark for each leg of the march. Remember when navigating, check your azimuth of march with the compass, select the best steering mark on that azimuth, then head for it.

Fig 13-36. Selecting and heading for steering mark.

For additional training in this area, references are provided below:

1. FM 21-26 — Map Reading
2. TEC Lsn 930-071-0014-F — Measuring Distances and Azimuths